ENLISTING MASCULINITY

*The Construction of Gender in
U.S. Military Recruiting Advertising during
the All-Volunteer Force*

Melissa T. Brown

OXFORD
UNIVERSITY PRESS

OXFORD
UNIVERSITY PRESS

Oxford University Press, Inc., publishes works that further
Oxford University's objective of excellence
in research, scholarship, and education.

Oxford New York
Auckland Cape Town Dar es Salaam Hong Kong Karachi
Kuala Lumpur Madrid Melbourne Mexico City Nairobi
New Delhi Shanghai Taipei Toronto

With offices in
Argentina Austria Brazil Chile Czech Republic France Greece
Guatemala Hungary Italy Japan Poland Portugal Singapore
South Korea Switzerland Thailand Turkey Ukraine Vietnam

Copyright © 2012 by Oxford University Press, Inc.

Published by Oxford University Press, Inc.
198 Madison Avenue, New York, NY 10016

www.oup.com

Oxford is a registered trademark of Oxford University Press

All rights reserved. No part of this publication may be reproduced,
stored in a retrieval system, or transmitted, in any form or by any means,
electronic, mechanical, photocopying, recording, or otherwise,
without the prior permission of Oxford University Press.

DISCLAIMER

The Marine Corps Recruiting Command has cooperated with the author in the creation of this work as a public service. The views/comments expressed by any government employee therein are those of the speaker/author and, except as expressly noted, do not reflect the official policy or position of the United States Marine Corps, Department of the Navy, Department of Defense, or the United States Government. Furthermore, it should be understood that the use of such views/comments does not constitute approval or endorsement of those views/comments, or the work itself, by the United States Marine Corps, Department of the Navy, Department of Defense, or the United States Government.

Library of Congress Cataloging-in-Publication Data
Brown, Melissa T., 1971–
Enlisting masculinity : the construction of gender in U.S. military recruiting advertising during the
all-volunteer force / Melissa T. Brown.
  p. cm. — (Oxford studies in gender and international relations)
Includes bibliographical references and index.
ISBN 978-0-19-984282-7 (hardback : alk. paper) 1. United States—Armed Forces—Recruiting, enlistment, etc.—History—20th century. 2. United States—Armed Forces—Recruiting, enlistment, etc.—History—21st century. 3. Advertising—Recruiting and enlistment—Social aspects—United States. 4. Masculinity in advertising—United States. I. Title.
UB323.B764 2012
659.19'355223620973—dc23   2011026846

9 8 7 6 5 4 3 2 1

Printed in the United States of America
on acid-free paper

CONTENTS

List of Illustrations and Tables   vii
Acknowledgments   ix

1. Introduction   3
2. Concepts and Context: Masculinity, Citizenship, and the Creation of the All-Volunteer Force   18
3. The Army   41
4. The Navy   74
5. The Marine Corps   104
6. The Air Force   130
7. Recruiting a Volunteer Force in Wartime   158
8. Conclusion   178

Appendix   187
Notes   195
Bibliography   205
Index   215

LIST OF ILLUSTRATIONS AND TABLES

Figure 3.1	1975 Army Ad	49
Figure 3.2	1990 Army Ad	54
Figure 3.3	1995 Army Ad	69
Figure 4.1	1972 Navy Ad	79
Figure 4.2	1974 Navy Ad	88
Figure 4.3	1994 Navy Ad	91
Figure 5.1	1990 Marine Corps Ad	115
Figure 5.2	2001 Marine Corps Ad	116
Figure 6.1	1972 Air Force Ad	136
Figure 6.2	1990 Air Force Ad	140
Table 1	Active Duty Military Personnel	187
Table 2	Female Enlisted Active Duty Military Personnel	189
Table 3	Female Active Duty Officers	190
Table 4	African Americans as a Percentage of Active Duty Enlisted Forces	191
Table 5	African Americans as a Percentage of Active Duty Officers	192
Table 6	African Americans as a Percentage of Female Active Duty Enlisted Forces	193

ACKNOWLEDGMENTS

My completion of this project has depended on the support of many people. I'd like to thank the Gender and International Relations series editors for giving me the opportunity to be a part of the series. J. Ann Tickner carved a path in feminist international relations for the rest of us to follow, and Laura Sjoberg has encouraged my work for several years, as indeed her tireless work within the discipline has provided opportunities for many feminist IR scholars. I also owe thanks to Angela Chnapko at Oxford University Press for leading me through the publishing process. This book started life as a dissertation, and I'm grateful to the members of my dissertation committee, Leela Fernandes, Edward Rhodes, and Cynthia Daniels, for the feedback and guidance they gave me throughout my time at Rutgers. The work of Cynthia Enloe, my outside reader, is an inspiration and a model; if I hadn't read *Bananas, Beaches, and Bases* as an undergraduate, I never would have gone to graduate school. And I never would have made it through graduate school without the support of many of my fellow students, some of whom formed ill-fated dissertation-writing groups with me, and all of whom provided me with friendship and a supportive intellectual community. They include Sarah Alexander, Molly Baab, Jon DiCicco, Martin Edwards, Jen Einspahr, Alexandra Filindra, Denise Horn, Krista Jenkins, and Nichole Shippen. I'd like to thank my colleagues in the Social Science Department at BMCC (and especially my officemates, Geoffrey Kurtz and Jacob Kramer) for their good humor and support; it's wonderful to be a part of such a collegial academic community. Alyse, Jill, Lisa, Aimee, Nicole, and the Whitemans always encourage me and can usually amuse me as well. My family has cheered me on, even though I've generally refused to talk about what I'm doing and when I'll be done doing it. Finally, my biggest debt of gratitude is to Sanford Whiteman. He's provided me with encouragement, affection, research help, and technical assistance, and he's good at identifying Air Force planes in recruiting ads.

Enlisting Masculinity

CHAPTER 1
Introduction

This book was inspired by a TV commercial. In early 1999, the U.S. Air Force was gearing up for Operation Allied Force. The United States had warned Serb leader Slobodan Milošević that if ethnic cleansing of Kosovar Albanians didn't cease, his military would be bombed by NATO forces. While serving Air Force pilots were on the verge of combat, American television stations began showing a recruiting commercial for the Air Force. Facing recruiting shortfalls, the Air Force was paying for television airtime for the first time in its history. The ad's focus on personal growth and fulfillment—young people were asking themselves what or who they wanted to be—was entirely disconnected from the impending military action by the Air Force. The commercial's portrayals also seemed far removed from the traditional masculine ideal of the warrior. The strong, heroic fighters of a World War II–era recruiting poster wouldn't recognize the kids in the Air Force commercial as brothers in arms. In the preceding decades, the U.S. military lost a war, Congress abolished the draft, Americans stopped thinking of military service as an obligation of male citizenship, and gender had become a contentious issue for the armed forces. In this context, the military branches have struggled with the question of how to depict themselves to convince potential recruits to enlist.

Military service has strong historical ties to masculinity and the transformation of boys into men. In the early 1970s, in the period when the U.S. military was making the transition to an all-volunteer force (AVF), masculinity was widely considered to be in crisis. Key elements of this crisis included the challenges to men's roles and male privileges by the women's movement; the loss of good-paying, blue-collar industrial jobs that gave working-class men status, economic independence, and the ability to support a family; and the loss of the Vietnam War. So, at the very moment when the military needed to begin finding ways to entice young people, and mainly young *men*, into military service, a key ideological component of the concept of military service, masculinity, was in a state of flux. The central question this book asks is whether, in the era of the AVF, masculinity is the underlying basis of appeals for military service, and, if so, what forms does it take? In a period when traditional masculinities have been discredited, and when women have gained importance as a source of labor for the military, a military institution faces a choice: it can move away from masculinity in its attempts to recruit, it can reforge the link between the military and masculinity but in ways that exploit and develop new masculine forms, or it can emphasize a traditional masculinity, establishing the military as a refuge for a traditional idea of manhood that is being challenged in other parts of society.

This question is important to understanding how standards of masculinity are shifting and what form or forms of masculinity are becoming dominant in American culture. The choices made by military branches about how they present themselves can also reveal how the relationship between masculinity and the military is evolving—whether it is becoming weaker, or stronger, or simply changing. They shed light on changes in the gender order both within and outside the military and on the evolving cultural meaning of military service in the United States.

There is a great quantity of both academic and popular literature on the links between masculinity and the U.S. military. It includes feminist, nonfeminist, and explicitly antifeminist versions.[1] Discussions of gender and the military tend to conceptualize masculinity too simplistically as either present or absent. A lot of the feminist variants seem to assume that the military is still intimately tied with masculinity and that the masculinity in question is a macho, warrior spirit, involving the denigration of women and connected to the abuse and harassment of women in the military, as well as some women outside of it. Much antifeminist literature assumes that feminists are destroying the military; that the military, perhaps with the exception of the Marine Corps, has gone soft and politically correct; and that, as a result, the recruiting materials produced by the services reflect an ethos of gender equality. In addition, much of the literature on masculinity and the military portrays the military as a monolith. To get a better grip on how the masculinity crisis and flux in gender roles are affecting the military requires both a more nuanced understanding of masculinity and a more careful look at the military as a set of interconnected institutions. While scholars, activists, and political commentators concerned with the relationship between gender and military service may talk about "the military," the military as a single entity does very little recruiting. It is the individual services, the Army, Navy, Air Force, and Marines,[2] that recruit. There are four different services, each of which needs to appeal to young men or young people and each of which faces similar external constraints, such as the level of funding for military pay and the national unemployment rate. Examining the individual branches allows an exploration of the relationship between aspects of the institutions, such as their histories, cultures, purposes, demographics, and personnel needs, and the specific constructions of gender they produce or privilege.

This book argues that masculinity *is* still a foundation of the appeals made by the military but that each branch deploys various constructions of masculinity that serve its particular personnel needs and culture, with conventional martial masculinity being only one among them.[3] Some military watchers would claim that over the course of the AVF, the service branches other than the Marines have pursued a recruiting strategy that focuses only on economic benefits, that they try to appeal to women at the expense of men, that the ads are carefully gender balanced, and that masculinity is not part of the pitch. Based on an examination of recruiting advertisements, these claims can, for the most part, be rejected. The Marine Corps does stand apart from the other branches in relying almost exclusively on a traditional, warrior form of masculinity, though other branches have also utilized that form to some degree. The Army, Navy, and Air Force draw on various strands of masculinity that are in circulation in the wider culture, emphasizing those that they believe will resonate best at a given time for a particular role, tailoring their appeals to the groups they most want to attract. The civilianized but still masculine offers made by the branches have included adventure and challenge—a modern analogue to the frontier masculinity that allowed a man to test his physical and mental abilities—economic independence and breadwinner status, dominance and mastery through technology, and hybrid masculinity, which combines egalitarianism and compassion with strength and power. The latter two sets of masculine traits have been growing in prominence during this crisis period, and the military's use of them reinforces their status and helps to make them socially dominant. The military branches, especially the Army, sometimes link militaristic imagery and the promise of success in the civilian economic world, blending masculine forms and creating a bridge between older forms of masculinity with which soldiering had previously been associated and newer forms gaining prominence in the wider culture. On the level of representation, recruiting materials do give women some access to these roles and to characteristics that are associated with men and masculinity, but they do so in such a tokenized way that the associations with manhood and masculinity are retained. Representations of military service also include pockets of warrior masculinity, mainly associated with direct combat, that are fully male and that preserve a more traditional masculine form.

THE STUDY OF MILITARY RECRUITMENT

The military is an important site of analysis, and it probably gets less attention from political scientists than it deserves. International relations scholars are concerned with the military and its role in national defense, and some political theorists examine it in relation to questions of civic obligation and the relationship between the individual and the state. As chapter 2 will show, the military is particularly important to scholars of gender because of its importance as a site for the creation and propagation of ideas about masculinity, as well as its position at the nexus of gender and citizenship. The military is a key institution in American society; it performs important national security functions internationally, carrying out foreign policy and projecting force, and it also performs various domestic functions, such as providing jobs, skills training, and economic stimulus; socializing young people (mainly young men); Americanizing immigrant groups; and standing as a national symbol and a source of national identity. Cynthia Enloe (1996) argues that the United States has what could be called "a 'militarized' concept of national loyalty and identity" because in the United States the military occupies "a special place in the public realm, somehow more intimately bound to patriotism, to the fate and dignity of the nation than, for example, public hospitals or even the national legislature" (261). The military is an embodiment of state power—when the state projects military force, it is generally, in one way or another, literally projecting the bodies of its soldiers[4]—a physical representative of the state *and* a symbolic representative of the people.[5]

Within the broader topic of the military, recruiting is a potentially productive area of study that can reveal a great deal about the interrelationship between society and the military. Recruitment is one of the military's most public faces. It is an attempt to legitimate service in the eyes of Americans, offering up reasons to serve and potential ideological bases for military culture. Recruiting images attempt to produce general support for military service and to build a positive image of the armed forces to domestic society at large. In particular, the military branches are trying to attract young people, and mainly young men, who are or will be high school graduates, to become enlisted personnel. The armed forces also need officers, but this much smaller group comes primarily from the service academies and from the Reserve Officer Training Corps (ROTC), and some separate, much more limited advertising campaigns are aimed at getting college students into ROTC programs. While high school students and recent graduates are the main audience, the military also needs to appeal to the people who are in a position to influence potential recruits, including parents, teachers, siblings, coaches, guidance counselors, and other members of the recruit's community. The images of soldiering presented in recruiting materials are created by military institutions for consumption by the general public. The military generates other images of soldiering, but these are mainly internal, for consumption by military personnel themselves, or they are directed at policy makers. (Recruiting materials do also offer reinforcement to current service members; for instance, Marines watching movies at a theater near their base are certain to cheer when a Marine recruiting commercial is shown before the movie.) Recruiting materials reflect an idea of what the military is for, what service members do, who should serve, and how those who serve will be affected by the experience. Recruitment involves overt image making and an attempt to sell particular pictures of military service, making it an especially fruitful site to study the construction of gender by the military.

Recruiting materials draw a picture of the military that is meant to appeal to the self-image of potential recruits, and they may not provide a highly accurate view of military life. Navy ads show thrilling images of fighter jets taking off from aircraft carriers, but a typical sailor is more likely to spend his days swabbing decks than piloting jets. Recruiting also does not necessarily reflect the way a service understands itself. A military branch may choose to deploy images of itself that don't fully comport with that branch's self-understandings in order to appeal to potential recruits and get them in the door[6]—those recruits can be socialized into the service during training. Recruiting materials, however, must in some way ring true to their audience, even if the image provided isn't a perfect reflection of reality. They also must resonate with the audience and its preconceptions of military service, gender roles, and America's national identity and role in the world. While the images can shape and alter perceptions, to be successful, they must also play off preexisting ideas and in some way reflect what the audience *wants* to be true of its military. The military has been an arbiter of masculinity, but in the era of the volunteer force, it must in some measure reflect back civilian trends to civilian society, building on ideas about gender from the civilian world as it constructs concepts of service and creates associations between soldiering and particular versions of masculinity, recirculating public attitudes in altered and reconstructed forms. This occurs at two levels: each branch wants to create a favorable impression of the service to the general public, and it also needs to attract particular segments of the population (such as risk takers or the technologically skilled) and must attempt to appeal to their desires and perceptions.

Recruiting must reflect back what the public, or particular sectors of it, wants to see, which is why the branches use advertising firms, attitude surveys, and focus groups. However, each branch also faces choices about how it presents itself, and each wants to shape the idealized images of service in ways that conform to its perceived notion of what is best or most functional for that military branch.[7] All of the branches use research on the youth market, all of them target a similar but not identical audience (despite some differences, they're all looking for people in roughly the same age range without felony convictions and preferably with high school diplomas), all of them do so in the same economic and social national context, and all of them are military institutions, but the messages developed by each branch differ, so it can't simply be the case that each service follows the research on social trends. Each branch cultivates its own distinct image, and each deploys constructions of gender in its own way as part of that project. There is no given way to appeal to a high school graduate with computer skills, and when a military institution does so by showing him he can have adventures as a world traveler, by talking about economic security, by calling on his patriotism, or by linking his computer use to advanced weaponry and control of the battlefield, it is making a claim about the meaning of military service and tapping into particular forms of masculinity circulating in the culture as the most salient.

Recruiting materials may be only a small factor in any individual's decision to enlist. Personal selling by recruiting personnel—the recruiter sitting down with a prospect and talking with him or her about the military—is a key factor in most recruits' decision to actually sign service contracts (Hanssens and Levien 1983). Individual recruiters have particular quotas they need to fill, say, a certain number of high school graduates or doctors, and they make pitches tailored to the individuals they need to recruit. Recruiters must first do a lot of legwork in the form of visiting schools, handing out business cards in public places, and making phone calls. They often need to have multiple conversations with both potential enlistees and their family members, and they offer up whatever enticements are at their disposal, from signing bonuses, to educational benefits, to any special incentive programs in effect. Recruiters give all of this individual attention and make their particular sales pitches, however, within the context of the larger institutional image that each service projects. Recruiters persuade individuals, while the national recruiting campaigns seek to reach large swaths of the population and more broadly shape the public image of the service.

The role that gender plays in military recruiting hasn't received much consideration in either the gender studies and feminist literature on the military or in the political science literature on military service. In addition to the literature on the connections between masculinity and military service (which is further discussed in the next chapter and includes Barrett 1996; Braudy 2003; Cohn 1998; Connell 1985, 1995; Elshtain 1987; Enloe 1983, 1989, 1993, 2000; Goldstein 2001; Herbert 1998; Higate 2003; Morgan 1994), there is a large body of literature on the relationship between women and the military (including Binkin and Bach 1977; Chapkis 1981; D'Amico and Weinstein 1999; De Pauw 1998; Enloe 1983; Francke 1997; Goldman 1982; Herbert 1998; Holm 1992; Katzenstein and Reppy 1999; Rogan 1981; Rustad 1982; Schneider and Schneider 1992; Skaine 1999; Stiehm 1981, 1989, 1996; Weinstein and White 1997; Zimmerman 1995). But in all of this analysis of the gendering of military service, there is a lack of attention to recruiting materials. Two works directly address the question of how recruiters manipulate ideas about gender, and both do so in a limited way. Megens and Wings (1981) examine the recruitment appeals of NATO countries and point out that even those militaries that promise equal opportunity and integrate women instead of segregating them into an auxiliary tend to portray men and women differently, depicting women in passive roles (receiving instruction from men), smiling, and wearing makeup. *Does*

Khaki Become You? Cynthia Enloe's (1983) groundbreaking book on women and military systems, includes a chapter on women soldiers with a short discussion of how recruiters attempt to appeal to women and what attracts women to the military. Both of these pieces lay important groundwork in calling attention to recruiting materials as a productive site of analysis and identifying some of the ways that recruitment materials are likely to feminize women soldiers; however, both are also quite brief and out-of-date, and both focus only on women.

Political science is concerned with issues of citizenship and obligation in relation to the AVF, including questions of who serves and whether the makeup of the forces should correspond to the makeup of society. In the United States, there is political competition over who should serve and what service means—whether women or gay people (and in the past, African Americans) have a right to fight, whether service should be an obligation or a choice, and whether military service is a job like any other or categorically different from civilian occupations. The images that the military branches put forward in recruiting materials implicitly take a position in these debates through the kinds of people they show and how they show them. However, political scientists haven't paid much attention to recruiting, leaving it mainly to military "manpower" analysts, economists, and sociologists, and even sociologists don't focus on the specific *content* of the appeals that are being made to potential recruits. The scholarship on recruiting that is done in these other fields generally focuses on such issues as how much money should be spent, recruiting standards (education and test score requirements) and the quality of recruits, the propensity of various demographic segments to enlist, the size of potential cohorts of recruits, the likely future needs of the military and whether a volunteer force can meet them, the potential of women to serve manpower needs, the role of the reserves, and similar kinds of manpower analysis. Scholars have focused on who is to be recruited, including the race and gender makeup of the forces. They do not, however, discuss ways in which appeals and recruitment materials have been gendered or racialized through the particular images of service they utilize. There are some studies (such as Faris 1984) of why people decide to join or to stay in the military—whether they are generally motivated by economic concerns or by normative factors, such as patriotism or family tradition—but they don't ask about recruiting materials and whether particular representations of military roles were appealing. There are also studies (such as Hanssens and Levien 1983) that examine the effect of advertising in terms of whether it generates leads or results in actual signed contracts; such studies might examine spending on different media and the impact of advertising, environmental factors, and factors having to do with recruitment staff (size of the recruiting force, motivational effect of quotas, etc.). The content of the advertising isn't considered relevant. These studies may be useful for budgeting decisions, but they don't reveal anything about the meanings produced by the ads and the various conceptions of military service they communicate.

The recruiting crisis of the late 1990s led to a spate of material on recruiting, mainly in the form of journalistic coverage and articles in military publications. There was widespread concern over the military's ability to recruit in a context in which service is simply one economic option among many, young people feel no obligation and have low propensity to enlist, and fewer people have personal contact with anyone directly involved in the military. Recruiting and the civil-military gap became the subject of symposia[8] and congressional hearings.[9] The concern over recruiting in this period, as discussed in chapter 2, often did frame the issue in terms of gender and masculinity. Some blamed the recruiting shortfalls on a demasculinization of the military and an erosion of its culture and traditions by the inclusion of women; they called for the Army, Navy, and Air Force to emulate the Marine Corps, which was meeting its recruiting quotas and which projected a masculine, warrior image (Bonat 1999; Keene 1999; Smart 2000; Strother 1999). These articles, however, tended more toward editorializing than scholarly study. The authors often seemed to be making assumptions about how the various military branches were presenting themselves without actually looking at recruiting materials, except, perhaps, for a single ad or TV commercial.[10] They are most interesting not for what they have to say about recruiting materials, but for the anxieties they reveal about the status of masculinity in society and the desire both for the military to retain its connection to masculinity and for warrior forms of masculinity to be more dominant in the larger culture.

The late-1990s debates about recruiting and the calls for the other services to act more like the Marines seem to take the view that there is one truly masculine approach, as exemplified by the Marines, and that the other services have all decided to forgo appeals to masculinity. I argue that recruiting materials utilize a variety of constructions of masculinity and male gender roles. Various inducements to service may have their roots in competing versions of masculinity—in different ways to be a man. In addition to the more traditional (or more recognizable) guns and toughness version of masculinity that each of the services has at one time or another used, recruiting materials have also featured learning a good trade that will allow economic independence, physical adventure and excitement, and technological prowess, which entails both mastery and control over sophisticated machinery and success in the civilian world. Each of these motivations for joining the military is tied to a masculine role.

CENTRAL QUESTIONS

So, the fundamental question that this book asks is: when the military appeals to potential recruits, does it present service in masculine terms, and if so, what form or forms does that masculinity take? More broadly, how do recruiting materials construct gender as they create ideas about soldiering? This section of the chapter elaborates on a few of the issues that underlie these two questions. The first of these is the nature of military occupations. Many military jobs have come to depend more on technical skill than on physical strength, and with advances in technology, many jobs are specialized and similar to civilian occupations. Such jobs are more readily opened to women, although any jobs outside traditionally feminine areas like nursing are still going to be done by more men than women; they also don't automatically have the clear association to masculinity that combat jobs do. The military branches can create appeals that try to masculinize noncombat jobs by associating them with warriorhood and combat by emphasizing their links to weaponry and defense; they can draw on various civilian forms of masculinity, particularly those that link technology to notions of dominance and control; or they can try not to impute any gender association at all to military careers. The military branches can also choose to highlight their specifically martial aspects and play down the civilianized facets of service. And of course, any branch can use different approaches at different times or in different contexts. By examining recruiting over the course of the volunteer force's thirty-five-year-plus history, I can examine how the recruiting strategies of each branch have developed and whether they have been consistent over time or how they have changed.

Another underlying issue is that of women's place in the military's gendering of service. The armed forces have struggled with the question of how to attract and utilize women while still keeping core military functions, namely, combat, exclusively male and how to integrate women without disrupting the association between military service and masculinity that might draw in men. The military needs to find ways to attract women recruits without alienating young men, who are still the main focus of recruiting efforts. Recruiting advertisements may try to reassure potential recruits and their families that women in the military don't lose their femininity, even though they are joining an institution known for conferring masculinity and making men out of boys. They may also offer women equal opportunity or the chance to have experiences and acquire traits that are typically associated with masculinity, like adventure, independence, and challenge. A military branch may also make no specific effort to reach out to women.[11]

Finally, each branch of the armed forces has its own history, institutional culture, and specific personnel needs. In the course of analyzing recruiting materials, I examine whether these differences lead the branches to utilize different constructions of masculinity or to deploy gender in their recruiting materials in significantly different ways. The differences among the services are drawn out in greater detail in the coming chapters, but a few key characteristics of their recruiting needs can be described here. The Army is the largest service, and it requires the largest number of recruits each year. Both the Navy and the Air Force need a large percentage of their recruits to fill technical positions, meaning that they need service members who will stay in the service long enough to justify the expense of training them and who have high mental aptitude scores. The Air Force needs the fewest recruits each year, and it is in the best position of any of the services to utilize the labor of women. The Marine Corps is the smallest service, but it needs a large number of recruits relative to its size. The Marines consciously keep turnover high because their leadership structure is smaller than those of the other services, so their need for career members is lower. The Marines have the largest proportion of combat-oriented jobs (the Navy, of which the Marine Corps is technically a part, provides much of their support services) and therefore the least number of women, both proportionally and in absolute terms. The size of the military has changed over the course of the AVF, dropping from around 2.3 million on active duty to around 1.4 million after the post–Cold War drawdown, and there have been some shifts in the size of the branches in relation to each other.[12] To give a sense of the relative needs of each of the services, in 2006, the Army needed 80,000 recruits, the Navy 36,656, the Marines 32,301, and the Air Force 30,750 (Shanker 2006). At that time, the Army had about 500,000 active-duty personnel, the Navy 350,000, the Marines 180,000, and the Air Force 349,000.

THE RECRUITING ADVERTISEMENT SAMPLE

This book examines how each of the branches of the military sells itself to various audiences. It asks how the advertising materials produced by each branch portray military service and how they use ideas about gender, and about masculinity in particular, in the process. I analyze the recruiting advertisements using an interpretive textual approach, which seeks to make explicit the meanings encoded in the published words and images. In the social sciences, content analysis is the more frequently used method for examining qualitative data like documents and transcripts, and it attempts to categorize the discrete elements of the data by coding schemes—words or images are put into categories and counted (Silverman 2003, 348). While this technique can yield valuable insights, and in fact has revealed much about the differential ways that advertisers portray men and women, "the counting or quantification of isolated elements in a piece of content cannot tell us everything about how meaning is produced in the text nor how the audience understands what is after all a complex piece of signification—the whole is often more than the sum of the parts" (Dyer 1982, 111). A textual approach makes use of semiotic and discourse-based analysis to examine how meaning is generated within a text (see Fiske 1982).

In analyzing the visual and verbal elements of the advertisements and the various potential meanings encoded in them, I examine factors such as the appearance of actors (including such elements as hairstyle, facial expressions, clothing, and bodily postures), the activities they perform, objects featured, settings, use of photographic techniques, forms of language, and rhetorical devices. However, much of my focus is on the gendering of the various factors (how these factors express ideas about masculinity and femininity) and on aspects that relate specifically to a military context. This includes the use of different types of uniforms (work uniforms, combat uniforms, or ceremonial dress); whether the activities being performed are combat oriented (like driving a tank, jumping out of an aircraft, or holding weaponry), ceremonial (standing in formation, saluting), technical (operating computer equipment, sitting in front of a radar screen), clerical, medical, physical (running, navigating an obstacle course), or leisure oriented; where the work or activity takes place (indoors or outdoors, in a military or civilian setting); the presentation of military hardware; the types of military personnel featured; the groupings of individuals and their apparent relationship to each other; whether actors are in active or passive roles, leading or instructing or being led or instructed; images of civilian life and interaction between military personnel and civilians; descriptions of service life; the descriptions of members of the military branches; and the descriptions of the benefits of service, both material and intangible. In addition to decoding the visual and linguistic elements of the advertisements, I also put them in historical context. My analysis shows how these various factors communicate messages about what service means and how it relates to particular forms or aspects of masculinity.

I collected print advertisements that were published between July 1970 (the beginning of fiscal year 1971 for the military) and December 2007. The all-volunteer force was officially inaugurated in July 1973, but the Project VOLAR volunteer Army field experiment began in fiscal year 1971 (Griffith 1996), and by 1972, the Army, Navy, and Air Force were advertising in earnest in anticipation of the AVF. I collected advertisements for each of the four armed services, excluding ads for the reserves, ROTC, and the combined forces, from the magazines *Life*, *Sports Illustrated*, and *Popular Mechanics* for the entire sample period and from *Seventeen* from 1994 through 2007.

I chose *Life*, *Sports Illustrated*, and *Popular Mechanics* because, for most of the period of the all-volunteer force, this is where the services were placing their ads. *Life* was a general-interest publication with a broad readership that included both men and women and potential recruits and their parents. *Sports Illustrated* and *Popular Mechanics* both have a readership that is predominantly male (though women's interest in sports and sports magazines has grown over the period of the AVF), while *Popular Mechanics*' demographics are skewed toward a more working-class population. According to Time-Warner, the company that owns *Sports Illustrated*, the magazine, which is "America's leading sports publication, is read by 21 million adults each week, more than any other men's publication" ("Digital Bridges" 2004). *Popular Mechanics* is a technology, science, how-to, and home-building magazine that has called itself

"The Must-Read Magazine for the Must-Know Man." Military hardware is a frequent subject of articles.

In the mid-1990s, the services began to advertise in a broader range of magazines, including *Rolling Stone, Entertainment Weekly, XXL* (a magazine about hip-hop music), and *Seventeen*, to better target the young demographic they need to reach. To see what ads the services were publishing specifically for the consumption of young women, and how and whether they differed from the ones published in magazines aimed at men, I collected advertisements from *Seventeen* from 1994 through 2007.

My recruiting print ad sample is a sample in terms of my choice of sources, but I attempted to collect every ad published in those magazines during the period under study. Some ads may have been missed due to human error, and in addition, some ads are missing because of gaps in the collections of the libraries from which I collected the materials.[13] My sample consists of 318 different advertisements, most of which were published multiple times, including 160 for the Army, 65 for the Navy, 54 for the Air Force, and 39 for the Marine Corps. I supplemented the advertisements I found published in the magazines with descriptions of advertising in news articles and scholarly work on the all-volunteer force. I also analyze the Internet sites that each of the services has maintained since the late 1990s. Recruiting Web sites, which generally share themes with print ad campaigns, have grown in importance for the armed forces because they are a preferred method of communication for the age group the services are trying to attract. They also allow the services to provide more content and information; they are easily updated, interactive, and cost-effective; and they provide the services with feedback about what types of approaches their visitors find most appealing, based on page hits and other data they can collect. In addition, I've gathered samples and descriptions of television advertising to fill out the image crafted by each of the services.[14]

THE PLAN OF THE BOOK

Chapter 2 provides historical and theoretical context for the examination of the recruiting advertisements. It discusses the concept of masculinity; explores the relationship among military service, masculinity, and citizenship; presents a brief history of the all-volunteer force; and introduces some of the issues raised by the end of the draft. Each of the chapters after that examines a branch of the armed forces and analyzes its recruiting ads up to the early 2000s. The recruiting advertisements that have appeared during the Iraq and Afghanistan conflicts are considered separately in the seventh chapter. In addition to providing some background material on the branch's recruiting practices and discussing the service culture, each chapter also includes a brief history of women's participation in that branch and a discussion of how women are portrayed or appealed to in the recruiting materials to complete the picture, mainly based on how each branch deploys masculinity, of how each branch genders military service.

Chapter 3 examines Army advertising, which at times has deployed a traditional warrior masculinity, featuring weaponry and soldiers who test themselves, but has also used other masculine models, like acquiring a good trade that will allow economic independence, learning discipline and self-confidence, and gaining technological prowess, which entails both mastery of sophisticated machinery and success in the civilian world. Army recruiting materials have forged links between civilian careers and self-development and militaristic imagery like weaponry and camouflage. In addition to promising the excitement of military action, these ads bring together more traditional forms of military masculinity with newer, business-world forms of masculinity that are gaining prominence in the larger culture. The Army's versions of masculinity, even its warrior type, tend to be accessible, personified by smiling, relaxed "regular guys." In the Army, which needs the greatest number of recruits each year, manhood seems to be a goal within reach of the average young man.

Chapter 4 shows that over the course of the AVF, Navy recruiting appeals have tended to shift back and forth between an emphasis on career and benefits and an emphasis on adventure and challenge. Each of these sets of appeals, however, contains a masculine subtext, if not an overt association with manhood. The career and benefits theme was presented first in terms of masculine pride in work that is physically and mentally challenging—"good, hard work"—later shifting to an emphasis on professional careers, personal success, and exposure to cutting-edge technology, more closely aligning the Navy with the high-status careers of the information age and its emerging dominant models of masculinity. The Navy's other main approach is to highlight adventure, offering young men the excitement of life at sea and challenges that allow them to test and prove themselves. In the 2000s, the offer of adventure became more explicitly militaristic, with ads that featured specifically martial forms of action and prominent displays of weaponry, layering a warrior masculinity on top of other kinds of appeals. The fact that the Navy fairly recently began utilizing what could be considered traditional military masculinity shows its lingering appeal and its continuing power to attract some sectors of the wider culture. The Navy is asserting that its commitment to masculinity hasn't weakened.

Chapter 5 examines the recruiting practices of the Marines. While military institutions in general are tied to masculinity, the Marine Corps in particular, with its focus on combat, has been seen as the force with the most macho and aggressive men. With the end of the draft and the challenges to traditional masculinity in the larger culture, the Corps didn't retreat from its association with masculinity, but sought to reinforce it. Over the course of the AVF,

Marine Corps advertising has remained remarkably consistent. The Marine Corps emphasizes its elitism and sends the message that the Marines demand that a recruit prove his worth, but once he has met the challenge, he'll be accepted into an exclusive brotherhood and be a part of a larger tradition. The Marines present a rite of passage into manhood. Marine Corps advertising isn't just masculine; it specifically presents a warrior masculinity. The Marines need to find young men who are more interested in combat jobs than in technical training, and the recruiting materials reflect that. Marine recruiting ads generally downplay benefits and economic incentives, so their appeals don't draw on models of masculinity tied to economic independence or mastery of technology. The Marines also have the strongest culture of any of the services, and they are concerned with finding recruits who are attracted to that culture and not just to military life in general.

Chapter 6 examines the Air Force, which has developed appeals based on its technological and career-related strengths and has drawn on conceptions of masculinity that are not particularly martial or militaristic. Air Force recruiting has emphasized job training and specifically offered respect and advancement to blue-collar, mechanically inclined young men, reinforcing a working-class masculinity that values skilled labor and economic independence. The Air Force has also made advanced technology a central draw; through association with this technology, the Air Force offers the masculine rewards of mastery, dominance, and control. In recent years, the Air Force has offered recruits not direct physical excitement, as the other services tend to do, but the vicarious thrills of the video gamer, who has extreme experiences through the mediation of technology. The recruiting Web site emphasizes the Air Force's humanitarian role, painting humanitarian missions as dramatic and important in a way that seems to reflect Steve Niva's (1998) concept of "new world order" masculinity, discussed in chapter 2. The Web site also depicts a comfortable lifestyle with a balance between work and other aspects of life, like leisure or family. The Air Force is the most civilianized of the armed forces, offering a work environment that is similar to that of a civilian bureaucratic organization, albeit one that uses a lot of sophisticated technology, with both offices and technical work areas. The Air Force offers technology-related forms of masculinity that don't demand a complete transformation or a new identity and allow the airman or officer to pass comfortably between the Air Force and civilian worlds and find status and opportunity in both.

While chapters 3 to 6 explore the gendered constructions of service developed by each branch over the course of the AVF, chapter 7 takes up the question of how these constructions are altered by the context of actual war fighting. War, as military traditionalists continually remind those who would raise questions about social issues like equality, is the ultimate purpose of military institutions, and the requirements of combat are the purported justification for the military's ties to masculinity. However, war can alter gender roles both inside and outside the military and reconfigure ideas about what is appropriate for men and women, based on military needs. Chapter 7 examines how the branches have responded to the Iraq and Afghanistan conflicts in their recruiting materials. For the most part, they have ignored the wars. When they do present combat imagery, it is mainly used to denote a masculine realm of challenge, excitement, and brotherhood and is disconnected from the conflicts at hand. Within the recruiting ads, women's roles are carefully contained. Even as the wars have expanded their military functions, the depictions of women continue to segregate them from any markers of war, keeping combat male in the military's self-representations.

The final chapter draws some broader conclusions from the other chapters and highlights the similarities and overlaps in the constructions of gender produced by the branches, as each mines a few key masculine models that are becoming dominant in the larger culture—professional-managerial forms, masculinity tied to mastery of technology, hybrid masculinity that combines toughness and aggression with compassion and egalitarianism—as well the more traditional warrior type. It argues that although most Americans believe they can ignore the military in the era of the all-volunteer force, when it comes to popular culture and ideas about gender, the military is not a thing apart from society, and it reflects on some of the implications of military recruiting materials for wider conceptions of masculinity and for our conception of military service.

CHAPTER 2

Concepts and Context

Masculinity, Citizenship, and the Creation of the All-Volunteer Force

THE CONSTRUCTION OF MASCULINITY

This text examines the relationship between military recruiting and masculinity, so some discussion of the concept of masculinity (and hegemonic masculinity in particular), the relationship between masculinity and soldiering, and the so-called crisis of masculinity is in order. In the 1970s, the women's movement shed new light on masculinity, and it began to get attention both from those who sought to reform it in the hopes of liberating men and those who sought to protect it from the threat of feminism. In the 1980s, in works such as *The Making of Masculinities: The New Men's Studies* (Brod 1987), masculinity started to receive sustained scholarly attention in ways that went beyond previous psychological studies of sex roles and that built on women's studies and feminist analyses of gender. Masculinity, very simply put, is the traits, behaviors, images, values, and interests associated with being a man within a given culture.[1] It is not a natural consequence of male biology, but a set of socially constructed practices.

In the Western philosophical tradition, meaning is made through difference and contrast. A positive definition depends on the negation or repression of something represented as its antithesis. Binary oppositions pair terms relationally. Many feminist theorists have pointed out that "masculine" and "feminine" are defined against each other and linked with other oppositional pairs, like hard-soft, culture-nature, rational-emotional, mind-body, strong-weak, public-private, active-passive, subject-object, and independent-dependent. This way of making meaning both defines masculinity and femininity as natural opposites and imputes value to masculine traits over feminine ones. Associations with masculinity or masculine traits can lend power in contexts that have no direct or overt relationship to men or women as men and women. As Joan W. Scott (1986) has shown, "gender is a primary way of signifying relationships of power" (1067); meaning is established through difference, and references to sexual difference—to commonly accepted male-female binary oppositions—can encode a hierarchical relationship or indicate a distribution of power.[2]

Masculinity is defined relationally to femininity in a way that privileges men over women, but just as feminist scholars have come to talk about intersectionality and the ways that gender is mutually constituted with other socially important categories like race and class, understandings of masculinity have also become more complex. The concept of hegemonic masculinity, which is generally associated with R. W. Connell, has become highly influential in the past twenty years (Connell and Messerschmidt 2005). Connell (1987) argues that any given social order includes multiple concepts of masculinity, that some forms of masculinity will have social dominance over others, and that the form of masculinity that inhabits the hegemonic position is not a fixed type but is contestable and can change. Hegemonic masculinity is constructed in contrast to subordinate masculinities, such as those associated with gay or nonwhite men, as well as to femininity.[3] Hegemonic masculinity may not correspond with the everyday lives of a majority of men, but it will require men "to position themselves in relation to it" (Connell and Messerschmidt 2005, 832), and it will "express widespread ideals, fantasies, and desires" (838). Nonhegemonic forms of masculinity, "which may represent well-crafted responses to race/ethnic marginalization, physical disability, class inequality, or stigmatized sexuality" may be actively oppressed and discredited, or they may be incorporated into the local gender order (848). Hegemonic masculinity changes over time and may adaptively appropriate aspects of subordinate masculinities.

Military Masculinities

Masculinity has strong connections to war fighting and to militaries, which are commonly perceived as institutions that confer masculinity and create men out of boys. According to R. W. Connell, "Violence on the largest possible scale is the purpose of the military; and no arena has been more important for the definition of hegemonic masculinity in European/American culture" (1995, 201). Morgan (1994) describes the specific masculine qualities that the military represents:

> Of all the sites where masculinities are constructed, reproduced, and deployed, those associated with war and the military are some of the most direct. Despite

far-reaching political, social, and technological changes, the warrior still seems to be a key symbol of masculinity. In statues, heroic paintings, comic books, and popular films the gendered connotations are inescapable. The stance, the facial expressions, and the weapons clearly connote aggression, courage, a capacity for violence, and sometimes, a willingness for sacrifice. The uniform absorbs individualities into a generalized and timeless masculinity while also connoting a control of emotion and a subordination to a larger rationality. (165–166)

Militaries have historically depended on female labor for a wide range of necessary support work, but with very few exceptions, men have been the combatants. The citizen-soldier ideal, as initially theorized by Niccolò Machiavelli, depended on masculine *virtu* vanquishing feminine *fortuna* (Pitkin 1984). Several scholars (including Burke 1999 and Francke 1997) have documented the gendered nature of U.S. military training, which has depended on violent hazing and the denigration of women and femininity. The connection between masculinity and war or the military has been traced out in particular historical contexts in America, such as the Civil War (Dubbert 1979), the Victorian age (Mrozek 1987), and World War II (Jarvis 2004). Braudy (2003) more broadly examines the changing perceptions of war and of masculinity and their interrelationship from the European knights of the Middle Ages to the terrorists of September 11, 2001. The relationship between soldiering and masculinity has been explored and discussed by feminists who want to expose and denaturalize the relationship, revealing how that relationship has been constructed (Cohn 1998; De Pauw 1998; Elshtain 1987; Enloe 1983, 1989, 1993, 2000; Goldstein 2001; Herbert 1998; Higate 2003; Stiehm 1989), and by other scholars and activists who take that relationship as natural and given (Gutmann 2000; Marlowe 1983; Mitchell 1998; van Creveld 2000). In theory and in practice, war making has been the province of men and a source of masculinity.

Americans' attitudes toward their armed forces have varied over the years, through war and peace and through conscription and volunteer forces. Throughout it all, and even in periods when military service has not served as a rite of passage for most males, the military has set a standard for masculinity. While Americans haven't always wanted to send their sons to the U.S. Army, they have supported their local military organizations and militias when they've existed. These militias were of questionable military utility, but, I would argue, they still performed masculinizing functions, allowing men to get together occasionally to put on uniforms and march or go out in the woods with their guns and see themselves as the guardians of their communities. Even when only a small number of men served in either the regular forces or the militia, men's relationship to the military was celebrated in parades and civic festivals. For much of the nineteenth century, political parties routinely staged militaristic spectacles, with companies of uniformed men parading to martial music, to generate men's enthusiasm for upcoming elections (Baker 1984; Snyder

1999). Men often pursue a vicarious relationship with the military, consuming pop-culture representations of the military in the form of movies, video games, novels, and popular histories on a massive scale, while their sons continue to play with a variety of war-themed toys. The United States has a large and diverse culture, with room for many localized gender orders. In the absence of conscription, the military's impact on masculine norms may be felt most strongly in particular locations and subcultures that are courted most directly by the various branches, while the military continues to affect the general culture and its notions of gender more broadly.

Militaries have historically been associated with masculinity, but what constitutes military masculinity changes with time and context, with new military roles and advances in technology, and with major political, economic, and social changes in the societies of which militaries are a part. Because constructions of soldiering and constructions of gender are interrelated, the recent inclusion of women in the military in larger numbers and in expanding roles makes the link between military service and masculinity more complex. According to David H. J. Morgan:

> The changes in the military and the changes in the gender order are mutually dependent. Changes in the military and the conduct of war have an effect on dominant images of embodied masculinities. Changes in the gender order, for example, in the widespread employment of women, in their turn have an effect on how the military is conceived and constructed. (1994, 179–180)

With the end of the draft and the inception of the all-volunteer force (AVF) in 1973, the U.S. military became dependent on women to fill at least some portion of its "manpower" needs. This need, along with political pressure and legal challenges, has forced military leaders to open up more job categories to women. Before the end of the draft, women made up less than 2 percent of the U.S. military. As of September 2010, women made up 13.5 percent of the Army (76,193 of 566,045), 16.0 percent of the Navy (52,546 of 328,303), 19.2 percent of the Air Force (64,275 of 334,196), and 7.5 percent of the Marine Corps (15,257 of 202,441) (Department of Defense 2010). Women comprise about 14.5 percent—roughly 208,000 service members—of an active duty force of just over 1.43 million. For so many women to be official members of an army (recognized as soldiers), and to be so when the state is not under a severe, direct military threat to its very existence, is historically uncommon. The presence of so many women has forced changes in military life, and it challenges the military's ability to confer masculinity on all of its members.

Masculine military cultures must also contend with changes in military functions. With the end of the Cold War, Western militaries have become more involved in "operations other than war." During the past twenty years, U.S. military actions have included peacekeeping missions, humanitarian aid, drug interdiction, and efforts to control ethnic cleansers.[4] Historian Linda Grant De Pauw points out: "In 1993, the army's basic operations manual, 100-5, introduced a separate chapter on 'operations other than war,' and began production of a special manual on peace operations. In March 1995, the National Military Strategy, the Pentagon's basic policy statement, added sustaining peace to the roles of American troops" (1998, 299). Changing military functions may change what types of masculinity are associated with soldiering. The idea of soldiers who "kill people and break things" may be dysfunctional for a military that is attempting to keep rival factions from violating a cease-fire agreement or training a national police force. Evolving international norms about how militaries should behave and growing concern for human rights may also alter the forms of masculinity that militaries encourage. For instance, a masculine sexualization of violence in military training can be problematic not only if sexual harassment of female fellow soldiers comes to be seen as unacceptable but also if rape of enemy women violates new ideas about rape as a war crime or if rape of local women is seen as an impediment to peacekeeping, counterinsurgency, or postwar reconstruction. War fighting itself changes, with the integration of new technologies and doctrines. Changing military roles and the inclusion of women don't mean that the military is becoming "emasculated" or ungendered; it means that military masculinities alter and new forms become dominant.[5]

In addition, different military roles can produce multiple forms of masculinity within a single military (Barrett 1996; Enloe 1988; Higate 2003; Morgan 1994). Barrett shows how officers in the U.S. Navy attempt to draw on different strands of hegemonic masculinity to validate themselves. While officers in general talked about discipline, perseverance, and toughness, naval aviators focused on their risk-taking behavior, and surface warfare officers emphasized their endurance of hardship and their ability to perform under pressure. Supply officers, who have lower status because their specialty is in the realm of support, not combat, and who are often denigrated as unmasculine by those in combat positions, try to frame their work as masculine in terms of their need to exhibit technical rationality and competence and their likelihood of achieving financial success in the civilian world. Connell (1985) outlines three forms of masculinity that have formed the basis of military organization. The first two interconnected forms—"physically violent but subordinate to orders on the one hand, dominating and organizationally competent on the other"—have been augmented by an increasingly important third type: "the professionalized, calculative rationality of the technical specialist" (Connell 1985, 9). This typology recognizes that not just masculinity but specifically military masculinity may take a variety of forms. Of course, the concepts that serve the functioning organization and those that are sold to potential members are not necessarily the same, and the three categories do not transfer neatly to the forms of masculinity used in military recruiting.

Many commentators (such as Leo 2001; Smart 2000; and Strother 1999), however, see military masculinity more monolithically, as the tough and aggressive warrior. In their eyes, when the military branches recruit or put out images of themselves, there is a masculine approach and nonmasculine approaches. The masculine approach, as exemplified by the Marine Corps, would be characterized by such visual markers as weapons and strong, unsmiling male bodies, either in postures of action or of rigid military bearing, as well as by ideals of physical toughness, testing oneself, and aggression. This failure to recognize any other masculine characteristics as appropriate to the military reveals anxiety about masculine roles and a desire, in the face of changing gender roles in the larger culture, to preserve a traditional ideal of masculinity in an institution that has been so important to the construction of masculinity.

The Crisis in Masculinity

Beginning in the early 1970s, around the time of the inception of the all-volunteer force, the perception began to spread that American manhood was in crisis. The growing women's movement, the defeat in Vietnam, the deindustrialization of the economy, and with it the loss of well-paying manufacturing jobs that could allow working-class men to be breadwinners all contributed to the idea that men could no longer be certain of their status or their roles.[6] The next few decades saw an outpouring of popular and academic literature on the problems of men and the uncertainties they faced. In 1973, George Gilder proclaimed in *Sexual Suicide* that if men lost exclusively male roles to the women's movement, the result would be the breakdown not just of the family but of society as a whole. Some profeminist men, like Marc Feigen Fasteau (1975), argued that men needed to dismantle the old concepts of masculinity because stereotypes of manhood damage men, cause them to cut themselves off from their emotions, and lead to misogyny, violence, and war. In 1979, in the introduction to his book on the history of masculinity in the United States, *A Man's Place: Masculinity in Transition*, historian Joe L. Dubbert could look back over the previous decade and see a new concern with masculinity and male roles. As one sociologist put it in 1987, "That men today are confused about what it means to be a 'real man'—that masculinity is in 'crisis'—has become a cultural commonplace, staring down at us from every magazine rack and television talk show in the country" (Kimmel 1987, 121). Best sellers ranging from Susan Faludi's *Stiffed* (1999) to Robert Bly's mythopoetic *Iron John* (1990) to *Real Men Don't Eat Quiche* (Feirstein 1982) have all proclaimed, in their own way, the insecurity of men's roles.

Anxiety over masculinity, to put the current crisis in context, is nothing new. Kimmel (1996) has shown that masculinity has repeatedly been in crisis when large-scale social transformations have affected institutions that undergird masculinity, like the economy and the family. In Kimmel's description of American masculinity, masculinity has always been troublesome—both difficult to achieve or to definitively prove and in a state of flux and uncertainty. Throughout our history, Americans have intermittently worried over the meaning of manhood and the virility of the nation, looking back on the era of their fathers as a time when the path to manhood was supposedly more certain, clear, and secure.[7] The present has always been a struggle and the past a golden age; "the search for a transcendent, timeless definition of manhood is itself a sociological phenomenon—we tend to search for the timeless and eternal during moments of crisis, those points of transition when the old definitions no longer work and the new definitions are yet to be firmly established" (Kimmel 1996, 5).

Kimmel argues that the periods when manhood has been thought to be threatened "were also crisis points in economic, political, and social life—moments when men's relationships to their work, to their country, to their families, to their visions, were transformed" (1996, 10). The responses to crisis have followed a general pattern: "American men try to *control themselves*; they project their fears onto *others*; and when feeling too pressured, they attempt an *escape*" (9). Elaborating on these responses, Kimmel explains:

> To some men, masculinity became a relentless test, demanding that it be proved in increasingly physical demonstration. From 19th-century health reformers to contemporary bodybuilders, some men have pumped up to regain lost confidence. Others have actively resisted women's equality; from 19th-century anti-suffragists to VMI cadets and promoters of "men's rights." . . . And finally, others have simply run away, escaping to some pristine homosocial world, whether mythic or real, as an all-male solace against encroaching dissolution. When the going's been tough, the tough have run away. (2005, xi)

There is also a fourth possible response: to attempt to resolve the crisis in masculinity by supporting equality for women. Some men have joined each struggle for women's rights "because they saw that gender equality was the only way that they, too, could live the lives they said they wanted to live—as men" (Kimmel 2005, xii).

One of the biggest crises in American manhood came at the end of the nineteenth century, in a situation with some economic and social parallels to the period when the all-volunteer force came into being:

> Three coincident processes shifted the terrain upon which manhood had been traditionally grounded—an unprecedented level of industrialization; the entry into the public sphere of large numbers of women, newly freed blacks, and immigrants; and the closing of the frontier—and the meanings of manhood were once again uncertain. The combined impact of these processes led many men to

feel frightened, cut loose from the traditional moorings of their identities, adrift in some anomic sea. By the last decades of the century, manhood was widely perceived to be in crisis. This fin de siècle crisis of masculinity was a popular theme for critics and experts. All agreed that it was increasingly difficult to be a real man. Who was a man? What did manhood mean? How could one tell that he was a real man? (Kimmel 1996, 78)

One of the major responses to that crisis was to create a new frontier through imperialist expansion (in 1898 the United States annexed Hawaii, the Philippines, Puerto Rico, and Guam) and to revive American masculinity through militarism. War was a potential way to reinvigorate a population that had grown "effeminate" through peace, office and factory work, and city life (Kimmel 1996, 111–112).

While the military was a way to salvage American masculinity in the years before World War I, in the post-Vietnam years, the military was itself a part of the problem, and the figure of the soldier in need of redemption. J. William Gibson (1991) argues that Americans have traditionally linked their military victories to moral superiority, and the U.S. defeat in Vietnam "created a cultural crisis in American national identity" and "raised fundamental questions about the dominant political and military paradigm of how war should be conceptualized, organized, and fought" (182). During the same period, civil rights and black nationalist movements questioned the racial practices of domestic society and U.S. foreign policies in the Third World, and the women's movement challenged traditional gender roles and the split between a masculine public sphere and feminine private sphere, giving new grounds for a critique of the military: "War as a particularly male activity, as opposed to a nongendered 'public' policy, became subject to scrutiny" (183). The combined impact of these social movements was "a serious challenge to traditional male military values," making the 1970s "a time of deep crisis for the cultural reproduction of war and the warrior" (183).

But while the military was discredited and a component of the masculinity crisis, by the late 1970s and into the 1980s, many men were turning to the military as a way out of the crisis and a means of escape. Men weren't, for the most part, literally enlisting in the U.S. armed forces; however, they looked to militarism as a redemption of masculinity. Gibson identifies two cultural strands that sought to redeem America's loss in Vietnam and "restore the nation's cultural heritage as the land of good men who always win" (183). In one, a paramilitary hero, like Rambo, goes outside the bureaucratized constraints of military structures to achieve victory.[8] According to these representations, politicians and military bureaucrats had restrained the military might of the U.S. soldier in Vietnam, leading to defeat, so the paramilitary hero exists outside of those bounds. In the late 1970s and through the 1980s, paramilitary culture was celebrated in "scores of movies, televisions shows, men's 'action-adventure' novels, magazines, war games, 'combat' shooting and 'mercenary' or 'survivalist' training schools, and the militarization of the domestic civilian arms market" (184). Within this culture, the warrior is "a gender ideal for all men; every man could be a warrior and should be prepared to fight his own private war against domestic and foreign enemies" (184).[9] While the paramilitary culture challenged military institutions and celebrated the individual warrior's skill over high-technology warfare, the other type of cultural production that tried to heal the wounds of Vietnam, the "techno-thriller" (as typified by Tom Clancy's novels), did validate the military and capital-intensive warfare by contrasting the values of Western society with those of the Soviet Union. The power of the Western forces comes not only from their technology but also from the organization of the military men into "extended male families" (188) that link the men through bonds of emotion and filial obligation. Susan Jeffords (1989) also argues that in the 1980s, cultural representations of the war in Vietnam, in the form of books, movies, and television shows, sought to heal the wounds of the loss of that war and "remasculinize" America.

In 1980, Americans elected Ronald Reagan to be their president, a man who was hostile to feminism (he actively opposed the Equal Rights Amendment), who was willing to stand up to communism and to use military force, and who declared it was "morning in America." He was photographed on his ranch, riding his horse and chopping wood. Reagan exploited the heroic myths of the American West and used displays of physical strength symbolically (Norton 1993). As Kimmel puts it, the 1980s was a decade "of the reassertion of pride, the retrieval of political and metaphoric potency for America and, hence, for the American man. In a replay of the frontier cowboy myth, America was once again sitting tall in the saddle" (1996, 291).

Still, for many men, the sense of crisis continued into the 1990s. The 1990 publication of Bly's *Iron John*, a lament for distant fathers, lost male initiation rites, and ancient masculine archetypes, was followed the next year by Sam Keen's *Fire in the Belly*, about men's need for new spiritual rites and new ways of defining their identities without looking to women for approval. As Kimmel notes, "All across the country in the first few years of the 1990s, men [were] in full-scale retreat, heading off to the woods to rediscover their wild, hairy, deep manhood" (1996, 316). Also in 1990, football coach Bill McCartney founded the Christian men's group the Promise Keepers, which held emotional rallies in football stadiums, where men were encouraged to—gently and lovingly—become the leaders of their families. While Bly worried about the wounds caused by distant fathers, and McCartney called on men to take their place at the head of the family, public attention began to focus on the role and importance of fathers. "Fatherlessness" became a politically charged concept and a subject of social policy (Daniels 1998). This concern over fatherhood in the 1990s "indirectly [expressed] profound male gender anxiety about the erosion of received definitions of masculinity" (Stacey 1998, 57).

Malin (2005) argues that the form of masculinity that was culturally dominant in the 1990s was a conflicted, hybrid masculinity that combined sensitivity with toughness. President Bill Clinton could be seen as the archetype for this form of manhood: "Sensitive to our pain, but tough on crime; wealthy graduate of Yale, but down-home Arkansas boy," Clinton's conflicted masculinity embraced "a kind of new, sensitive nontraditional masculinity at the same time that it sought to demonstrate a powerful, thoroughly established sense of 'real American manhood,' the sort conventionally depicted in advertisements for pickup trucks by Ford, Dodge, and Chevy" (Malin 2005, 7).

While Malin sees hybrid masculinity as conflicted, Steve Niva (1998) describes a similar form of masculinity as an emerging ideal. According to Niva, the 1991 Gulf War was a turning point for American masculinity, finally putting to rest the ghosts of Vietnam and ushering in a "new world order" masculinity "that combined toughness and aggressiveness with some tenderness and compassion" (111). A benevolent United States would lead the post–Cold War world, upholding international law and serving as a model of democratic government and enlightened gender relations.[10] While enemies in wartime are conventionally feminized, in this war, Saddam Hussein was portrayed as hypermasculine. American manhood, by contrast, was progressive and sensitive, as well as tough, and America's military might was also advanced and technologically sophisticated, allowing U.S. soldiers to project lethal force while also, supposedly, sparing innocent lives with their precision. Niva argues:

> In addition to emphasizing the contrast with Saddam Hussein and his regressive model of manhood, the new hegemonic vision of U.S. masculinity also accentuated the technological and civilizational superiority of the U.S. military and society. The military's new "technowar" paradigm for capital-intensive, high-technology warfare highlighted the differences between economies and political systems and, thus the superiority of Western men over other men. The old John Wayne image of the warrior was replaced by blending the technologically sophisticated heroes of Tom Clancy's "technothriller" novels with the megamasculine Rambo. Infantrymen took a backseat in war coverage to computer programmers, missile technologists, battle-tank commanders, high-tech pilots, and those appropriately equipped and educated for new world order warfare. (119)

Technological power in service of benign might and strength tempered with compassion make the American man and his new form of manhood the putative superior to his rivals.

While new world order masculinity was coming to the fore on the stage of global politics and war, global markets and economics formed another arena for the development of a transformed masculinity. In 1998, Connell suggested that a new hegemonic model of masculinity might be developing among managers in the global corporate economy, and he named this emerging pattern "transnational business masculinity." Like older forms of business masculinity, the new form "is involved in exercising and legitimizing collective power, institutional power, and personal authority in the workplace," but it also includes "a self-conscious modernity in relation to nationality, sexuality, and gender" and a "conscious endorsement of gender equity" (at least in theory, if not in practice; the vast majority of international managers are male) (Connell and Wood 2005, 359). It also includes "an uncertainty or provisionality" about the position of men in the world, both in terms of men's position vis-à-vis women and the place of individual men within corporate structures, where no loyalty binds employer and employee, and one's job, no matter how well paid, is never secure (360). As a response to uncertainty, the businessman treats both his body and his life as things to be managed; he views himself as a corporate entity or enterprise and applies the types of reasoning used in the office and in business decisions to his personal life. Both transnational business masculinity, which is linked to an economic elite, and new world order masculinity, which is specifically tied to and grows out of the U.S. military, may, like other models of masculinity, be sources on which military recruiters can draw or against which they can measure military service when crafting their appeals for recruits.

This discussion of masculinity, its relationship to the military, and the playing out of the crisis in masculinity since the early 1970s is not meant to be exhaustive, but rather to provide some background for the coming chapters by showing the context in which the U.S. armed forces faced the prospect of attracting volunteers and the complexity of that task; masculinity and the military are closely interrelated, and the AVF commenced in a period when masculinity was in flux, in part because of the military loss in Vietnam. However, while military masculinities were to some degree discredited in the immediate aftermath of that war, militarism—perhaps in some new form or associated with different masculine characteristics—was still a potential way to redeem or reinvigorate American masculinity.

THE MILITARY, CITIZENSHIP, AND GENDER

One reason that the military should be considered a vital subject of study for political scientists is that it has a special relationship both to masculinity and to the nation and citizenship. The military stands not only at the nexus of the domestic and the international but also at the nexus of citizenship and gender, helping to create a gendered conception of citizenship. In the United States, except for the military, every aspect of citizenship, including voting, holding office, and jury duty, is formally accessible to women on the same terms as to men. The military, however, remains fundamentally gendered as masculine because of the exclusion of women from ground combat and the resulting requirement that only young men are obliged to register for Selective Service and a potential draft.[11] The military has also institutionalized a heterosexual idea of citizenship, since homosexuals have been barred from serving or from serving openly in the era of "don't ask, don't tell" (which was coming to an end as this book was being written). This, too, however, is tied to gender. The gay ban was in large part about what constitutes proper manhood, and as Cohn (1998) argues, it helped to preserve the masculinizing function of the military.

After the American and French revolutions, the mass army made up of citizens came to replace the mercenary system, and with this democratization of war, the nation and the military were linked. In various national contexts, participation in the military has been a requirement of citizenship. The mass citizen army may only come into being at rare moments; in practice, the military may be a separate class from the rest of society. Since the democratization of war, however, the relationship between the people and the military has come to matter, and the appropriate link between a democratic society and the people who defend it is a subject for debate. In the United States, only a small percentage of the population ever dons a uniform, but since the revolution, Americans have been worrying over the proper relationship among the people, the military, and the state.

The founders of the American republic were committed to the idea of the citizen-soldier as a safeguard against tyranny. The mobilization of citizens to defend the republic, a form of self-rule, would prevent the ills of a standing army, engage the citizen in civic practices, and inculcate the citizen-soldier with the virtues required for responsible citizenship in the republic. Under the Militia Act of 1792, every free, white, able-bodied male citizen was required to enroll in his state's militia.[12] Citizen-soldiers were of questionable military utility, and military reforms, beginning with the Dick Act of 1903, nationalized the militias and then transferred men's military obligations from their local communities to the nation, but the citizen-soldier concept lingered on, even into the all-volunteer force.

At the conclusion of the Peace of Paris in September 1783, at a ball to celebrate the establishment of the United States of America, Sarah Livingston Jay, wife of treaty negotiator John Jay, offered the following toast among others: "May all our Citizens be Soldiers, and all our Soldiers Citizens." According to historian Linda Kerber (1990), "American men, listening to the toast, knew they were citizens and might be soldiers; . . . American women, however, upon hearing the toast, knew that they had fought for and supported the revolution in many ways but as yet were denied full rights as citizens" (90). The survival of the American republic had depended on the willingness and ability of men to fight; "the connection to the Republic of male patriots (who could enlist) was immediate; the connection of women, however patriotic they might feel themselves to be, was remote" (92). Military service and citizenship were conceptually linked from the beginning of the republic, and since then, various groups—African American men, women, gays and lesbians—have fought to participate in the military on an equal basis with white men, in order to claim the rights and benefits of both service and of first-class citizenship.

Since the Revolutionary War, fighting in the armed forces has been a way to earn American citizenship, and naturalization has been used as an incentive for immigrants to serve. In the United States, the welfare state's beginnings lay in the Civil War pension system, a benefit based on military service (Segal 1989, 80), and through much of the twentieth century, major social benefits, like educational assistance, were tied to military service (2–3). The Twenty-Sixth Amendment to the U.S. Constitution, which lowered the voting age to eighteen, was justified on the grounds that the young men between eighteen and twenty-one being drafted to fight in the Vietnam War deserved a political voice. In addition to the relationship between service and voting, Americans have presumed that military service makes one worthier of a public voice, and veterans have particular clout in national security debates. Participation in war is considered to be good preparation for political leadership. According to Charles Moskos, "For at least the first three decades after World War II, military service (or at least a very good reason for having missed it) was practically a requirement for elective office," though the end of the draft and the unpopularity of the Vietnam War weakened this view (1993, 86). As Sheila Tobias notes, "To be sure, women have made great strides in politics, but they remain handicapped because men have one insurmountable advantage—experience in war—that matters a great deal in politics" (1990, 164). Tobias found that whether men participated in popular wars, like World War II, or unpopular wars, like Vietnam, wartime military service has a great deal of political value. Aside from the duty and heroism represented by war service, participation in war, especially a morally questionable one such as Vietnam, leads to "moral ripening" that is a qualification for political leadership. After Vietnam, even prisoners of war, who could be considered unsuccessful warriors, and veterans who protested the war could use their experience as political currency: "While the parameters of heroism may change, the basic phenomenology appears to remain the same: war is the vital playing field, the grooming ground for politics" (167).

The United States entered World War I during a period of activism in the struggle for women's suffrage. Prosuffrage women recognized the connection between military service and the rights of citizenship, and many of them took the opportunity opened to them by the Navy to serve in the Naval Coast Defense Reserve Force, in the hopes that it would bolster their claims for voting rights. In March 1917, Secretary of the Navy Josephus Daniels received a postcard that made that link:

> I am sure your proposal to recruit women in the U.S. Navy will meet with great success. The women in this country are eager to do everything they can to help the government—and they are also anxious to become citizens of the U.S.A. I hope you will help women to get the vote and women will show what they can do. "Women are people." (Quoted in Ebbert and Hall 1993, 8)

The active role of women in supporting the war, including the work they did in factories, helped them win support for the Nineteenth Amendment.

In the years before President Truman signed Executive Order Number 9981, which declared a policy of racial equality (a policy which was not immediately or easily implemented), African Americans (mainly men)[13] were at times excluded from service entirely and at times allowed to serve in segregated and/or menial positions. During World War II, civil rights organizations demanded the "right to fight" (Moskos and Butler 1996, 29). This demand was both a claim to the rights and obligations of citizenship and a claim to the privileges of manhood. African American men, in asserting a right to fight, were proclaiming their masculinity and their equality to white men.

The literature on citizenship and military service from the past several decades has mainly been concerned with the effect of the end of conscription. Surprisingly, most of this literature ignores questions of gender, although the end of the draft has important consequences for gender. State armies do not, as a general rule, draft women.[14] Conscription ties all males to the military and makes men, as a group, ultimately responsible for the security of the state. Women may be allowed to volunteer in some form or another, but their service is not required. Ending conscription, so long as both women and men can volunteer for service, breaks the automatic link between masculinity and soldiering. Professional armies allow for the inclusion of greater numbers of women and on more equal terms.

The literature on citizenship and military service frequently expresses concern that service is no longer viewed as an obligation but only a possible economic choice. Commentators fret over the composition of the forces, in terms of socioeconomics and race, and over how society is impacted when middle- and upper-class young men don't serve. With the end of the draft, concerns over who participates and issues of civic obligation are a matter of concern, but only in relation to men. That this whole question of civic obligation completely excludes the half of the citizenry not subject to the draft, women, is basically a nonissue. For example, Charles Moskos asks "what has been lost?" as the end of the draft has led to new attitudes toward service and a differently composed military:

> The answer is simple. Universal military service was the one way in which a significant number of Americans discharged a civic obligation to their nation. If this fact is obvious, its significance has been obscured by a political culture that

ignores the importance of individual obligations while virtually enshrining individual rights—possibly to the detriment of our civic health. Universal military service did something else: It brought together millions of Americans who otherwise would have lived their lives in relative social and geographic isolation. No other institution has accomplished such an intermingling of diverse classes, races, and ethnic groups. (Moskos 1993, 87)

Moskos sees great value in compulsory military service but implicitly argues that the participation of women isn't necessary to the achievement of this social good. He talks about "Americans" and "universal" service, without any acknowledgment that "American" means only American men, and "universal" isn't.[15]

Similarly, in discussing the demise of the actual citizen-soldier (even if the ideal continues), Eliot Cohen paints a picture of the diversity of earlier forces:

The true army of citizen-soldiers represents the state. Rich and poor, black and white, Christian and Jew serve alongside one another in similarly Spartan surroundings—at least in theory. The idea of military service as the great leveler is part of its charm in a democratic age, one of whose bedrock principles is surely the formal equality of all citizens. The voluntary military, by way of contrast, is very rarely representative. To be sure, in the contemporary United States recruiters attempt to maintain some rough balance among ethnic groups, although even here it is clear that minority groups are overrepresented. Recruiters pay no heed, however, to socioeconomic, religious, or other kinds of ethnic diversity in the ranks. That the children of millionaires almost never serve or that a bare handful of Ivy League graduates don a uniform is not even a matter for comment. (2001, 24)

Rich and poor, black and white, Christian and Jew, but not male and female. The concern for diversity and formal equality is, without being acknowledged, only among men. (Elsewhere in the same article, Cohen makes an offhand reference to "the inevitably male-oriented world of military service" [25].) In terms of gender, the all-volunteer force, with its greatly increased participation of women, becomes more representative of society, not less, but this isn't seen to have value, the way that the mingling of various classes of men does. The discussion of women's participation still centers on their potential liabilities or whether they have a right to greater opportunities, not whether they have an equal responsibility, leaving intact the concept of a masculinized citizenship obligation.[16]

The questions of whether citizens/men should be compelled to fulfill a military obligation to the state and of how much the military should "look like America," in terms of race and class or in terms of gender, are part of a larger debate over whether the military, in a democracy, needs to itself be concerned with issues of democracy, citizenship, and citizen participation and civic engagement, or whether it simply needs to protect that democracy from outside threats. James Burk (2002) delineates these two main approaches, which can be associated with Morris Janowitz (1960) and Samuel Huntington (1957), respectively. In Huntington's view, civilians should decide on the objectives of security policy and then allow the military to decide autonomously how to fulfill those objectives. Janowitz, on the other hand, was concerned with preserving the citizen-soldier ideal in an age when war no longer requires the participation of the majority of (male) citizens but rather a large, standing professional force. Janowitz believed that military service "demonstrated and enhanced one's citizenship, and fulfilling the obligation [to serve] improved democratic life," and so he argued for a national service program, including military service, that would give (male) youth a chance to serve and participate. He was also concerned that "professional soldiers continued to think of themselves as citizen-soldiers rather than as mercenaries or just another politically partisan occupational pressure group" (Burk 2002, 11–12). So, "the liberal theory, underwriting Huntington's work, is primarily concerned that civil-military relations preserve the military's ability to protect democratic values by defeating external threats," while the "civic republican theory, underwriting Janowitz's work, is primarily concerned that civil-military relations sustain democratic values—especially the value of civic virtue—by bolstering civic participation through the citizen-soldier's role" (12). The question, then, is whether the military itself needs to advance and embody the values of society. In the era of the AVF, this has played out in debates over whether the military should engage in "social experimentation" with the integration of women and gay people, potentially threatening military readiness (as those in the Huntington camp might put it), or whether a commitment to equality and democratic values requires concern about who participates in the military, whether the issue is the expansion of participation or the racial and socioeconomic makeup of the force. It can also lead to questions about how the military should present itself, what picture of service it should project, and what types of people it should attempt to appeal to in its efforts to recruit.

There is political competition over who should serve and what service means—whether there is a right to fight and all groups must have equal access in order to reap the benefits of service, or whether the military (or technically, Congress, acting to protect the military's interests) may put restrictions on service to best serve the cause of military readiness. The images that the military branches put forward in recruiting materials provide some answers to this question through the kinds of people they show and how they show them. More broadly, the military branches make choices about how to portray military service and the link between service and citizenship, including whether service is specifically gendered, either as masculine or also as potentially feminine, and if so, in what forms. The next section of this chapter describes the inception of the all-volunteer force, which forced the service branches to make these choices and to articulate conceptions of military service in recruiting materials.

THE ALL-VOLUNTEER FORCE

For much of its history, the United States experienced cycles of mobilization and demobilization, with large recruitment efforts and conscription during periods of war, followed by a fairly rapid demobilization to a small peacetime standing force. Between the two world wars, the United States fielded an all-volunteer force that was the largest peacetime army in the nation's history up to that point, but it was still small by today's standards; the National Defense Act of 1920 authorized a maximum force of 280,000 for the Army, though enlisted strength remained far below 200,000 until 1940 (Griffith 1982, 22).

After World War II, the U.S. role in the world, the growing Cold War rivalry, new technologies like nuclear weapons, and a new dependence on air power meant that the United States needed a larger peacetime standing force than it ever had before. Although the new technologies vastly reduced the number of men needed to wage war, they altered war's time frame. While past conflicts had allowed time for a small standing force to be built into a mass army, new international challenges and new forms of warfare required a quick response and a larger force in being. To man that large standing army, except for a period from April 1947 to June 1948, American men were subject to a draft from World War II to 1973. However, while the United States needed a larger standing force than ever before—more than 2 million men on active duty for most of the period and higher numbers during the Korean and Vietnam conflicts—the changes in warfare also meant that truly mass mobilization wasn't necessary, and only a small portion of the draft-eligible population was actually needed for service. A mass mobilization on the scale of World War II was an unlikely future prospect. Large numbers of draft-motivated volunteers enlisted to exercise control over when they served and to get their choice of service. These volunteers, along with an expanding population of draft-age men, kept draft calls low. (Conscription was more important for motivating enlistments than for actually producing draftees.) Because few conscripts were needed, deferments expanded—for certain occupations, for education, and for family responsibilities. Because of the deferments and the ability of local draft boards to select inductees, by the early 1960s, the draft was coming to be seen as inequitable. Based on the shrinking number of call-ups, being called to serve through conscription came to be seen less as an ordinary, expected obligation and more like bad luck. In 1964, when Barry Goldwater was seeking the Republican presidential nomination, he promised to end the draft, and President Johnson ordered the Department of Defense to conduct a study of the draft. If not for the Vietnam War, conscription might have ended in the mid-1960s (Segal 1989).

During the Vietnam War, call-ups increased, along with opposition to the draft. After World War II, new technologies required that military personnel meet higher mental aptitude standards. The results of aptitude tests tended to correlate with socioeconomic status, meaning that many poor young men were considered unfit for service. The poor who did qualify were more likely to be drafted (and this includes a disproportionate number of African American men, since African Americans are disproportionately poor) because they were less likely to be eligible for educational and occupational deferments. Once drafted, poorer inductees were also more likely to be channeled into combat forces, and thus more likely to be wounded or killed, than those with stronger educational backgrounds who were more likely to be given jobs requiring technical skills (Segal 1989). Socioeconomic factors may have driven conscription and casualty trends, but there was a perception among African Americans, who had earlier pursued the right to fight, that they were unfairly bearing the costs of this war. Concern over the unfairness of the draft increased. In 1966, President Johnson appointed a commission to make recommendations on reforming the system, and that same year various other conferences on the draft were also held to consider possible alternatives, including an all-volunteer force. In 1967 and 1968, Congress limited educational deferments, and in 1970, the power to select inductees was taken away from local draft boards and replaced by a national lottery. By 1969, draft calls were beginning to decrease with the Vietnamization of the war, which shifted the military burden from the U.S. forces to the Army of the Republic of Viet Nam, the South Vietnamese forces.

Richard Nixon made a campaign promise to end the draft, and after being elected, he appointed the Gates Commission to develop a plan for instituting a volunteer force. The Gates Commission presumed that a marketplace philosophy, focusing on soldiers' pay and benefits, could attract recruits (Griffith 1996, 35–36). Many military sociologists were opposed to the idea that economic incentives would be the basis for service. They feared that traditional service values would be undermined, and they argued that if military service came to be seen as just another job, it would be bad for the military and for society, leading to a mercenary force disconnected from American society and values. Charles Moskos (1982), for instance, was concerned that the military was shifting from an institutional framework to an occupational one. An institution "is legitimated in terms of values and norms, i.e., a purpose transcending individual self-interest in favor of a presumed higher good. Members of an institution are often seen as following a calling, captured in words like 'duty,' 'honor,' and 'country'" (137–138). An occupation, by contrast, "is legitimated in terms of the marketplace. . . . Supply and demand rather than normative considerations are paramount" (138). Soldiers in a volunteer force would be motivated by self-interest and feel no sense of identification with the institution and its purposes; the notion of citizen obligation would be undermined.

The Gates Commission rejected such arguments. It claimed that military compulsion undermined patriotism and respect for government more than a force that allowed individuals to freely choose service. Volunteers were not mercenaries, and the choice to serve was based on many factors, including a sense of duty; no one had claimed that career officers were mercenaries (Rostker 2006, 79). Nixon accepted the commission's findings and asked Congress to change the law. Congress approved the AVF in 1971. The draft was set to expire in July 1973, but draft calls had been declining, and all of the forces were preparing for the volunteer force. By January of that year, conscription had ended.

The AVF appeared to be a success in its early years. Military pay was comparable to entry-level civilian wages, and youth unemployment was high, making the AVF an attractive option, despite young people's reservations about the military in the wake of the Vietnam War. During this period, however, the demographics of the military began to change. The Gates Commission had claimed that ending the draft wouldn't change the composition of the force. They were mainly talking about issues of race and educational background. The Gates Commission hadn't even considered the possibility of expanding the recruitment of women. The commissioners assumed that women would continue to make up less than 2 percent of the military and even discussed replacing many of the positions that women tended to fill, like clerical jobs, with civilian workers to reduce costs (Binkin and Eitelberg 1986). The volunteer force succeeded in large part, however, because of the increasing participation of African American men and of women. According to military sociologist David R. Segal:

> With unemployment particularly high among young black males and with the women's movement coming to regard the military as a channel for mobility, enough people were brought in. Contrary to the expectations of the Gates Commission, however, the social composition of the force did change. It became increasingly dependent on the poor, the black, and to a lesser extent, women. (1989, 38)

The end of conscription and these demographic shifts had potential ramifications for the relationship between military service and masculinity, and for the specific constructions of gender, and masculinity in particular, that the military branches create and deploy. The link between masculinity and the military was potentially weakened: women became a more regular part of the force, men were no longer automatically linked to service by conscription, and military service was also less associated with middle- and upper-class white males, the group of men that, due to its privileged social position, is most likely to be associated with hegemonic masculinity. However, the association has deep historical roots, and with the end of both the draft and the Vietnam War, the military would get the chance to rebuild and to craft portrayals of itself that could remake the connections between service and masculinity, perhaps on new terms. The differing ways that each of the services attempted to do this are explored in the chapters to come.

In addition, while the military became less relevant for elites, the military branches began to make a concerted effort to attract other men and to take advantage of their needs and desires, constructing masculine ideals that could be locally hegemonic in the process. The military can attempt to shape both wider cultural conceptions of military service and those of particular groups. In discussing the postdraft relationship between masculinity and the military, it's also important to note that even if only a portion of eligible young men actually enlist, and even if those of the highest socioeconomic status are unlikely to consider enlisting, the military can still help to define masculinity in society. The young men who don't join the military are still exposed to a large amount of recruiting advertising, along with other representations of the military that can have an impact on their understanding of the military and their ideas about masculinity. As noted earlier, men who don't serve may still enjoy consuming various cultural productions tied to the military (which can include not just books, movies, games, and clothing but also recruiting commercials), in large part for their associations with masculinity. Even men who resist the military's masculine norms may still use the military as a negative referent, the representative of a culturally dominant idea of masculinity *against* which to define themselves.

Another potential effect of the transition to a volunteer force was that the marketplace model of service embraced by the Gates Commission could affect ideas about masculinity in the larger culture or within targeted groups. The military's role as a standard-bearer of masculinity means that its acceptance of free-market values could help make the aspects of masculinity related to earning more socially prominent and those tied to collective values less so. In other words, if recruiting materials emphasize individualism, rationality, and career advancement over duty and honor, this may help make masculinity related to those concepts hegemonic. In fact, the service branches have drawn on a variety of masculine attributes, including those associated with individual economic advancement.

Since those early years, the AVF has gone through periods when recruiting faltered, quality dropped, and some called for a return to conscription. Funding for military pay and benefits has also risen and fallen. In 1996, General Maxwell A. Thurman delineated several distinct eras of the AVF. The first AVF, from 1973 to 1976, was the period of transition and initial success, and it came to a close with the end of the GI bill. The second AVF, from 1976 to 1979, was marked at the end by the failure of all the services to achieve their recruiting goals. Military pay and benefits had begun to fall behind those of entry-level civilian jobs, and for several years, the scoring system for the Armed Forces Qualifying Test was miscalibrated, and a large number of unqualified recruits were allowed into the military, degrading the quality of the force. This period saw calls to declare the AVF a failure and return to the draft. The forces rebounded during the third AVF, from 1979 to 1983. This period included an increase in military pay and the introduction of the Army College Fund but also a reduction in the resources devoted to recruiting. The fourth AVF, from 1983 to 1991, ended with the fighting of Desert Storm and the beginning of force reductions. Thurman characterized the fifth AVF, the period during which he wrote, as a time of reduced forces, reduced recruiting resources and little advertising, a lower recruiting mission, regional threats, and peacekeeping missions (Thurman 1996).

In the years after Thurman's analysis, the AVF again faced major recruiting shortfalls. In the late 1990s, all of the forces except the Marines struggled to meet their recruiting quotas. The recruiting shortfalls were blamed on a number of factors, the most important of which seemed to be a healthy economy and low unemployment rates. Media coverage also attributed recruiting problems to a drop in the recruitable population of eighteen- to twenty-four-year-olds; the increasing propensity of young people to go to college and the growth of nonmilitary sources of educational assistance; a cohort whose fathers came of age after 1973 when the draft ended or whose parents may have developed negative feelings toward military service during the Vietnam War; a lack of direction, purpose, and leadership in the armed forces; longer deployments and more work for members of the downsized military; and an erosion of military tradition and changes in military culture, including expanded roles for women and the perception that gays were being permitted to serve under the "don't ask, don't tell" rule.

Discussions of the military's recruiting problems during this period often focused on the military's culture and whether the military, in integrating women and performing operations other than war, had undercut its war-fighting ethos and abilities and become too soft to attract young men, and possibly also to still be an effective fighting force. The Marine Corps, which continued to meet its recruiting goals as the other services faltered, was held up as an example for the other services to emulate. The Marine Corps is the smallest branch of the service; it has the smallest percentage of women (less than 8 percent) and the fewest jobs open to them. Although the recruiting materials of the other three services have often highlighted the tangible benefits of service, the Marine Corps has emphasized challenge, elitism, and self-transformation, using overtly masculine imagery and celebrating war fighting. While a variety of solutions to the recruiting crisis were posed, including targeting recruitment efforts and advertising more efficiently, emphasizing service and patriotism, developing more distinct "brand identities" for each of the services, accepting lower quality recruits, shortening terms of service, and changing economic incentives and retirement benefits to better fit with the times, many commentators (e.g., Bonat 1999; Keene 1999; Smart 2000; Strother 1999) argued that the other services should be more like the Marines and appeal to a masculine, warrior spirit. They blamed recruiting problems on a demasculinization of the other branches.[17]

Some academics took this view as well. Military historian Martin van Creveld (2000) linked recruiting shortfalls to a degradation of the military caused by women. Elliott Abrams, a political scientist and former assistant secretary of state, and Andrew J. Bacevich, a political scientist and former Army officer, didn't blame women for the recruiting trouble but looked to masculinity as a solution. The two cochaired a conference, "Citizens and Soldiers: Citizenship, Culture, and Military Service," in 2000. Based on the discussion at that conference, they made a number of suggestions (reported in Abrams and Bacevich 2001), including that the military overtly use claims about masculinity to improve recruiting:

> In a society in which male adolescents find it increasingly difficult to discern what it means to be a man or how to become one, we should *promote military service as a rite of passage to manhood*. Young males yearn to leave boyhood behind and to become men. But in a society in which fathers are increasingly absent, in which gender roles have blurred, and in which adolescents increasingly trade activities once thought to be "manly" in favor of becoming mere spectators, opportunities for the individual to demonstrate to himself that he is indeed a man have dwindled. The rigor and purposefulness of military service can offer just the opportunity to do a man's work, something that the Marine Corps has long recognized and effectively exploited. The other services and above all the Army need to do the same. There are more than enough men out there to fill the services' needs. [Emphasis in original.] (22)

Brian Mitchell, a strong opponent of women in the military, writing before the late-1990s problems about the AVF more generally, goes so far as to argue that the military would have no problem meeting recruitment goals if women were excluded from the armed forces, not just from combat-related roles, but entirely. Like many of the women who have fought for increased opportunities in the military, Mitchell rejects the distinction between combat and noncombat roles as artificial. He argues that in today's gender-confused culture, young men would flock to an all-male military, more than enough to make up for the loss of female labor:

> The AVF might still exploit the need for young American men to prove themselves, and easily make up the number of women now in service, if it aggressively portrayed itself as a place for men only. By highlighting its integrated aspects

> and aggressively pursuing young women, however, the AVF is actually working to eliminate any remaining attractions that the military might hold for young men. Recruiting commercials with cute coeds bragging about being "airborne" are guaranteed to turn away men more effectively than they attract women. Men simply do not aspire to be women or to emulate women, and whatever women are, men will seek to be anything other. (Mitchell 1989, 218)

Mitchell implies that military recruiting highlights gender integration, targets young women, and features them as military personnel. There is a fairly common assumption (Gutmann 2000; Strother 1999) that the armed forces, in a bow to political correctness, are using women to represent themselves to the public. As the coming chapters show, this is not a highly accurate portrait of recruiting advertising. Many of these same commentators who laud the Marine Corps' approach make reference to the slogan "We're looking for a few good men"; the Marines have occasionally used the phrase in advertisements, but they stopped using it as their regular slogan in 1976. The commentators who still refer to the sentence as the Marines' slogan seem to think it's what it should be. There is sometimes a difference between what the services are doing and what people assume or fear they are doing, and it reveals their anxieties about the links between the military and masculinity.

Those who extol the masculine approach of the Marines may really be bemoaning the decline of the cultural power of a particular form of masculinity and the rising dominance of other varieties (business related, tied to technology, hybrid forms like Niva's new world order masculinity). There is an idea that the military should remain the bastion of a certain form of masculinity—one whose characteristics include physical strength, aggression, courage, toughness, and a willingness to sacrifice for others that will be rewarded with special privileges—even and especially if that form is no longer dominant outside the military. It is a desire for a masculinity that seems more certain and more truly masculine; it involves nostalgia for a time when masculinity was supposedly more secure and men's prerogatives less endangered by women's demands. The culture wars over the military involve an effort to fix a gender order that has been in flux and to use the military to shore up a version of masculinity under threat. The military branches, however, need to appeal to young men growing up in the post-Vietnam, post–women's movement, post-industrial gender order, and so they draw on a variety of masculine constructions to appeal to a wide range of these young men and to serve their own specific needs.

CHAPTER 3
The Army

This chapter examines how the Army, the largest of the service branches, has confronted the challenge of recruiting a volunteer force. Over the course of the all-volunteer force (AVF), the Army has frequently made economic appeals, showcasing service as a path to economic security and upward mobility. Army recruiting ads have offered good jobs, technical training, and, increasingly, access to professional careers. Army recruiting materials in the second half of the AVF have sometimes forged links between civilian careers and militaristic imagery. In addition to promising the excitement of military action, these ads bring together more traditional forms of military masculinity with newer, business-world forms of masculinity that are gaining prominence in the larger culture. In this way, I would argue, the Army is making a bridge between the older forms of masculinity with which Army service had been associated and forms that are becoming hegemonic in the civilian world, a bridge that serves both to revitalize Army masculinity, making it seem more up-to-date, and to validate the business world as a source of status and prestige for young men.

The Army has also promised character development and personal transformation, developing a soldiering masculinity that involves young men testing and proving themselves. While this form of masculinity relies on the traditional warrior trope of facing a challenge and demonstrating strength and courage, and it involves displays of weaponry and other visual markers of warriorhood, the Army's version of soldiering masculinity is accessible and personified by "regular guys." As fits a military branch that needs to attract large numbers of recruits, in the Army, manhood seems to be a goal within reach of the average young man. The Army, more so than any other service, has also created many ads—especially those touting specific educational benefits—that could be read as gender neutral. In addition, the Army has used images of women more frequently than the other services and has gone the furthest in framing them as normal, unexceptional members of the institution, though they are never associated with the still fully masculinized realm of ground combat.

This chapter provides some background material on the Army's culture and how the Army was positioned going into the all-volunteer force, before presenting an analysis of the recruiting materials and the forms of masculinity they construct. The source materials include 150 print advertisements published by the Army between 1970 and 2003, twenty-one television commercials that aired between 1980 and 2003, and two different incarnations of the Army's recruiting Web site. The chapter also examines how the Army genders women's military service in recruiting materials, while giving a brief history of women's participation in the Army.

ARMY CULTURE

Beneath any changes undergone by the military branches with the transition to the AVF, each service has retained central elements of a core culture and institutional worldview. The influential RAND military analyst Carl Builder explored the "enduring personalities" of each of the services. According to Builder:

> The altar at which the Army worships is less apparent than the altars for the other two[1] services. That may be because its ideals are more diffuse or variable or subtle. Several consistent themes surface, however when the Army talks about itself: They have to do with the depth of its roots in the citizenry, its long and intimate history of service to the nation, and its utter devotion to country. . . . Of all the military services, the Army is the most loyal servant and progeny of this nation, of its institutions and people. If the Army worships at an altar, the object worshiped is the country; and the means of worship are service. (1989, 19–20)

The Army is the service branch that sees itself as the most closely tied to the citizenry, however citizenship is defined at any given historical moment. More important than the Army's self-perception here may be that the Army's links to citizenship, through the citizen-soldier ideal and the Army's ties to the militia system, may make it the biggest political target of the armed forces in the competition over the meaning of military service or for concerns about who serves. Discussions of military service often focus on the Army and soldiers, rather than on the other branches. The Army is the branch most emblematic of military service; within common usage, the generic service member is a soldier, that is, an enlisted member of the Army. It is the biggest

[42] *Enlisting Masculinity*

service, and it needs to attract the most recruits each year. (The numbers shift depending on the authorized end strength and how many soldiers reenlist but have been somewhere in the range of 70,000 to 90,000 new recruits each year during the AVF.)

Builder also claims that the Army is more concerned with people—how many of them it has and their skills—than with hardware and technology. The Army divides itself into the three traditional combat arms: infantry, artillery, and armor. The three combat arms are a source of pride and identification, but intraservice competition among them is minimal, and the three branches on the whole recognize their dependence on one another. Another division within the Army is more salient in terms of status, power, and promotions. According to Builder: "In the Army, the basic division is between the traditional combat arms (e.g., infantry, artillery, and armor) and all others, who are seen in (and fully accept) support roles to the combat arms" (1989, 26). This has had a significant effect on the status of women within the Army. The Army privileges the combat arms over supporting roles, and women are prohibited from serving in direct ground combat. Women as a group are excluded from what the Army perceives as its core function and what is certainly its main source of prestige.

Gender integration is still an issue for the Army, as it is for all of the armed forces, but during the AVF, racial relations have been less of a problem. African American men have fought with the Army in every major American conflict (as well as on the British side in the American Revolution), generally in segregated units under white leadership, often in menial positions, and usually with a great deal of controversy. However, in the years since President Truman ordered the desegregation of the military, the Army has made the greatest strides in achieving integration and equality. Moskos and Butler (1996) characterize racial relations in the Army as a relative success story in comparison with the larger American culture. According to the Center for Strategic and International Studies:

> The Army routinely receives high marks in human relations. Since its slow start in the early 1950s, the Army has become a model for the other services in the successful integration of racial minorities into its ranks and promotion of minority officers. Fully 40 percent of the active Army is composed of minority personnel, and 21 percent of the active Army's officer corps comes from minority populations. (2000, 11)

African Americans have found better opportunity and more of a meritocracy in the military than in the civilian world and have entered the volunteer Army in disproportionate numbers. In the 1970s, some military observers worried that, as seemed to be the case with integration of neighborhoods, once the Army reached a certain tipping point of 30 to 35 percent black, in an occupational version of white flight, young white men would no longer enlist (Nalty 1986, 339). These fears proved to be unfounded—white men's propensity to enlist has had much more to do with their prospects in the civilian economy than with the racial makeup of the force. Recruiting ads regularly depict African American men, both on their own and as part of groups of soldiers.[2]

THE RECRUITING BACKGROUND

The U.S. Army, surprisingly, has a more limited recruiting history than either the Navy or the Marine Corps. This is mainly because for much of U.S. history, a substantial federal force came into being only for specific, brief periods of time. In the early years of the American republic, military service was tied to local militias and state, not federal, government. In 1784, after the Revolutionary War, Congress discharged George Washington's Continental Army, except for "twenty-five privates to guard the stores at Fort Pitt and fifty-five to guard the stores at West Point, with a proportionate number of officers," none of whom could hold a rank higher than captain (Millis 1956, 46). The states were responsible for recruiting, training, and arming their militias, and in times of national emergency, the federal government called on the states to provide troops, both conscript and volunteer, for a national army. This system created a host of problems during times of conflict, but it lasted through the nineteenth century (though for a period during the Civil War, there was a federal draft). A small, national Army that ranged in size from about 5,000 to 10,000 volunteers manned frontier posts and fought Native American Indians during the periods when the country was generally at peace in the years before the Civil War, and 25,000 to 35,000 men did so in the period afterward.

From 1919 to 1940, the United States had a peacetime standing Army, manned by volunteers. As the Army began recruiting that force after World War I, it turned to paid advertising to attract recruits. The Army placed ads in the "help-wanted" sections of newspapers, and a typical ad read: "Men Wanted for Enlistment in the U.S. Army from 18–40 yrs. of age for a 3 yr. period with every Opportunity to Earn, Learn, & Travel" (quoted in Griffith 1982, 31). Army posts offered educational and vocational training to enlistees, including classes in agriculture, mechanical arts, and academic subjects (33). In March 1920, the War Department launched a major recruiting campaign:

> The campaign, patterned after wartime bond rallies, sought to combine patriotism with the functional benefits of army service. In a telegram to all recruiters General Harris said that the campaign would "insure immediate recognition that the Regular Army is not only in theory but in fact a part of the Nation and not a thing apart," and that the result "will make not only for the welfare of the Army's lasting benefit, but for the welfare of the nation as a whole." (Griffith 1982, 37)

The drive failed, and the Army learned that patriotic appeals didn't work well in peacetime—service benefits were the draw (38–39).

In the 1920s, the economy was strong and enlisted pay low, and the Army had trouble finding enough recruits (a lesson, perhaps, for the critics of the all-volunteer force who blamed the recruiting shortfalls of the late 1990s on a degradation and demasculinization of military culture). During that decade, the Army "built athletic facilities, theaters, recreational centers, and, beginning in 1929, improved barracks in an effort to increase service attractiveness," but it took the stock market crash and Great Depression to solve recruiters' problems (Griffith 1979, 172). An "A-Board" recruiting poster from 1931 shows the range of inducements that the Army used to attract recruits (reprinted in Mitchell 1967). Over the course of four panels, a young man and a recruiter talk about the benefits of Army life, next to a series of changing Army posters, as the young man's suit transforms into a soldier's uniform. In the first panel, the young man says he's "always wanted to see more of the world before [he] [settled] down," next to a poster advertising travel in the Army. The second panel includes a poster that says "Earn and Learn in Army Schools: Qualify for a Better Job!" In the third panel, the recruiter lists the tangible benefits of Army life: "good food, quarters, clothing, and medical attention in addition to pay of $21 to $157.50 monthly," while the poster in that panel says "Retire at Middle Age." In the final panel, the civilian, now wearing a uniform, shakes the recruiter's hand and agrees to serve, next to a poster that proclaims "The US Army Builds *Men*." Travel, education and advancement, pay and benefits, and manhood were all bases of the Army's recruiting appeal.

In the early 1970s, the U.S. Army once again had to attract recruits to a volunteer force. The end of conscription posed the biggest challenge to the Army. Of all the services, the Army was the most reliant on conscripts, it needed the largest number of recruits each year, and it suffered from the worst reputation, even aside from the antipathy generated by the Vietnam War. The Army had an authoritarian, institutional character that was typical of a military service; the other military branches had similar natures, but they were mitigated by other factors that made those services more attractive to enlistees. The Air Force had its technology, the Navy offered the romance of life at sea, and the Marines were the most macho service, while the Army was considered "tradition-bound and routinized" by its own personnel, who considered the Air Force the "most modern and glamorous of the services" (Moskos 1970, 18). Military sociologist Charles Moskos reports:

> Attitudinal surveys conducted during the Cold War period showed Americans consistently giving highest prestige to the Air Force followed, in order, by the Navy, Marine Corps, and Army. These surveys also found specific stereotypes associated with each of the services: Air Force, technical training and glamour;

Navy, travel and excitement; Marine Corps, physical toughness and danger; Army, ponderous and routine. (1970, 18)

As the Gates Commission, appointed by President Nixon, studied the creation of an all-volunteer force, the Army quietly conducted its own study of how it could meet its manpower needs in the absence of a draft. The study, known as Project Volunteer in Defense of the Nation, or PROVIDE, uncovered some disturbing news for the Army:

> One of the fundamental revelations of the PROVIDE study was the extent to which the Army's public image had declined. Butler's group cited surveys which indicated that veterans rated the Navy and Air Force ahead of the Army as the service of preferred enlistment and that the general public and educators ranked the Army last. More troublesome was the discovery that 70 percent of Army veterans advised prospective volunteers to join services other than the Army. Given such attitudes, the study group concluded, rebuilding the Army's public image was a prerequisite to achieving an all-volunteer force. (Griffith 1996, 22)

The Modern Volunteer Army Program attempted to make life in the services more attractive, with such changes as relaxed haircut regulations, an end to hated KP (kitchen police) duty, and dormitory-style rooms instead of open barracks, and it tried to highlight those changes in the media. The Army also developed various service options, like training guarantees and delayed entry. In anticipation of the all-volunteer force, the Army began advertising heavily in the beginning of fiscal year 1972 (summer 1971). In addition to the specific pitches, the Army tried more generally to rehabilitate its image. To demonstrate that it was changing, the Army adopted the slogan "Today's Army Wants to Join You,"[3] and ads told potential recruits that the Army "wants to accommodate" them.

THE RECRUITING ADVERTISEMENTS

Over the course of the AVF, Army recruiting has followed several different tracks, allowing the Army to appeal to different sectors of the population. Each type of ad has recurred during the AVF, though the prominence of each type has shifted as the economy has changed or the Army has had new benefits or programs it could advertise. All of these categories, which are illustrated and discussed in detail later, draw on different sets of masculine models and characteristics. The concept of hegemonic masculinity posits that various forms of masculinity exist within any gender order (Connell 1987), and the Army implicitly makes use of this. Different styles of masculinity may be salient to different subgroups of men, so by deploying several forms of masculinity, the Army may be able to attract men from a variety of groups that it finds desirable. A given advertisement may use more than one type of appeal or may not fall clearly into one category or another. In general, however, the ads either follow the economic track, promising economic independence and security or upward mobility and the chance for advanced training or a college education (which can provide access to hegemonic forms of masculinity for a working-class population),[4] or they offer character development and personal transformation, developing a soldiering masculinity that makes reference to traditional warrior traits like strength and courage but in an accessible, unaggressive form, softer than that offered up by the Marine Corps; less frequently, and mainly in television commercials rather than print ads, they follow a service and patriotism-oriented track, which allows the potential recruit to imagine himself in the traditional role of the protector.

The 1970s

Economic benefits have always been part of the appeal of military service when it has been done on a volunteer basis, and this was certainly the case with the all-volunteer force. In the early 1970s, most Army ads promoted benefits, money for education, skills training, and good jobs. In addition to emphasizing jobs and benefits, they feature regular guys hanging out together. In fact, they make explicit references to "the guys." Many show smiling, approachable young men in civilian clothes. Some of the ad headlines from this period that reflect this benefits-based approach read as follows:

> "Now the Army starts you at $268.50 a month. And you may not even have to spend it."
> "We've got over 300 good, steady jobs."
> "We'll pay you $288 a month to learn a skill."
> "The job you learn in the Army is yours to keep."
> "Lots of people have jobs we taught them."
> "Mike, Leroy, Rocky, Vince and Bunts are taking the Army's 16-month tour of Europe. Together."

Throughout the 1970s, some portion of the ads published talk about specific benefits like the Project Ahead program, which allowed soldiers to attend college while they served, or about jobs and skills training. These ads show soldiers doing various kinds of work, and most of these ads also make some mention of less tangible perks, like challenge or pride. The Army is presented as a place for a young man to get his start in life by developing his character and learning a skill or getting ready to go to college. The Army is a place to become a man but not in the sense of an initiation rite—more in the sense of growing up, becoming responsible, gaining an economic foothold, and maturing.

While most of the ads at the inception of the AVF focused on benefits and economics, a small number of ads from the early 1970s, and more from the mid-1970s, use more overtly masculine enticements and fall into the character development and soldiering masculinity track I identified. An ad from 1973 mentions the Army's new Adventure Training program. It pictures an expanse of desert, with brush and a cattle skull in the foreground and mountains in the background, next to the heading: "You get 12 matches, a knife, some twine, and 3 days to enjoy yourself." The ad promises an exciting adventure that allows a soldier to test himself, though, it's important to note, the ad makes it clear that this type of adventure is an option, not a requirement. (It's another way the Army is being accommodating; this isn't the Marine Corps.) An ad from the same period focusing on Airborne says, "When you jump, it's just you," and it talks about "the jolt in your gut." Another ad features the M60-A1 Tank under the title "Think Enormous," contrasting the size and power of the tank with a small, gas-efficient car.

In several ads from the mid-1970s, the Army appears as a place to serve, be challenged, and prove oneself. Basic training is presented as "8 weeks of physical and mental conditioning that'll push you to limits you never thought you could reach." Another ad warns recruits: "The Army offer reads well, but it doesn't come easy"; to be soldiers, they'll need "intelligence, courage, discipline, teamwork, pride in self and love of country." A third ad from this period refers to the pleasures of testing oneself against the Army's heavy equipment:

> Step on the throttle. And 750 horsepower jumps to your hand. Ahead is a 60° gradient of mud and rocks. Although your stomach wants to bail out, you're ready. You're riding in an M60-A2 tank. 54 tons of armored steel. Months of training, as rugged as the Texas terrain you're rumbling through, have put you here. Smack in the middle of our proving grounds. When you make it, you'll be a proud, proven member of Armor.

These ads promote a warrior masculinity, with their references to courage, ruggedness, and enduring physical challenges—attributes that Goldstein found to be associated with warriors and thus tied to masculinity across a range of cultures (2001, 266–267). Also, unlike the ads promoting benefits, with the exception of what appears to be a mother at her son's graduation from basic training, they show only men. The soldiering masculinity on offer, however, isn't extreme or intimidating. The "Think Enormous" and "12 Matches" ads both have a lighthearted tone, and the "Step on the throttle" ad uses explicitly masculine language and pictures two men in a tank, but the men, while militarized, don't look fierce—they are smiling at the camera (see figure 3.1).

> Somehow you get the feeling it's not the tank they're testing.
>
> Step on the throttle. And 750 horsepower jumps to your hand. Ahead is a 60° gradient of mud and rocks. Although your stomach wants to bail out, you're ready.
> You're riding in an M60-A2 tank. 54 tons of armored steel. Months of training, as rugged as the Texas terrain you're rumbling through, have put you here. Smack in the middle of our proving grounds. When you make it, you'll be a proud, proven member of Armor.
> And you'll be earning rewards as exciting as the job. Good pay, travel, and in-service educational opportunities. For more information, write to Army Opportunities, P.O. Box 5510, Dept. 6AB, Philadelphia, PA 19143. Or call 800-523-5000 toll free. In Pa., call 800-362-5696.
>
> **Join the people who've joined the Army.**

Figure 3.1. Army ad reprinted from *Sports Illustrated*, July 28, 1975. Army materials courtesy of the U.S. Government.

In the late 1970s, the Army ran a series of ads in which a soldier reflects on a word. Those words include "Challenge," "Country," "Decision," "Drive," "Direction," "Discipline," "Growing," "Honor," and "Skill." Most of them show men in fatigues in an active role, performing some task. All of them also feature a small paragraph in the upper right corner titled "Pay & Benefits." These ads talk about a variety of intangible benefits that come from serving in the Army, mainly having to do with personal growth, accomplishment, and character development, though a few of them (like "Skill" and "Europe") are focused on tangible benefits. These ads combine approaches: some of the imagery and language offers a soldiering masculinity, while they also include an economically based appeal.

By the late 1970s, however, entry-level military pay began to lag behind civilian pay, and in 1976, the GI bill (an educational benefit) ended. The military had trouble meeting its recruiting goals (in 1979, the services were short 20,000 recruits, 7 percent of their target), and the quality of male recruits became a concern (Segal 1989, 39). Challenge and personal development were not enough to make potential recruits sign contracts under the highly unfavorable economic circumstances. After the recruiting failures of the "hollow Army" of the late 1970s, the Army developed a research program on the attitudes of young Americans, involving N. W. Ayer, the Army's advertising agency, the RAND Corporation, the Department of Defense's Youth Attitudinal Tracking Survey, the Army Research Institute, and the Military Academy at West Point (Thurman 1996, 60).

The 1980s

In 1981, the Army switched its slogan from "Join the People Who've Joined the Army" to "Be All You Can Be." N. W. Ayer also created several alternative campaigns, based on its research. In addition to "Be All You Can Be," the agency offered the slogans "The Advantage of Your Age—Join the Army," "Join Tomorrow's Army Today," and "Army—We'll Show You How" (Thurman 1996, 60). The Army introduced the "Be All You Can Be" slogan in a TV commercial. The debut ad is very slick, with constantly shifting images and a variety of camera angles, backed by a soundtrack featuring electric guitar. The ad shows a young, white, blond man in the final stages of putting on his dress uniform, lightly polishing a boot, buttoning his jacket, and adjusting a shining belt buckle, as details of the uniform are interspersed with shots of the soldier's face and a flag flashing over the screen. A voice intones:

> To most people, this is just a uniform, but to me, it's something more. Every time I put it on, it makes me feel better and stronger than I was yesterday. When I'm in this uniform, I know no limits. You've got to see the pride in my mom's eyes or the way my friends look up to me. But none of that matches the satisfaction I feel inside. That's the pride of being a soldier in the U.S. Army.

Then the voice of an announcer asks if the listener is "interested in wearing this uniform" and explains some of the benefits, including college money or an enlistment bonus. While the announcer speaks, the viewer sees shots of a young white woman and a young black man in uniform, tanks rolling, parachutists jumping out of a plane, helicopters, and soldiers climbing a net, paddling a small boat, and creeping along in combat gear. At the end, we hear the voices of the three individual soldiers saying that the Army can "bring out the best of what's inside you," before the announcer says, "Be all you can be." The ad mentions some of the new tangible economic benefits of service the Army could offer—a key factor in the rebounding of the AVF in the early 1980s—but, as fits the new slogan, it puts more emphasis on development and improvement of the self. The ad uses militaristic imagery, emphasizing the military aspects of Army life, not other potential types of work soldiers do, and the focus of the ad is a strong, handsome young man, looked up to by his friends. His dress uniform is an emblem of his difference from and implied superiority to his civilian counterparts; one of the roles that uniforms have historically played is to set soldiers off from other men while lending them a masculine prestige (Braudy 2003).

Another TV commercial, from 1983, that's part of this strand of soldiering masculinity shows a young African American man making a parachute drop with his unit. The soldiers collect their gear and then enjoy breakfast; the featured soldier greets the large man who pushed him out of the airplane at the beginning of the ad with a cheerful "Hey First Sergeant, good morning." A voice-over announces: "In the Army we do more before 9 A.M. than most people do all day." The Army's new jingle plays over most of the ad, with lyrics about "stretching out," having a "future to find," "reaching," and "growing."

While these ads offer a personal growth and development that's directly tied to soldiering, other ads from the period follow the economic track. A 1982 TV commercial shows a conversation between a father and son about the son joining the Army. A young man in a letter jacket talks to his father as the older man works in his TV repair shop. The father expresses some concern when the young man says he's joining the Army, because he thought the son was going to go to college and become an electrical engineer. The son says that he's still going to be an engineer; he'll be learning about electronics in the Army, and the Army College Fund will help pay his tuition, so that the son can help out the father for a change. The commercial ends with the father's acceptance and a hug. The Army is going to give the young man upward mobility, raising him from his TV-repair roots into engineering and letting him do it independently, without having to rely on his father. Here, the Army is offering economic advancement to working-class young men, with a subtle but distinct masculine undertone, communicated through the framing of the young man as an athlete, the machinery in the shop, and the emphasis on the father-son relationship. The Army gives the son independence from his father, and it enables him both to gain his father's approval and to rise above him in social class.

The Army had a new educational benefit to advertise, called the New GI Bill Plus the New Army College Fund, and in the print ads, it also returned to an emphasis on job training. Unlike the campaign of the early AVF, however, this time the Army was specifically marketing interesting, exciting job skills (as opposed to just a good trade) and advanced technology. These job opportunities included "96 Bravo," also known as intelligence, "one of the biggest mental challenges the Army offers," as well as "98 Golf" or signal intelligence, which is a soldier who "translates and analyzes foreign radio communications." The soldiers in these ads are all young men (with one exception, discussed in the section on women) wearing battle dress uniforms (camouflage) or, in a few cases, a service uniform, pictured with or using some type of military equipment, and they are all smiling, projecting competence, accessibility, and friendliness.

Some of the ads in this series that appeared in *Popular Mechanics* but not in *Life* or *Sport Illustrated* focus on the maintenance of military hardware, such as aircraft structural repair (68 Golf), avionic mechanics (35 Kilo), and helicopter repair (67 Victor), perhaps reflecting the idea that readers of that publication would be likely candidates for jobs that feature advanced technology but are also based on the traditional, blue-collar masculine skill of repairing machinery. Other ads that appeared in *Popular Mechanics* later in the 1980s also feature high-tech military hardware and forge a link between the fighting prowess of the military and the technical skills needed to keep the weapons working. For instance, one ad shows a photo of a helicopter under the title "the Army has the fiercest helicopter in the world," along with a mechanical drawing of the same helicopter with its weapons systems labeled and the tag, "here's what's in it for you." The ad promises: "It can see in the dark. And attack without being seen. Rain or shine, it can strike like lightning. It's fast, mean, and smart. But the Apache attack helicopter doesn't fly by itself. It needs trained experts to keep it at its most ferocious. You can be one of those experts." The ad features the technician, not the pilot, as the necessary human element. Not only does the ad indicate that the soldier will have expertise but also it associates that technical expertise with military ferocity, offering the readers of *Popular Mechanics* a masculinity tied to both technical skill and martial strength. The ads for these technical jobs in particular combine elements of the economic draw, with the Army promising good technical jobs and advanced training to people who might otherwise be mechanics, with a special military slant that imbues these jobs with a sense of power, importance, and military muscle.

In the mid- and late 1980s, the Army published ads that focus on upward mobility and promise that the Army helps soldiers decide what they want to do, as well as ads that feature the character development and, implicitly, the transformation into manhood that comes with facing challenges and testing oneself mentally and physically (development that will, incidentally, also help a soldier succeed in the world). For instance, in one ad, a member of a Ranger battalion explains, "If you can succeed as a Ranger, you're bound to succeed in life," because Rangers face mental challenges like overcoming fear, and they must train hard physically so that they can "move faster, go further, work harder." One of the ads in this series is notable for featuring a woman instead of a man. SP4 Michelle Kowalski of Signal Intelligence declares, "I thought I could test myself here. But I've practically reinvented myself." The Army took her on an "inner journey to [her] independence," letting her "find out what [she's] made of." Here, as will be discussed further, women, too, are given the chance to "be all [they] can be," and access to some traditionally masculine experiences, like proving oneself by meeting a challenge.

The 1990s

This theme of character development was generally linked to men, however, and to specifically martial images, and it continued throughout the 1990s. Images of soldiering are linked to characteristics like adventure, pride and confidence. A photo of soldiers rappelling down a rock face carries the headline "Meet the Greatest Challenge of Them All. Yourself." Another ad promises: "You'll be the one others look to. You will be a leader." Soldiers who drop out of a helicopter straight into water "swim in the deep end," with all the mastery that implies. These ads further developed the theme of soldiering masculinity grounded in self-development and the transformation of one's character.

The other major trend of the 1990s, one that I think is particularly significant for conceptions of hegemonic masculinity, was the linking of militaristic imagery to the idea of professional success. Many print ads combined a textual emphasis on civilian careers or, in a few cases, educational attainment, with explicitly martial visual references, such as camouflage-print backgrounds, weaponry, and soldiers in battle dress, often captured in a moment of action. One such ad is headlined "Before you start your career, it pays to learn the ropes" and goes on to claim that attributes sought by employers, like "Making decisions," "Handling responsibility," and "Working with others," are developed in the Army. The accompanying picture is of several soldiers dangling on ropes hanging from a helicopter (see figure 3.2). Several of these ads mention national surveys about the traits businesses look for. One calls the Army a "management training program that's been endorsed by hundreds of American companies." An ad that appeared several times in the mid-1990s says "The best place to start a business career isn't always in business." This phrase captions a picture of a man in battle dress in midair, leaping from one giant boulder to another, holding a rifle above his head, his mouth open in a shout. Several TV commercials also link civilian business-world success or educational attainment to imagery of military action. In one of the ads the Army broadcast during the summer of 2000, soldiers with camouflage face-paint rise out of the water with their rifles aimed in front of them; they ride a small watercraft into the open back of a helicopter, while the voice-over intones: "Someday, at a job interview, they'll ask, 'do you work well under pressure?' Try not to laugh." Masculinized, militaristic adventure is combined with civilian job prospects.

A few of the print ads specifically mention high-tech training or working with technology from the future, and they indicate that the recruit will be qualified for jobs requiring technical skills. Most, however, are looking for recruits to fill positions, like combat-oriented jobs, with no clear civilian counterparts. The Army is promising that these jobs will also lead to civilian-world success. Although he won't have learned a specific skill, the soldier will be prepared, because of the traits he's acquired, for the corporate world. These ads promise the excitement of military action, but they seem to recognize that while excitement and adventure are appealing, they may not be enough for a young man who would like to be able to compete in the business world and who looks to that world for models of status and success. (Those young men who are mainly interested in the combat aspects of service and see them not just as a type of adventure but as markers of status and success in and of themselves and an end in themselves may be more likely to join the Marine Corps.) These ads, then, bring together more traditional forms of military masculinity,

Figure 3.2. Army ad reprinted from *Sports Illustrated*, February 19, 1990. Army materials courtesy of the U.S. Government.

with their imagery of combat action, with newer, business-world forms of masculinity that had been gaining prominence in the larger culture (see Connell and Wood 2005); they conflate martial and corporate masculinities.

While most Army recruiting followed the two tracks discussed so far (economic and personal transformation), alongside the melding of the martial and the professional that the Army was promulgating, there was a third strand to the Army's approach: a patriotic appeal to service that put the soldier in the traditionally masculine role of the protector or defender. As both feminist Jean Bethke Elshtain (1987) and antifeminist Brian Mitchell (1989) would agree, serving as a protector of women (or of an idea of home or a set of values represented by women) and earning or demonstrating one's manhood by doing so are fundamental motivations for going to war. The soldier-as-protector theme is most directly exemplified in a late-1980s TV commercial titled "Freedom Isn't Free." Three types of images are interspersed: martial action (soldiers—all male—riding tanks, moving through rain and mud, running with rifles, and dropping out of helicopters), footage of civilians (kids getting on a school bus, a couple sitting on a car, a pregnant woman, Boy Scouts, a wedding, a boy in a football uniform, old men at a diner, guys playing basketball, a little girl with her hand over her heart), and patriotic scenery (a farm, a flag being raised, hands touching the Vietnam Veterans Memorial, and the Statue of Liberty). In the background, a song with the following lyrics plays:

> I'm from a town, where things are as good as they come, and it's pictured in my mind just as clear as the midday sun. Now I'm out here in the darkness and the rain is coming down, never was like this in my hometown. My hometown is not like this, but that's all right with me. See I'm out here for my hometown, 'cause freedom isn't free. We walk through the wind, we move through the rain, we ride the skies above to make this world a better place for the ones we love. And freedom, oh freedom, I'd gladly pay the price, 'cause you can't have your freedom without sacrifice. My home time is not like this, but that's all right with me. See I'm out here for my hometown, 'cause freedom isn't free.

This song lays out the protector role explicitly. The men suffering in the mud and wielding weapons make the idyllic American life possible.

Other TV commercials carried this same theme, though some of them pictured a few women as soldiers along with the men. The women do not do anything that appears combat oriented, though they might stand in formation or march. These ads tend to alternate between footage of soldiers, usually dramatically lit to help them appear heroic, with shots of civilians or idealized scenes of civilian life; often, the civilians form a literal appreciative audience at a parade. There may be stirring music in the background. In one commercial from the summer of 2000, the voices of soldiers intone a few of the lines from the soldier's creed, intertwined with the voices of individual civilians praising and thanking the troops. They say: "You are my brother"; "You are my sister"; "You are brave"; "And full of courage"; "You're my son"; "You are my daughter"; "You're a peacekeeper"; "You stand tall"; "You make me proud"; "You keep your promises"; "You keep me safe"; "You are my hero"; "You keep freedom alive." This 2000 version of the ad includes references to women and to peacekeeping but still frames soldiers as heroic protectors and thus implicitly as part of the masculine protector tradition.

This type of ad appeared much less frequently than the others, but it offered a distinct variant of soldiering masculinity. One print ad in the sample from the late 1970s and one TV commercial from 1987 called on the idea of the soldier as a defender in the Cold War context—both picture a soldier in Berlin. The soldier in the print ad talks about looking over at the "other side" at Checkpoint Charlie, which "gives a soldier a very clear sense of his duty—which in [his] opinion is to protect certain beliefs and a way of life." The rhetoric and imagery of the soldier as protector, however, is more fully developed after the 1991 Gulf War, which seemed to reinvigorate or relegitimize the idea that the American soldier plays this role, allowing recruiters to make use of it.

In addition to print ads and television commercials, in the late 1990s, the Army began to utilize the Internet as a recruiting tool. In the year 2000, the Army's Web site, www.goarmy.com, was built around the TEAMS concept: Training, Education, Adventure, Money, and Service. The section on training links the military and civilian job markets, focuses on technology, and makes occasional references to the excitement of combat roles. The Army claims:

> High-tech training makes our soldiers more marketable in an information-based society. Much of it is either directly transferable to a civilian career, or builds character traits that employers are looking for. So, basically, wherever a soldier wants to go in life, he or she can get there from here.

The page goes on to describe several specific occupational areas, including aviation, air defense, infantry, medical, armor, artillery, signal corps, and chemical. The description of infantry encourages the idea that we are moving into an age when the infantry soldier is above all a technologist:

> Soldiers toting M-16s, crouched in foxholes, shivering in the rain . . . that's the Hollywood image that probably comes to mind when you think of the Infantry. The truth is, today's Infantry soldiers are smart and very well trained. They use hand held computers to collect and relay data about their positions and that of enemy units to commanders miles away, all in near real-time. And as we draw closer to the 21st century and technology makes its way further into the field, infantry soldiers will be even better trained . . . for careers in the civilian world.

Air Defense Artillery soldiers sound a lot more like warriors. They "venture where the action is—up alongside our battle tanks," and they "prowl the battlefield in a Humvee-mounted Avenger, ready to unleash lethal Stinger missiles against intruding aircraft." The air defense occupational specialty offers up "a world of excitement and a crucial role to play on new millennium battlefields." In all of the four basic areas (Combat Arms, Combat Support, Combat Service Support, and Health Services), however, the Web site notes how skills in each specialty can be transferred to the civilian world or, where there isn't a direct correspondence, how employers appreciate the traits acquired. Military service can either be understood in terms of advanced technology and success in the information-based economy or in terms of the excitement and adventure that can be linked to combat and to soldiering masculinity.

While adventure (the "A" in TEAMS) comes generally from "facing new challenges, being awed by their magnitude and overcoming them," the Web site gives the specific examples of basic training, which all recruits will experience, Infantry, Army Rangers, Airborne, Air Assault, and Parachute Rigger. The education page describes several educational programs available to recruits, and the money page talks about bonuses and benefits. The final component of TEAMS, service, doesn't receive much attention—it merits only three paragraphs. Those three paragraphs, however, frame the soldier as a protector who "stand[s] between our nation and anything that threatens its freedom" and is "the one the nation turns to in times of need." The brief section also talks about tradition; about the code of "Duty, Honor, Country"; and about badges, medals, and insignia, which "remind soldiers of the values their unit holds sacred, the victories it has won and the pride that comes with serving." With its brevity, and its bringing together of so many broad concepts with so little discussion or explanation of them, this page implies that the job/benefits/economics and excitement and adventure themes are what service is really about.

By the end of the 1990s, the Army, along with the Navy and Air Force, was struggling to meet recruiting quotas. In fiscal year 1999, the post–Cold War troop level reductions, which had masked recruiting problems from 1993 to 1998, came to an end. In those years, the Army had failed to meet recruiting missions, but these failures were "forgiven" in relation to the mission requirement numbers by applying them to the annual reductions required by the drawdown (Hauk and Parlier 2000). In 1999, the Army's recruiting goal was 74,500 soldiers; it fell short by 6,290.

The 2000s

In January 2001, in an effort to turn around the recruiting situation, the Army radically altered its public face when it retired "Be All You Can Be" and rolled out a new advertising campaign, created by Leo Burnett USA, built around the slogan, "An Army of One." The Army hoped to counter the perceptions of young people that soldiers are, as an Army public relations official put it, "nameless, faceless people in green uniforms crawling through mud" (Leo 2001, 13). The Army wanted to encourage the idea that young people have the chance to be a part of something larger than themselves, while still retaining their individualism. Although Secretary of the Army Louis Caldera claimed that the campaign would de-emphasize benefits, the

Army also coined a secondary slogan, "212 ways to be a soldier," which refers to the number of training specialties that are potentially open to recruits. To enhance its brand identity, the Army also created a new logo, a white star outlined in gold and black.

In the debut TV commercial, a soldier jogs in the desert as the voice-over narrates:

> I am an army of one. Even though there are 1,045,690 soldiers just like me, I am my own force. With technology, with support, with training, who I am has become better than who I was. And I'll be the first to tell you the might of the US Army doesn't lie in numbers. It lies in me, Corporal Richard Lovett. I am an army of one, and you can see my strength.

The ads appeared during the NBC sitcom *Friends*, Fox's *The Simpsons*, and WB's *Buffy the Vampire Slayer*, as well as on cable stations MTV and Comedy Central. The bulk of the Army's TV advertising had traditionally been broadcast during sporting events and during football games in particular. By debuting the ads on *Friends*, the Army hoped "to help broaden its audience and also shake off its stodgy male-only image" (Dao 2001). The Army bought airtime on Spanish-language TV networks Univision and Telemundo as well. With this campaign, the Army began making a concerted effort to reach out to Hispanics (a politically questionable term, but the one used by the U.S. military). Hispanics have been underrepresented in the military, and as they've become a larger share of the U.S. population, the Army has become concerned with finding ways to reach this sector of the market (Clemons 2005; Porter 2002). In addition to broadcasting ads in Spanish, the Army coined a bilingual slogan for the campaign, "Yo Soy el Army" ("I Am the Army"). Several of the advertisements in the campaign—which use real soldiers instead of actors—feature soldiers from a variety of ethnic and racial groups. Corporal Lovett of the first TV commercial comes from a Panamanian and Native American background (Dao 2001).

The new slogan met with a great deal of derision. An editorial in the *VFW, Veterans of Foreign Wars Magazine* criticized the slogan on the grounds that "defying logic, it makes no appeal to the foundations of service: camaraderie and patriotism" ("Army's New Slogan" 2001). (Of course, the "Be All You Can Be" slogan was based not on camaraderie or patriotism, but on self-development, putting the focus on what the Army could do for the recruit more than what the recruit could do for his country.) Critics pointed out that the military is based on group work and unit cohesion, not individuality (Derbyshire 2001; Garfield 2001a). John Leo of *US News & World Report* complained about the new campaign's (and along with it, the Army's) de-emphasizing of masculinity, in contrast to the Marines' approach. He claims that the decision to debut the ad on *Friends* instead of during the Super Bowl was not based on the age range of the viewers of each, but on another reason:

> The Super Bowl features macho males, while the Clinton administration has been working for a gender-fair, androgynous Army that seems to downplay aggressiveness and bravery as too macho. (Even weapons may carry a new stigma. So far, no soldier has been shown carrying a gun in the "Army of One" ads.) Meanwhile, the Marines, who have no trouble meeting their recruitment goals, keep stressing the old values. (Leo 2001, 13)

Despite this criticism, the ads in the campaign show no softness. The print ads use a dark visual palette and are framed in the stark black and gold of the new star logo. And while most of the ads show the head and shoulders of a soldier, some do show weapons. One ad from the summer of 2001 shows the upper body of a soldier, identified in small print at the top of the page as Sgt. Joseph Patterson, Enlisted Liaison Operational Forces Interface Group. He is encased in body armor, his face is obscured by a helmet, and he holds a rifle. It is a stark image in shades of gray and black, without any text infringing on the image. Small print along the side of the photo says: "What you see is a Soldier system that gives me 360 vision in pitch black. Makes me invisible to the naked eye. Lets me walk up a mountainside. And run in a desert. You've never seen anything like me. But don't worry. They haven't either. I AM AN ARMY OF ONE. And you can see my strength." It's an image of a faceless, impenetrable military machine that presents a technologized warrior masculinity, and it's more hard-edged and aggressive than most of the ads in the sample. There is a second version of the ad that shows Sgt, Patterson, viewed from below, in an action shot, leaping with his weapon pointed in front of him. Other ads show a Bradley armored vehicle "blasting through a sandstorm" and Special Forces soldiers in snowy terrain. A minority of "Army of One" ads show a warrior masculinity (and one that, if anything, is harder than earlier versions used by the Army), but it is still one strand of the Army's approach.

Some ads in the campaign seem like a clear continuation of the character development theme, with taglines like "Most job training teaches you how to make something. Mine taught me what I'm made of" and "This uniform didn't change me. Earning the right to wear it did." Other ads include a description of the pictured soldier's specialty. These may include advanced skills that seem sophisticated, implying high-level, important work. For instance, one ad that specifically mentions the Special Forces shows three soldiers in free fall, with text along the top stating "The HALO jump wasn't the hard part. Knowing which Arabic dialect to use when I landed was." This ad does not feature "aggressiveness and bravery," as John Leo complains, but it does feature a subtler masculinity that involves mastery of difficult intellectual skills, as well as taking for granted the physical prowess and courage required to jump out of an airplane.

Although the campaign faced a lot of criticism, its debut was considered highly successful—the Army recruited its yearly quota a full month early (shortly before the terrorist attacks of September 11, 2001). There was a downturn in the economy, which generally boosts military recruiting, but the Army claimed that the improvement in recruiting happened too soon to be attributed to the economy. There is usually a time lag before a rise in unemployment is reflected in recruiting (Teinowitz 2001).

The new ad campaign also included a redesign of the Army's Web site. The new site reflected the aesthetic of the Army of One campaign. Along with information on Army life and Army careers, it included several personal stories from individual soldiers and video segments following recruits through basic training, because research had shown that many potential recruits fear basic training. The site included downloadable wallpaper—pictures to use for the background of a computer's desktop—each of which featured a single stark image, including a parachutist, a tank, and a helicopter, with slogans such as "Become Your Own Force," "You Can See My Strength," and "16,600 lbs of Anti-Gravity." The Web site presented these images of power, but it also offered several profiles of recruits talking about why they decided to enlist, what they hoped to get out of the Army, and their concerns about basic training. The personalization of the Army experience through these individual soldiers and their hopes and fears makes the hard images in the wallpaper seem achievable.

Along with a more interactive Web site, the Army's revamped recruiting strategy included the development of a highly sophisticated video game, "America's Army," available free online (www.americasarmy.com). The Navy and Air Force have also provided games on their Web sites, but they are fairly simple, small-scale games, while "America's Army" is a long-form game to which players can devote hours. The initial version of the game, which debuted on July 4, 2002, includes a role-playing basic-training segment called "Soldiers: Empower Yourself" and a combat segment called "Operations: Defend Freedom," which allows various players to engage in virtual warfare together over the Internet. The game includes highly realistic details, particularly in terms of how the weapons look, sound, and function. It does not, however, aim for realism in the depiction of killing itself—deaths are indicated only by a red splotch (Hodes and Ruby-Sachs 2002). According to a description of the game in the *Nation*, "There are four combat missions included in the 'Recon' version of 'Operations': defend the Alaskan oil pipeline against terrorist saboteurs, safeguard an enemy prisoner of war, raid a terrorist training camp and cross a bridge held by enemy forces." In November 2003, the Army updated and expanded "Operations" into "Special Forces," in which players undergo virtual training and attempt to qualify for the Special Forces. Players who fail to achieve the status of Green Berets, "the masters of unconventional warfare," can play the game only in the role of indigenous forces, "local militants who are familiar with the mission area [and] help SF teams" (www.americasarmy.com/aa/intel/versions.php?id=12). Since then, the Army

[60] *Enlisting Masculinity*

has released several updates and new versions of the game with new missions and scenarios.

A "Frequently Asked Questions" page available on the early versions of "America's Army: Special Forces" claims that the game is not just focused on combat and is not about killing. However, in each version of the game, the characters are all combat soldiers of one kind or another, and much of the game seems to be about training for combat and learning to use weapons. The Web site lists the possible roles a player can fill in the game, assuming that he or she passes the virtual training required. The characters pictured on the "Squad Roles" are all portrayed as men. The skills, weapons, and role of each squad member are described, and each description contains a link to a description of the job on www.goarmy.com, the Army's recruiting Web site, merging the characters in the game with real Army soldiers. All of the squad roles in the game, with the exception of medic, are marked "closed to women" on the recruiting Web site.

The "America's Army" Web site includes an extensive collection of images (screen shots) from the game in a video gallery. The gallery from early versions of "America's Army: Special Forces" included groups of photos from twenty-seven different scenarios, such as "Blizzard," "Oasis," "Village," "Camp MacKall," and "Rifle Range." In all of the photos in all of the scenarios, the only female characters are in the "Combat Medic" section. These female characters are not players in the game, but characters that the players interact with, and they include a female instructor, female medical personnel, and a female receptionist, whom the players are told not to bother on their way out. While women may certainly play the "America's Army" game, the game focuses on male characters and glorifies combat soldiers.

The video game medium itself may affect its audience quite differently than other marketing tools used by the Army, such as print ads or television commercials. Cultural anthropologist Charles Piot describes some of the various theories about video games and violence, including this common view:

> Some scholars suggest that the bodily violence of video games performs the same role that scatological humor has long performed in boys' culture generally—allowing maturing males to explore what it is like to live in masculine bodies and to reject maternal constraint. Moreover, the "phallicism" of the characters—the weaponry that appends itself to and extends, often doubling the size of, the bodies of its predominantly male protagonists—is seen as providing a form of identification for an otherwise emasculated male suburban youth deprived of the old socializing institutions. (Piot 2003, 353)

This raises the question of whether violent video games are in and of themselves a source of masculine identification for young men, whether playing them gives the players a feeling of manliness or masculine bodily power, which the Army can then tie directly to soldiering through its video game. Piot himself, based on conversations with teenage informants, understands video game violence in terms of "bodies and agency":

> The body is experienced as detachable/combinatory and porous rather than bounded and whole, and the self as "intensity"—and site of intense action—rather than as "emotion." Living in an increasingly technologized cyborg culture where the boundary between human and machine becomes ever more blurred, these games play with the border not only between self and other but also between one type of self and another. In so doing, they offer players an opportunity to explore new subjectivities they find exciting and enhancing and they enable a re-imagining of human possibility and action in a post-contemporary world. (2003, 361)

In this case, the "re-imagining of human possibility and action" is linked to a figure that the player could one day inhabit in the nonvirtual world, the U.S. Army soldier. The pleasure of video game combat, of the melding of self with powerful, destructive (phallic) machines, is linked with the real-world role of soldiering.

Having described and analyzed Army recruiting over the course of the AVF and how recruiting materials construct several different strands of masculinity, while occasionally noting how women fit into or are absent from these tropes, the chapter now considers more directly how the Army genders women's military service in recruiting materials, while giving a brief history of women's participation in the Army.

WOMEN, THE ARMY, AND RECRUITING

As noted, of all the services, the Army faced the biggest challenges in fielding a volunteer force. As a result, the Army has been more willing than the Navy or the Marine Corps to utilize the services of women, and of all the services, the Army's recruiting materials have pictured women the most frequently. Throughout the AVF, the Army has tried to tempt women into joining by offering them equal opportunity, but it has also at times attempted to reaffirm the femininity of female soldiers. Overall, however, the Army is the service most likely to present women as a regular part of the institution.

In World War I, women served in the Army nurse corps but could not enlist in the Army, despite pressure from some women's groups like the Young Women's Christian Association and the Women's League for Self Defense. It was only because of severe personnel shortages that the War Department, with some reluctance, allowed Army posts to hire women for *civilian* positions (Holm 1992, 13–14). Late in 1940, as the war in Europe led to the reinstitution of male conscription, many women's organizations began lobbying for women to be a part of the mobilization. Congresswoman Edith Nourse Rogers—who had tried to gain benefits for the women who served overseas in World War I, all of whom lacked military status—introduced legislation in May 1941 to open the Army to women. After negotiation with the War Department, the resulting law, which finally passed in May 1942, created an auxiliary corps for women, the WAAC. The auxiliary status caused administrative and recruitment problems—the lack of full military status gave Army women fewer legal protections overseas and fewer benefits than male soldiers, making the other services' new women's programs more attractive in comparison—so, in 1943, the Women's Army Auxiliary Corp became the Women's Army Corp (WAC). The Army decided it would be highly selective and take only an elite group of women, requiring them to meet standards for moral character and technical skill or education that did not apply to men; it cherry-picked its first group of 400 white and 40 black female officers out of 30,000 applicants (Holm 1992, 22, 28).

The Army initially planned to recruit 12,000 women the first year and reach a maximum strength of 25,000 within two years, but there was an immediate rush to enlist; field commanders and agencies began requesting thousands of women, so the Army made quick plans to expand the program and even envisioned an eventual women's force of 1.5 million, an unrealistic goal that would hurt the program (Holm 1992, 30). With new civilian employment opportunities for women rapidly expanding and widespread resistance to women's participation in the military among both women and men, there was no way the Army could attain so many women without conscripting them (46). The WAAC/WAC was plagued with problems, from its initial auxiliary status, to inappropriate recruiting practices (hostile male recruiters stationed in recruiting offices in the worst areas of cities), to poorly designed and badly stocked uniforms, to a vicious slander campaign against the WACs, waged mainly by U.S. troops.

The Women's Army Corp was created with the idea that women would serve in a limited number of roles that were customarily filled by women in the civilian sector, such as clerical and administrative work. As manpower shortages increased, women began filling roles that had previously been considered unsuitable, such as radio operator and repairman, gunner instructor, parachute rigger, and engine mechanic (Holm 1992, 60). By the summer of 1945, there were about 100,000 WACs in uniform (and 57,000 Army nurses); virtually all of them were demobilized at the end of the war.

Looking ahead to a future conflict in which the United States might once again need to mobilize women, in 1948, Congress passed the Women's Armed Services Integration Act, which allowed women to serve in the active peacetime forces but limited their numbers to no more than 2 percent of the total force, capped the number of women officers at 10 percent of the 2 percent, limited the promotion of women, and denied spousal benefits to husbands. Military policies also prohibited women from having command authority over men.

Between World War II and the inception of the all-volunteer force, the only time the military attempted to increase the number of women in the services and aimed recruiting efforts specifically at them was during the Korean War. To reduce draft calls for men, the Pentagon decided in October 1951 that in the next ten months, it would try to add 72,000 women to the armed forces, increasing their numbers from 40,000 to 112,000. The Women's Army Corps was to grow from 12,000 to 32,000. President Truman kicked off the recruiting drive in November 1951. The campaign attempted to appeal to women's patriotism with slogans like "Share Service for Freedom" and "America's Finest Women Stand beside Her Finest Men" (Holm 1992, 151–152). The drive was a failure and came nowhere near its goals. Public opinion was turning against the war, and the services' pay and living standards were not competitive in a tight labor market. In addition, as Jeanne Holm suggests, "The public's attitude toward women serving in the armed forces had not mellowed since World War II. If anything, the frantic recruiting campaigns of 1951–52 had reawakened the old accusations of immorality and masculinity as attributes of women who joined the services" (153–154). Because soldiering has historically been tied so firmly to masculinity, women associated with militaries have been condemned either as unnaturally mannish or as camp followers of low moral character—women who have served militaries in support roles have often been assumed to be prostitutes (De Pauw 1998).

Throughout the 1950s and 1960s, the number of women in the military never came close to reaching the 2 percent limit mandated by Congress. The services were highly concerned with the quality of female recruits, holding them to higher educational, mental, and physical standards than the male recruits (Holm 1992, 154, 179). The range of jobs women could hold was seriously limited; by 1965, 70 percent of enlisted women performed clerical and administrative duties, and an additional 23 percent worked in a medical capacity (183–184). In 1963, the Army eliminated defensive weapons training from the women's basic training program when the M14 rifle replaced the carbine; Army trainers didn't believe women would be able to handle the heavier weapon (Morden 2000, 282). In that same period, members of the Women's Army Corps also stopped receiving the bivouac training that teaches soldiers how to live in the field. They did, however, learn how to apply makeup during their military indoctrination. Uniforms and hairstyle regulations aimed for a neat, feminine appearance (Holm 1992, 181–182). All branches of the military were highly concerned with the image of their women service members and the retention of their femininity. The limits on women's roles and the concerns about their appearance exemplify Cynthia Enloe's (2000) claim that military officials who rely on women's labor try to

[64] *Enlisting Masculinity*

harness it in ways that won't threaten masculinized military culture. Keeping women feminine and out of "male" jobs supports the masculinity of military men. The women who directed the WAC also enforced gender roles to make women soldiers more acceptable to both the public at large and to the Army men with whom they had to serve and to protect their reputations against charges of masculinity or promiscuity.[5]

The Army had no plans to send women other than nurses to Vietnam, but the commander of U.S. forces in Vietnam, Gen. William Westmoreland, wanted WACs assigned to his headquarters to help deal with the war's paperwork (Holm 1992, 209). Over the course of the war, about 500 WACs served tours in Vietnam. With resistance to the Vietnam War and the draft growing, in 1967 the Pentagon decided that it would increase the size of the women's programs for the first time since the Korean War by adding about 6,500 women. That same year, the 1948 legislation on women's integration was modified; some of the restrictions on the promotion of women officers were lifted, as was the 2 percent ceiling on women's participation. Both the Armed Services Committee and the Defense Department made it clear during the congressional hearings that the legal changes were not meant to change the type of jobs that women filled in the military or to expand their roles in any way (201).

As the military began to explore how it might successfully achieve an all-volunteer force, it looked to women as potential substitutes for male draftees. The 1969 Army study known as PROVIDE, Project Volunteer in Defense of the Nation, found that to increase the number of women serving, the Army would have to change the image of the Women's Army Corps. Lieutenant Colonel Jack R. Butler wrote: "Although today's women are ranging further into fields of employment previously reserved for men, they hesitate to enter military service" because of "traditionalism by parents, males, and women themselves" (quoted in Griffith 1996, 190). Butler recommended a publicity campaign that would demonstrate to women that "their true value to the service is not that they are capable of replacing men, an unfeminine connotation, but that they are women and the feminine touch is required to do the job better." It would also emphasize that in the Army, women and men receive equal treatment when it comes to pay, benefits, and responsibilities (190–191). Women were limited to certain jobs, but military pay and benefits are determined by rank and length of service, so within the larger framework of the extreme restrictions on their careers, Army women were, indeed, formally equal to men.

In response to an order by the secretary of the Army to reduce dependence on male soldiers, the Army's Office of Personnel Operations completed a study that recommended opening more military occupational specialties to women. The chief of the Office of Personnel Operations advocated the implementation of the study's recommendations to "improve the Army's image as a pioneer and leader in equal opportunities and the 'women's liberation movement,' to place the Army in a stronger recruiting position in competition with our sister services, to enrich the morale of the members of the Women's Army Corps, and, more importantly, to help the Army transition to a volunteer force" (Griffith 1996, 193). The Army planned to increase the size of the WAC incrementally from 12,400 in fiscal year 1972 until it reached 23,500 in fiscal year 1978.

Thus, at the inception of the AVF, the Army's research indicated that it should try to appeal to women's desire for equal opportunities and keep up with women's entry into nontraditional fields, at the same time that it tried to reassure women and men that women could serve and retain their femininity. It is ironic that this male-dominated institution, so tied up with masculinity, might claim that women's "feminine touch is required to do the job better"—a claim that presumably applied to the pink-collar jobs that Army women had mainly been doing until that point—as the Army was allowing women to perform jobs that had always been done by men and that men would continue to do. None of the recruiting materials in my sample claimed that women have special feminine talents that make them good soldiers, but there were ads specifically aimed at women, some of which sought to reinforce the femininity of women in the Army.

In 1972, an Army ad instructed young women on "how to tell your parents you want to join the Army," which seems to presume that the Army expected female potential recruits to face some resistance from their families. The ad mentions job training, salary, vacations, education, and the chance to mature. It presents several possible job fields—"medical, dental, personnel management, communications, stock control, data processing, or administrative procedures"—all of which are fairly traditional for women.

Another ad from 1972 posed the question "What's new for women in today's Army?" The answer included new job opportunities, "over 300 in all," because "almost every job open to men is now open to women"; new travel opportunities; and new uniforms. The Army promises:

> We're working on a whole new uniform wardrobe, including some things you can wear right now. A black felt beret, white shirt, gloves and scarf. Smart patent leather, low-heeled shoes, clutch handbag, and a matching umbrella and raincoat.

So even if Army women are exploring new career territory and performing jobs previously restricted to men, the Army has ensured that they'll be wearing feminine clothes. Women are offered atypical experiences and roles, but their femininity won't be diminished if they accept them. The Army may also be sending a signal that it is interested in attracting only the type of woman who takes an "appropriate" interest in her appearance, not one who is looking to escape gender roles entirely or who looks or acts in ways society codes as masculine. Enloe has shown that uniforms are an area of gendered concern for the military; women service members' uniforms are meant to convey a feminine respectability, with no hint of gender bending or "mannishness," to provide a contrast to the men's appearance that promotes the masculine culture of the military (Enloe 2000, 263).

While most ads from the early 1970s are aimed at young men, a few of them do make textual references to "young men and women" and include women among groups of men pictured. For instance, an ad from 1972 that claims "We've got over 300 good, steady jobs" shows a crowd of Army personnel, including not only two female nurses but also a woman in uniform. The Army made visual references to women as soldiers earlier and more frequently than the other branches pictured female service members.

Over the course of the 1970s, women's participation expanded rapidly, with their numbers rising and their job opportunities increasing. Congress opened the service academies to women in 1976. In 1978, the Women's Army Corp was dissolved, and women were integrated into other Army units instead of all belonging to a separate unit together. By the next year, women were no longer being held to higher enlistment standards than men. In the coming decades, the expansion in women's participation would be accompanied by backlash, attempts to roll back women's participation, and political controversy.

The 1980s began with new military benefits and a new Army slogan—Be All You Can Be—and with an attempt by the Army and the Air Force to scale back the number of women they recruited. The services wanted to limit women's recruitment until their impact on readiness, which had already been the subject of study in the 1970s, could be further studied. Even before the conclusion of the Women in the Army Study, in 1982 the Army barred women from twenty-three military occupational specialties that had previously been open to them because of potential proximity to combat operations in wartime (Holm 1992, 402). Retired Air Force Maj. Gen. Jeanne Holm attributed the attempt to limit the recruitment of women to both resistance to female incursions into previously male areas and to a desire to undermine the AVF and convince the incoming Reagan administration to return to a draft (395). The Pentagon, however, was not considering conscription and didn't support new restrictions on women's roles. In fact, later in the decade, the Pentagon studied ways to address various issues faced by women in the services and to achieve some consistency among the services in their application of combat restrictions. The result was the Department of Defense's 1988 "Risk Rule," which established uniform criteria for closing noncombat positions to women, based on the risk that they would be exposed to direct combat, hostile fire, or capture, and which allowed thousands of new positions to open to women.

Despite the attempt to limit women's participation, in the mid-1980s, the Army began to produce ads that feature women and that are similar to ads that picture men. The series of ads bearing job codes like "96 Bravo"—there are nine of them in the sample—includes "93 Juliet," air traffic radar control, which is illustrated with a smiling woman sitting at a radar console and wearing a headset. The ad featuring Specialist Michelle Kowalski talking about testing herself and finding out what she's made of is from this same period. While Kowalski is feminized to the extent that she is clearly wearing cosmetics along with her camouflage cap, the ad's textual content does not put her into a special or different category in relation to other ads in the campaign. From this point on, one or two ads in any series might show a woman instead of a man, but with basically the same message or theme. While women aren't pictured nearly as frequently as men, when they do appear, they seem to be a legitimate part of the service.

Two ads from the 1990s make a direct pitch to women as women. These ads share the general look of others from the same period, with text superimposed on a camouflage-print background. The first, from 1995, bears a text box with the words "there's something about a soldier," and then continues:

> Especially if you're a woman. Because you'll find yourself doing the most amazing things. Like being a flight Crew Chief or a Topographic Surveyor, or any one of nearly 200 skills the Army offers. You'll also find yourself doing some very familiar things. Like getting into aerobics, going to the movies or just being with friends. The point is, a woman in the Army is still a woman. You carry yourself with a little more confidence. And you may find yourself shouldering more responsibility than you ever dreamed, but that's because, in the Army, you'll gain experience you can't find anywhere else. You could also find yourself earning as much as $30,000 for college. . . .

The ad pictures the head and shoulders of a serious-looking young woman, lightly made up, wearing a helmet with a radio headset, with a helicopter in the distance behind her. A smaller picture inset in the text shows the woman in civilian clothes and jewelry with her hair down; a young man in a bolo tie has his arm around her (see figure 3.3).

In some ways, this ad is like others in the same series, with its overall look, the picture of the soldier in some sort of military gear, and the references to educational benefits and the value of Army experiences. On the other hand, several aspects both visually and rhetorically serve to reinforce the female soldier's femininity and to reassure a potential female recruit that becoming a soldier won't compromise her feminine identity and make her unrecognizable to herself or undesirable. A woman in the Army is still a woman.

The other ad, from 1996, isn't as overtly concerned with the female soldier's gender presentation and identity. The ad states in large, boxed print, "If you have the will to succeed, we have about 200 ways." The rest of the text reads:

> As a woman in the Army, you will receive training in one of 188 military specialties. It's training that could prepare you for a career in high technology. You could learn guided missile technology or work with complex computer systems. You could manage communications and intelligence systems—all while working

as a vital part of a team. And, if you qualify, you'll earn money for college, too. So come with the will to succeed. Today's Army will make a way.

The accompanying picture, captioned "Patriot Missile Team," shows a woman and two men in front of a control panel. One man sits at a keyboard wearing a headset. The woman, standing above him, holds a clipboard and points to a

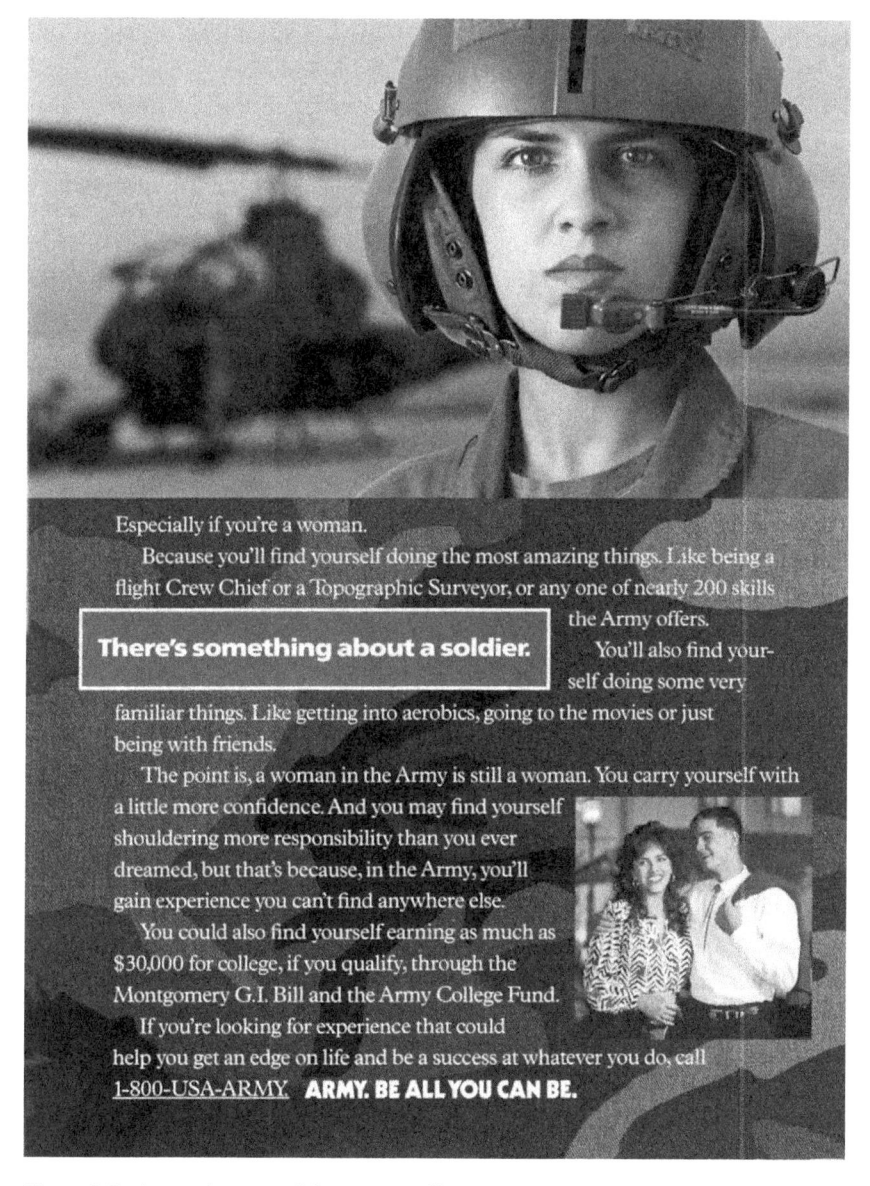

Figure 3.3. Army ad reprinted from *Sports Illustrated*, June 5, 1995. Army materials courtesy of the U.S. Government.

THE ARMY [69]

screen as the other man, leaning over her shoulder, looks on. The image of a missile launching and lines of computer code are superimposed over the picture. The woman is subtly feminized, with makeup, a ring, and manicured fingernails, but she is clearly in a position of some authority, and she is linked to militarized technology.

Although the ad's imagery prominently features a woman, without looking carefully at the ad copy, a viewer wouldn't necessarily think this is an ad aimed at women and, by glancing at the picture and the most prominently displayed text on "the will to succeed," might just absorb a general message about the Army, technology, and success that isn't clearly linked to gender. In some ways, then, this ad affirms that women are a regular part of the Army. It also sends the message that Army women are authoritative and technologically skilled, but still feminine.

Women, in fact, could theoretically be a more regular part of the Army after changes in policy in the early 1990s. While small numbers of women soldiers had participated in the invasions of Grenada (Operation Urgent Fury) in 1983 and of Panama (Operation Just Cause) in 1989, more than 40,000 women (about 30,000 of whom were in the Army), or a little more than 7 percent of the total U.S. forces, were deployed in the 1991 Persian Gulf War. The military's experiences in that war and the election of the Clinton administration led the Pentagon in 1994 to rescind the Risk Rule, which had set the parameters for women's military participation. The rule change allowed women to serve in more combat support positions, including more than 32,000 new positions in the Army, while still keeping them from direct ground combat (Women's Research and Education Institute 2003). In the 1990s, women served in "peace operations" in Somalia, Haiti, Bosnia, and Kosovo. The 1990s also brought allegations of rape and sexual harassment at the Army's Aberdeen Proving Grounds, as well as concerns in Congress over whether gender-integrated basic training was weakening the military.

The Army's advertising campaigns of the late 1990s rarely used images of women (though television commercials might show a few women soldiers among the men). The print ad sample, in fact, includes only a single ad with a woman from 1997 to 2000 (the ad appeared three times in 1997 and 1998). This ad was one of a series about what the potential recruit will be in the Army. The ad picturing a woman reads: "You'll be pushed to the limit. And discover you have no limits. You will be a soldier." Three pictures accompany the text: a row of parachutists trailing behind an airplane, a closer shot of a few parachutes and one parachutist, and the parachutist, now on the ground in a dress uniform, with a very small caption reading "Cpl. Patricia Burdette. Age 23. Parachute Rigger." In this ad, the soldier just happens to be a woman. As in the 1980s ads with women, there are no textual references to her femaleness, but unlike those earlier ads, the picture of her face doesn't dominate the page, so the casual reader might just see an Army ad with parachutes, without really noticing the soldier's sex. On closer inspection, Corporal Burdette is an attractive woman, lightly made up and impressive in her dress uniform, with its ribbons and badges. The Army, in pushing her to discover that she has "no limits," is offering women a boundlessness more traditionally associated with masculinity, just as earlier ads, mentioned previously, promised them masculine traits like independence, authority, and the ability to face challenges.

Women appeared in a few "Army of One" print ads, some of which were published in *Seventeen* magazine (the only Army ads I came across in *Seventeen*). The women talk about their interesting jobs and how they've personally developed in the Army. One ad, which pictures Specialist Robin Ingram, a transportation management coordinator, reads: "This uniform didn't change me. Earning the right to wear it did." Exactly the same copy appears on another ad that pictures an infantryman, Specialist Marc DeCarli. The ads that depict women use the same dark tones and overall aesthetic of the campaign as a whole, and the women are feminized only to the extent that they wear subtle makeup. (However, in a couple of them, the women's faces are in close-up, so you don't see that they are in uniform, making them look less militarized.) As with the earlier campaigns, women aren't pictured with weapons.

This campaign follows the pattern set by the Army over the course of the AVF. In any given advertising campaign, one or two print ads in a series are likely to show a woman instead of a man, with basically the same message or theme, or ads might include a woman or two among a majority of male soldiers. Although a few ads have directly addressed women as women and referred to their perceived potential concerns and desires, the Army, at least in its public representations, has mainly been offering to women the same things it has been offering to men, including roles, behaviors, and characteristics that have been associated with masculinity. However, women are never associated with combat and never shown wielding a gun.

While the Army made some use of women's magazines, publishing Army of One ads in *Seventeen*, it also published ads that feature women and ads that make a direct pitch to them as women (including "There's Something about a Soldier" and "If You Have the Will to Succeed") in *Sports Illustrated*, which is mainly read by men. The Army may have guessed that athletic women or those interested in sports were likely targets, but it also means that the Army didn't fear that it would alienate young men by presenting women as soldiers. The Army presents women as a normal part of the service.

CONCLUSIONS: MASCULINITY AND ARMY RECRUITING

During the late 1990s recruiting shortfalls, commentators accused the Army, Navy, and Air Force of abandoning masculinity and the concept of the warrior in their recruitment pitches. There was a common assumption that the armed forces, in a bow to political correctness, had been using women to represent themselves to the world (e.g., Gutmann 2000; Strother 1999). Gutmann, a critic of gender-integration of the armed forces, described Army recruiting efforts as follows:

> There are very few ads—some aired during the NBA playoffs, for instance—that show a man's world; most are scrupulously gender-balanced. In some of its displays and literature the Army even uses the image of a woman wearing a helmet, BDUs [battle dress uniforms—camouflage], army boots, carrying a rifle, walking forward, shoulders hunched menacingly. The Army is about 22 percent female and none are "ground-pounders," but the Army still uses a lone female to represent itself to the world! (2000, 278)

Not only does Gutmann overstate the percentage of women in the Army but also she misrepresents Army advertising. While some Army ads include women, the great majority of soldiers pictured are men. The Army does *not* "[use] a lone female to represent itself to the world," and the women who have been shown are unlikely to be pictured as Gutmann describes, with helmet and rifle and "shoulders hunched menacingly." Anyone so pictured will be a man.

The Army did not abandon masculinity in its recruiting materials with the transition to a volunteer force. As this chapter has argued, the Army has used a number of masculine appeals, though some of the inducements are connected to economics, which some commentators refuse to recognize as having anything to do with masculinity because it isn't part of a warrior masculinity based on such factors as strength, courage, and aggression. What the economic appeals do offer is the earning potential and economic independence that are prerequisites for manhood in American culture. The Army may also use visual or textual markers of masculinity to underline the masculine aspects of the economic appeal.

In addition, the Army offers upward mobility and the chance for advanced training or a college education, which can provide access to hegemonic forms of masculinity for a working-class population, particularly as good-paying factory jobs have disappeared and threatened the social position of blue-collar men. During the AVF, there is a shift in the way that job-training benefits are framed, and this happens to some degree with Air Force and Navy recruiting as well. Ads from the 1970s and into the 1980s talk about learning a skill, which will give the recruit future economic independence and security in the civilian world, or about getting a good job in the Army. A few early ads list traditional blue-collar skills, as well as a few more aspirational ones. (One ad claims the Army has "jobs in construction, transportation, communications, computers" and "jobs for photographers, printers, truck drivers, teachers, typists, TV cameramen and repairmen. Cooks, electricians, medical aides, meteorologists. Motor and missile maintenance men.") Often, it's specifically technical skills that are on offer, like data communications specialist, teletypewriter operator, or computer technician. In the 1980s and especially the 1990s, the language changes from a blue-collar offer of job training and skills to the use of terms like *career* and *professional*. The term *skills* is still occasionally mentioned, but only in relation to using highly advanced technology. As the economy's manufacturing base continued to decline, the ability of blue-collar work to confer economic security and social status on men diminished. In the larger culture, knowledge-society, information-based careers had become the main route to a comfortable lifestyle and to social prestige and, thus, to masculine achievement.[6] In the past, middle- and upper-class men had careers, while working-class men could still act as breadwinners and achieve economic independence and status in their communities through blue-collar work. Without good-paying factory jobs, working-class men who can't move up into careers or into highly specialized technological fields find themselves slipping down into low-paying, low-status service industry or retail work, fields that employ a preponderance of women.[7] Linking military service to careers and professionalism taps into the masculine model that has achieved dominance in the economic realm.

The other main thrust of Army recruiting is a soldiering-based masculinity, to a small degree using the role of the protector but mainly in terms of character development and personal transformation, with reference to such traditional warrior traits as strength and courage and with frequent use of militaristic imagery. However, there is no doubt that overall the soldiering masculinity offered by the Army is of a less aggressive and more accessible form than that offered up by the Marine Corps. The Army can make a man out of a boy, but he needn't undergo an extreme rite of initiation or a trial by fire to achieve that transformation. While soldiers are often depicted in military contexts, in combat uniforms, riding tanks and carrying weapons, they are also often pictured out of uniform, going to school, socializing, or playing sports. Even in uniform, they are often smiling and relaxed, projecting a good-natured competence. Soldiers are often named, giving the potential recruit an individual with whom to identify.

The Army needs to attract the most recruits and appeal to the widest possible audience. The Army has varied the bases of its appeals but overall has presented an accessible version of manhood, showing regular guys, just like the readers of *Popular Mechanics* or *Sports Illustrated*, only better, stronger, prouder, and more skilled for having joined up.

CHAPTER 4

The Navy

This chapter examines the Navy's efforts to attract recruits once it could no longer rely on draft-motivated volunteers. Naval recruiting advertisements during the AVF have promised the travel and adventure of a seagoing life, mental and physical challenges, and career advancement and skills training. The Navy has responded to the challenge of recruiting a volunteer force by focusing its efforts almost exclusively on young men. While recruiting materials have made token references to female sailors, the Navy presents itself as a male world where women mainly represent the pleasures of travel and shore leave.

Navy recruiting pitches have made use of various markers of masculinity. The Navy has relied on specifically militarized forms of masculinity (and interestingly, it has made this appeal to what could be considered traditional warrior masculinity recently in its history, showing that its commitment to overt masculinity isn't weakening), as well as forms that have conventionally been linked to the sailor's life, with its physical demands and privations and opportunities for exciting experiences. But the Navy has also looked to the civilian world repeatedly over the course of the AVF, tapping into the evolving masculine forms of the economic sphere, with offers of good job skills giving way to promises of professional accomplishment and technical prowess.

The analysis in this chapter is based on sixty-four print advertisements published by the Navy between 1970 and 2003, eighteen television commercials that aired between 1980 and 2003, and two different incarnations of the Navy's recruiting Web site. After a brief discussion of Navy culture, this chapter presents an analysis of Navy recruiting materials from the first two decades of the all-volunteer force, pauses to consider the role of women in recruitment materials and provide some background on women's participation in the Navy, and then continues with analysis of recruiting materials in the 1990s and early 2000s.

NAVY CULTURE

According to RAND analyst Carl Builder, while the Army is concerned with the concept of service and with its ties to the citizenry and the nation, the Navy's institutional worldview is linked to tradition:

> Tradition has always been an important part of military life, but the Navy, much more than any of the other services, has cherished and clung to tradition. The US Navy was born and bravely fought its way out from under the massive shadow of the British Royal Navy and its rich traditions. . . . This reverence for tradition in the US Navy has continued right to the present, not just in pomp or display, but in the Navy's approach to almost every action from eating to fighting—from tooth to fang. In tradition, the Navy finds a secure anchor for the institution against the dangers it must face. If in doubt, or if confronted with a changing environment, the Navy looks to its traditions to keep it safe. (1989, 18)

Builder also characterizes the Navy as concerned about its size as measured in ships (as opposed to the Army's concern with the number of people in uniform and their skill level). It is not a particularly "toy-oriented" service, however—members of the Navy are not specifically devoted to a particular type of ship or a technology, but to the institution as a whole. Builder notes that "whereas the things the Navy owns and operates are clearly a source of interest and pride for those who serve in them, Navy personnel are more likely to associate themselves with the Navy as an institution" (1989, 23–24).

Despite service members' identification with the institution as a whole, there is also a great deal of intraservice rivalry among the various branches:

> The Navy is the most elaborate in its distinctions among, and the relative ranking of, its various components, branches, or activities. The implicit intraservice distinctions within the Navy provide an extensive, fine-structured, hierarchical pecking order from top to bottom. At the pinnacle of this structure, since World War II, has been carrier-based fighter aviation. At (or very near) the bottom is mine warfare. Submarine and surface warfare specialties, in that order, lie in between. (Builder 1989, 25)

Dunnigan and Macedonia agree that "the major branches of the Navy don't get along very well" and that "among the Navy branches, there is a more visible pecking order than in the Army" (1993, 220). However, they rank the branches slightly differently than Builder does, putting the nuclear submarine crews ("squids") just above the carrier aviators ("Airedales"), with surface-ship sailors coming in last. Certainly both aircraft carriers and submarines are proudly and frequently displayed in recruiting ads, more often than other types of ships.

The nature of naval life has historically allowed commanding naval officers at sea great independence. Independent command at sea is another hallmark of Navy culture, and it is one that may influence the Navy's relationship to the larger society. According to a report by the Center for Strategic and International Studies, "In one sense, the Navy's fierce streak of independence may insure its world-renowned professionalism, but it also may have insulated the service from social trends and sensitivities felt more keenly by the other services and society in general" (2000, 12). The combination of tradition, independence, and elitism may have led to conservatism and resistance to change in terms of women's participation in the Navy and historically, as discussed later, African American men's participation as well.

The Navy's resistance to women's participation is partly attributable to a conservative culture that resists change and to an idea of life at sea, filled with homosocial traditions and rituals (like the Shellback ceremony that initiates sailors when they cross the equator for the first time), that envisions the ship as a male world.[1] It can also be ascribed to the Navy's institutional needs. The Navy has had trouble utilizing women's labor. When women were barred from serving on most ships, placing them in shore billets caused problems because it required men to spend more time at sea. To allow sailors some semblance of a home life, they generally rotate between sea billets and shore billets, alternating periods of time at sea and in port. Putting women into shore billets disrupted this sea-shore rotation system. When women's opportunities to serve at sea expanded, the Navy worried about sexual relations between male and female sailors and about the reactions of sailors' wives to the news that their husbands would be spending six-month deployments at sea on ships with women. Opponents of gender integration gleefully dubbed the USS *Acadia* "The Love Boat" because of reports that on its return to San Diego in 1991 after deployment to the Middle East, apparently 36 women of the 360 on the crew were missing because they had been airlifted to shore earlier in the cruise due to pregnancy (Gutmann 2000). Whether for reasons of practicality, tradition, or both, women have not been a focus of Navy recruiting efforts during the AVF.

THE RECRUITING BACKGROUND

The U.S. Navy has long experience with recruitment. In the eighteenth and nineteenth centuries, when many nations depended on a draft or impressment of sailors to man their navies, the United States relied entirely on voluntary enlistments (Shulman 1995, 39). The Navy recruited only experienced seamen to fill its ranks, and it restricted recruiting efforts to coastal areas. These limitations, combined with low pay and poor shipboard conditions, led to a force that was approximately half foreign-born, with immigrants from all over the world. At the turn of the twentieth century, with a nativist desire to create a more "American" force and with technological changes in ships requiring more highly trained sailors, the Navy began recruiting young men from the American interior without experience at sea who would be trained in their duties (40). The drive to Americanize the Navy can be tied to the late-nineteenth-century crisis in white masculinity, described by Kimmel (1996), which was partly rooted in the expanded public roles of immigrant men. Imperialist military expansion, conducted in large part by the newly American-manned Navy, helped to resolve the crisis. The practical effect in terms of recruiting is that from the end of the nineteenth century, the Navy has been trying to appeal to young men across the country who may have had no direct exposure to life at sea.

In the late 1800s, the Navy attempted to raise its public profile through expositions and displays, articles in both magazines aimed at boys and those aimed at adults, and statues and memorials (Shulman 1995, 46). In 1906, the Navy hired a New York advertising firm to prepare its first illustrated, professionally produced recruiting brochure. The thirty-two-page pamphlet, *The Making of a Man-o'-Warsman*, offered an attractive account of the training and opportunities offered by the Navy. Historian Frederick Harrod notes that "the title evoked romantic images of deep-water sailors on high-masted frigates; yet, ironically, the booklet was issued when the traditional 'man-of-warsman' was rapidly becoming a part of the past and was giving way to a new breed of sailor-technician" (1978, 3). The title also suggests a particularly naval form of masculinity—the strong, salty man-o'-warsman. Around this time, the Navy began to advertise frequently in the "help-wanted" section of newspapers. A typical ad read:

> WHAT THE NAVY OFFERS YOUNG MEN. For the young man between 17 and 25 years of age, who has a good character and sound body, not afraid to leave home, the Unites States Navy offers excellent opportunity for steady employment; work is not severe, and plenty of time for recreation; athletics of all kinds encouraged. Pay $16 to $70 a month, according to ratings, with no expense for food, lodging, doctor's attendance and medicine. A complete outfit of clothing furnished gratis on first enlistment. (Quoted in Harrod 1978, 42)

From its inception, Navy recruiting in peacetime used appeals to tradition, the romance of life at sea, and the masculine character of naval service, but it also offered recruits economic opportunities and concrete benefits.

Men were not drafted into the Navy in the post–World War II period, but the end of conscription still had an impact on the Navy and its recruiting practices. During the period of Project Volunteer in the early 1970s, as the draft-dependent Army tried to figure out ways to fill its ranks without conscription, the Navy estimated that somewhere above half of its enlistees were true volunteers. The rest were draft-motivated, joining the Navy to avoid being called up for the Army (Griffith 1996, 56). With the loss of that source of recruits, the Navy needed to expand and revitalize its efforts to sell itself, and those efforts needed to appeal to a Vietnam-era public that was wary of military service.

THE RECRUITING ADVERTISEMENTS—PART I: THE FIRST TWO DECADES OF THE AVF

At the beginning of the AVF, the Navy, like the Army and the Air Force, used an economic appeal, highlighting training and good jobs, and it also layered on top the vision of an exciting, challenging life. Naval recruiting during the AVF has made two central offers, sometimes in combination and sometimes separately: one economic, with the promise of good jobs or high-tech training, and one related to adventure and the traditional benefits of life at sea—excitement, challenge, travel, getting away from home and finding oneself, and, through all of these things, becoming a man. The evocations of life at sea are also sometimes tied to tradition and patriotic calls to service that suggest a romantic vision of the Navy and its glorious past with which the potential recruit can associate himself. Faced with competing forms of masculinity within the larger culture (Connell 1987), the Navy, like the Army, calls on more than one masculine model in its recruiting efforts.

One of the first advertising campaigns of the AVF used the tactic of celebrating the past while extolling the advantages of naval life. In 1972, the Navy began publishing a series of ads that juxtapose early recruiting posters with pictures of modern life in the Navy (see figure 4.1). Two of these ads read: "1919 Join the Navy and see the world. 1972 Join the Navy and find your place in the world" and "1919: Join the Navy and see exotic places. 1972: Join the Navy and get job training that will take you places." These ads claim that the old benefits of Navy life, like world travel, haven't disappeared, but now new benefits and good job training are also available. They end with the slogans "Be someone special in the New Navy" and "Be a Success in the New Navy." The Navy tries to evoke nostalgia for a rich past and the traditions of sailing, while appealing to young men in need of good jobs. Nostalgic and patriotic appeals reappeared in 1975 when the Navy commemorated its bicentennial and its role in American history.

Continuing with the "be someone special" theme, the Navy ran a series of ads that focused on training and skill development but stressed that the kinds of jobs one would get in the Navy were interesting and fulfilling, and they frequently differentiated naval life from civilian life, painting Navy life as more challenging and worthwhile. Some of these ads announce:

> "Life's too short to waste time wishing you were somewhere else. Get moving."
> "Don't just make a living. Make a life for yourself."
> "Life's what you make it. Make it great."
> "A Navy career. Because there's more to life than a paycheck."
> "Get out of the ordinary. Get into the Navy."
> "The Navy won't hand you the same old routine."

These ads characterize the Navy as "a place to grow" that offers "challenge," "hard work," "high standards," "leadership," and "personal responsibility."

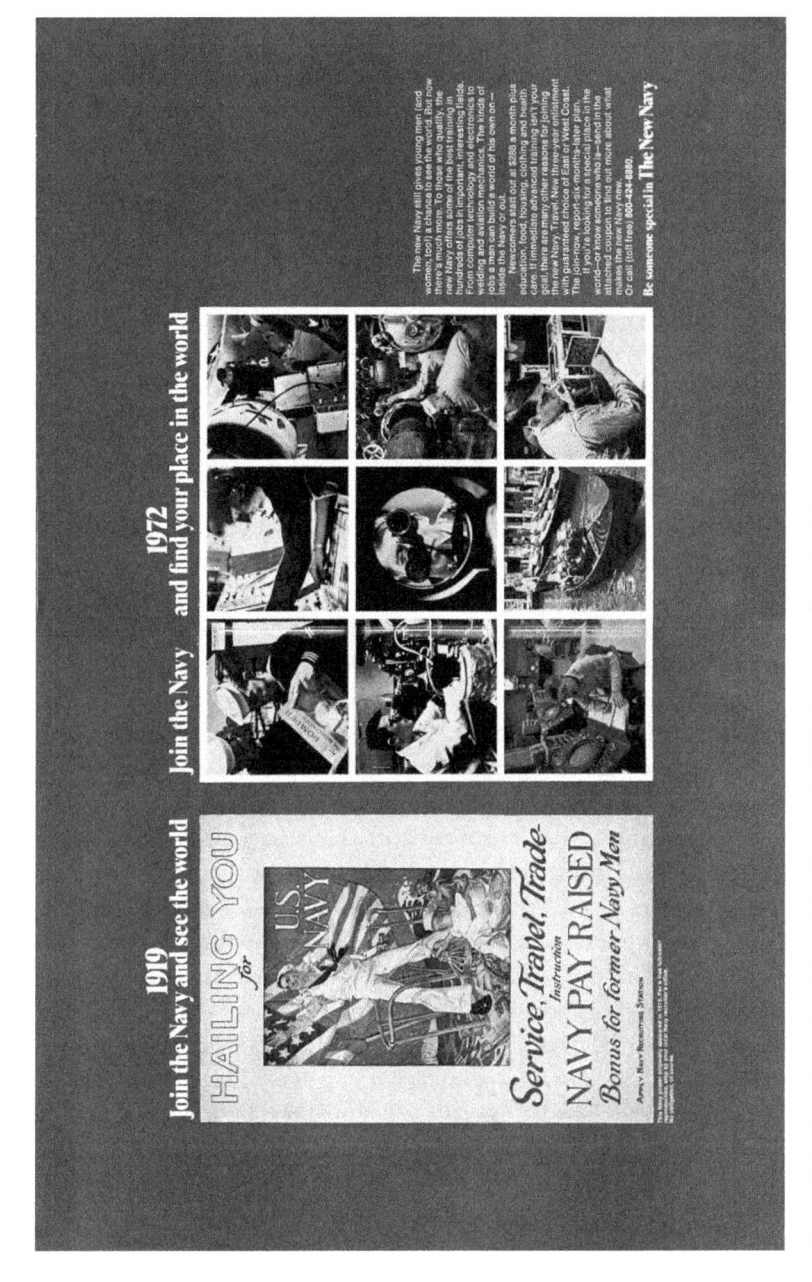

Figure 4.1. Navy ad reprinted from *Life*, October 6, 1972. Courtesy of the U.S. Navy.

Civilian jobs are disparaged as leading to "nowhere." The worker may be just "punching a time clock" or "following some other routine [he is] bored with." Most of the ads include multiple pictures, showing sailors engaged in a variety of work and leisure activities—on the decks of ships, working with technical equipment, socializing, and traveling. Some of the ads focus on the advanced electronics and nuclear power programs as challenging options with great potential for future success in the Navy or the civilian world. The ads in this series also promise travel, educational benefits, the chance to make friends, and an exciting new life. The references to punching a time clock and jobs leading nowhere imply that the potential recruit's other option is some form of blue-collar work, and the Navy is implicitly offering upward mobility and access to a better, broader kind of life than the recruit could have at home.

Several of the ads from the first half of the 1970s offer a masculine pride in work that is both physically and mentally challenging. The Navy is "a profession that lets you stand a little taller" and a place to "master a skill." Navy work is "Good, hard work. With your own two hands. And the wind in your teeth." The Navy offers "jobs that keep your head busy," as well as "action-filled jobs" and "active jobs that that keep your muscles moving." And while Navy life is good (according to the Navy), they're "not saying Navy life's a snap. Far from it. It's hard toughening work." Standing tall, mastery, hardness, action, muscles, and toughness are all signifiers that connote masculinity. In addition to such descriptions of work, one of the ways these ads demonstrate that Navy life is demanding, surprisingly enough, is by reference to the "chores" that are a part of that life. Men who join the Navy for advanced technical training not only need such attributes as "good hands," "a good mind," and a "strong desire to learn and achieve" but also must have "a willingness to do [their] share of the housekeeping chores." Other ads mention swabbing decks, "dealing with your fair share of chores," and "the nitty-gritty housekeeping chores." *Housekeeping* is a term generally associated with women, and the performance of housekeeping chores was a contentious issue in America at that time, as women demanded a more equitable distribution of household labor. In the context of the ads, however, a willingness to do one's fair share of chores does not signal a loosening of gender roles or a concern for gender equity. Rather, in the (then) all-male world of the Navy ship, housekeeping loses its association with femininity and becomes a way to signal that Navy life won't be soft or easy. The references to chores, especially when modified by a rough-sounding adjective like *nitty-gritty*, emphasize how physically demanding the life of a sailor can be and turn the difficult, routine, unpleasant tasks of maintaining a ship into badges of masculine toughness.

While the chance to "be someone special" was, implicitly, mainly being offered to men, this offer was not limited to white men. With the shift to an all-volunteer force, the Navy of the 1970s seemed to be making a concerted effort to reach out to African American men. In the sample, most of the ads that pictured sailors included African American men. The only ad in the entire sample that profiled an individual sailor in depth, published in *Sports Illustrated* in 1975, told the story of a black naval flight officer from New Jersey. The Navy created a series of recruiting posters in the early 1970s that featured African Americans.[2] Some of these posters appeal to an idea of racial pride and promise individual and group advancement, with captions such as "we'll take you as far as you can go," "you can study black history and go out and make it"—which alludes to a World War I recruiting poster with the caption "The Navy Needs You! Don't READ American History—MAKE IT!"—and "join the Navy and see the world change," a play on the historic offer to join the Navy and see the world, offering new opportunities rather than travel. Other posters claim that being in the Navy won't conflict with or detract from African American racial identity. In particular, one with a picture of two men wearing dashikis states, "You can be Black, and Navy too," and a companion poster shows a young man with an afro hairstyle next to the words, "Your son can be Black, and Navy too."

This effort to reach out to African American men was a shift from earlier, racist Navy policies, dating back to the Navy's efforts to "Americanize" the service at the turn of the twentieth century. From the 1880s to the 1890s, under the new recruiting policies, the percentage of African American men in the Navy dropped from 14 percent to below 10 percent, and the opportunities for service narrowed to servantlike positions as cooks and stewards (Shulman 1995, 41). From 1919 to 1932, African Americans were completely prohibited from enlisting (Harrod 1978, 168). During World War II, black men in the segregated Navy could serve on ships only as messmen and stewards, and they weren't commissioned as officers. In 1945, the Navy began allowing integrated crews to serve on noncombat ships, with the proportion of black personnel on any ship capped at 10 percent (Segal 1989, 107). President Truman's directive to integrate the military after World War II was resisted by the Navy. According to Admiral Elmo Zumwalt, while the other services honored Truman's order more quickly, the Navy, seeing itself as an elite service, attempted to keep itself "lily white or to have the minimum possible integration."[3] In the late 1960s and early 1970s, all of the armed services experienced racial tensions and disturbances, and for the Navy this included race riots on the aircraft carriers *Kitty Hawk* and *Constellation* in 1972 (Segal 1989, 111). The larger social pressures of the civil rights movement and a desire to decrease racial tensions in the service probably pushed the Navy to overcome its conservatism on race and persuaded it to include African American men in its public representations of itself and its construction of the figure of a masculine sailor. I suspect that an even bigger factor was that with the challenge of recruiting an all-volunteer force, the Navy needed to expand the pool of potential recruits, and increasing the number of African American men in the service seemed preferable to increasing the number of women, black or white, which was another possible alternative. Greater racial integration would be less disruptive to the Navy's culture and less problematic than greater gender integration.

The emphasis on physicality, toughness, and mental challenge in Navy recruiting materials continued in the late 1970s and was joined by a new focus on adventure and testing oneself. The Navy offers the ocean itself as a road to masculine achievement. One ad shows an expanse of water with the caption "the toughest proving ground on earth." The text continues:

> Since the beginning of time, men have tested themselves against the sea. At sea, there are no free rides. Every mile you travel is paid for in skill, courage, grit and ingenuity. There are no excuses or second bests. The sea asks the limit of your ability and accepts nothing less. . . . Proving yourself is worth some effort.

Many ads from this period show dramatic pictures of a ship in an open expanse of ocean or a submarine surfacing, and they begin to use the slogan "It's not just a job, it's an adventure."

In the early 1980s, the Navy continued to use that slogan, but the tenor of the ads changed. Instead of emphasizing challenge and adventure, they highlight career opportunities, technical skill, and personal development, especially in the ads running in *Popular Mechanics*. (The Navy may have needed more people with the aptitude for technical training and assumed that it might find them among that magazine's readers.) A series of ads from the early 1980s used their headlines to explain some potential definitions of the word *adventure*:

> "Making the Most of Yourself Is What the Navy Adventure Is All About."
> "A Job Important Enough to Become a Career Is Part of the Navy Adventure."
> "Choosing the Career You Want Is Part of the Navy Adventure."
> "Pride in Being One of the Best Is Part of the Navy Adventure."
> "New Challenges Are Part of the Navy Adventure."
> "A Career You Can Be Proud of Is Part of the Navy Adventure."

The Navy attempted to reframe the "adventure" of its slogan as a journey to self-development and personal success. The ads update the figure of the sailor (which the Navy itself promulgated just a few years earlier) from someone who has an exciting life at sea doing challenging physical labor to someone who has an exciting life performing technical work and making use of advanced training. Copy in one ad reads: "Accept the challenge and you'll never be the same. In the Navy you will become an experienced professional with a job skill you can build a career on. And you'll posses the pride, maturity and self-confidence only the Navy Adventure can give you." Another promises "You become a top-notch professional and achieve a level of skill second to none."

Technology is mentioned frequently, with references to "modern equipment," the "most-up-to-date equipment and methods," and "today's hottest technologies [including]: micro-electronics, state-of-the-art computers, advanced communications, nuclear power and more." Most of these ads picture a young man in uniform working with technical-looking equipment or at a control panel. One ad states: "There's no prouder moment than when you master a highly technical skill." This claim is a bit surprising coming from a branch of the U.S. military—one might think that someone serving his country in the armed forces, sworn to defend the nation, might have prouder moments than mastering a technical skill. In these ads, however, the Navy gives a young man a chance to feel pride by allowing him to become a technical professional, with the word *professional* recurring frequently. As is discussed shortly, this was the beginning of an effort to tap into a masculine model that was becoming dominant in civilian life. This focus on technological professionalism could also resonate well in a culture where the "techno-thriller," featuring militarized, masculine professional types who use advanced technology to vanquish America's enemies, was becoming a popular genre for male readers (Gibson 1991).

In the mid- and late 1980s, Navy advertising frequently mentioned career opportunities, travel, adventure, and pride. Some of the ads were dominated by spectacular images, like a ship silhouetted by the setting sun or a submarine surfacing, inside the outline of the word *Navy*. These ads use the slogan "live the adventure" and contain less text than the other ads, highlighting the drama of the images. One such ad, picturing a submarine, states "Break through to adventure. The Navy adventure is new challenges. New opportunities. And a sense of pride you've never had before. If you're ready, it's all out here waiting for you." Other ads from the late 1980s are tagged with the slogan "You are Tomorrow. You are the Navy." They emphasize career training, but they also talk about personal development, with words like *challenge*, *responsibility*, *discipline*, *confidence*, *teamwork*, and *leadership*.

A series of television commercials from 1986 that use the "live the adventure" slogan imply that a sailor will gain the masculine traits of mastery, confidence, and control of his future through his Navy training and experiences. Each is a montage, including scenes of sailors at work, either on a ship, submarine, or carrier deck; dramatic shots of anchors rising, jets taking off, and submarines surfacing; scenes of training, like men running on a beach; and a few images of travel, including sailors sitting with kimono-wearing Japanese women in a garden. In one, the narrator declares: "To break free, to reach new heights, master new skills, to meet the world, on its terms and yours, feel the pride, show the world you're US Navy." Another says, "To rise, to meet the challenge, to master the most advanced skills, to meet the future with new confidence, to break through, show the world you're US Navy." The ads mention "advanced skills," but the emphasis is on sailors rising to a challenge and gaining control of their own destinies.

Throughout the 1980s, Navy recruiting materials offered adventure, challenge, and discipline, which are the traditional masculine rewards of the sailor's life, but they also promised young men the more modern masculine achievements of mastery of complex technology and career advancement. The accomplishment of career and personal success could give young men both economic independence and social status. As the economy continued to shift its emphasis from manufacturing to service and information, status and economic success were tied less and less to a good trade and more and more to knowledge-society careers. As American culture in the Reagan 1980s celebrated the Yuppie (young urban professional)[4] and Wall Street (both the financial sector and the movie, which trumpeted that "greed is good"), some strands of Navy advertising emphasized career, professionalism, and technology. The Navy, like the Army, began to include this type of appeal in its repertoire during a period when new hegemonic forms of business masculinity were emerging.[5]

WOMEN, THE NAVY, AND RECRUITING

During the first two decades of the AVF, Navy recruiting expressed ambivalence about women, making token reference to the possibility that they might be sailors but mainly using them, when they pictured them at all, as a way to attract potential male recruits. The Navy has relied on women's labor in limited contexts and used their images as a recruiting tool, but it has also tried strenuously to keep women off ships and thus away from the core of the service's culture and functions.

Several World War I recruiting posters by Howard Chandler Christy used the image of a young woman to entice young men into joining the Navy. One showed an attractive young woman dressed like a sailor next to the words "Gee!! I Wish I Were A Man. I'd Join the Navy." The poster girl is cute and feminine in her sailor's outfit, with its collar blowing open and her throat exposed. She's clearly not meant to be taken seriously as a potential recruit, but to serve as a contrast to the "real man" who could enlist or to suggest that being in the Navy has sex appeal. Below her, the poster reads, "Be A Man And Do It. United States Navy Recruiting Station."

During this period, women actually could join the Navy, though their service life was drastically different from the men's. In fact, Bernice Smith, the young woman who modeled for the "I Wish I Were a Man" poster, became the first woman in California to enlist (Williams 1999). In the spring of 1917, Secretary of the Navy Josephus Daniels feared that the Navy was heading into war without enough manpower. Having discovered that the wording of the 1916 Naval Act, which authorized a buildup of naval forces, did not specifically exclude women, the Navy decided to invite women to enroll in the Naval Coast Defense Reserve Force. Most of the women performed some form of clerical work. The women were enrolled as Yeomen (F), with the designation "(F)," for female, ensuring that they wouldn't inadvertently be assigned to sea duty. The way the term "Yeoman (F)" sounds when spoken aloud led many in and out of the service to refer to Navy women as "Yeomanettes" (Ebbert and Hall 1993). All Navy yeomen had to be assigned to ships, but Navy regulations prohibited women from serving on Navy ships. The Navy solved this problem by assigning the Yeomen (F) to tugs at the bottom of the Potomac River (Holm 1992, 12).

The Naval Reserve Act of 1925 limited enlistment to "male citizens of the United States," in part because some senators feared that allowing women into the peacetime Naval Reserve could open the door to women's service in the Army Reserve. The sex-restrictive language was carried over into the Naval Reserve Act of 1938, meaning that at the beginning of World War II, women were legally excluded from the Navy (Ebbert and Hall 1993, 19). The Navy initially believed it would not need to recruit women for World War II and that the civil service would be able to supply additional personnel to perform any tasks that women naval personnel might. Shortly after Pearl Harbor, the Navy came to realize that it was mistaken and began months of struggle with Congress over whether the Women's Naval Reserve would be an auxiliary force, like the Army, or whether women would be members of the Navy, as the Navy preferred (30). (As it turned out, the auxiliary status of women was unworkable for the Army.) The Navy won the battle in July 1942, and the new women's service was created. To stop the newspapers from using terms like *sailorettes* and *goblettes* to describe the naval women (*gob* was a slang term for a sailor), Elizabeth Reynard, a special assistant to the head of the Bureau of Personnel, came up with the acronym WAVES, Women Accepted for Volunteer Emergency Service (38).

In 1948, the Women's Armed Services Integration Act made women permanent members of the Navy, but it restricted women from serving on ships other than some transports or hospital ships. Very few women served on ships, and most who did served in a medical capacity. Early in the Vietnam War, transport ships that had been carrying dependents became troop transports, making women ineligible to serve on them, and when the Navy decommissioned its last hospital ship in 1971, even nurses could no longer go to sea (Holm 1992, 328). By the time Martin Binkin and Shirley J. Bach completed a study for the Brookings Institution in 1976 on women in the military, they could report that "since there are currently no hospital or transport vessels in the fleet, all seagoing jobs are closed to women" (1977, 24).

Naval policy makers felt that the most cost-effective way to use women was to congregate them in a few locations and limit them to traditional fields, and over the course of the Cold War, the Navy restricted the ratings (job categories) in which women could serve. In 1952, enlisted women were eligible to serve in thirty-six ratings (about 60 percent of all ratings). In 1956, the number dropped to twenty-five ratings, and by 1962 twenty-one ratings could be filled by women (Ebbert and Hall 1993, 141). During the Cold War, women served overwhelmingly in the traditional fields of clerical-administration and health care. The Navy, like the other services at the time, worried about its female members projecting a feminine appearance to the world. Women who present a respectable feminine image can suitably contrast with male service members, emphasizing their masculinity (Enloe 2000). Navy regulations required that women's hair "shall be arranged and shaped to present a conservative, feminine appearance," and when Navy women, following civilian trends, began neglecting to wear their hats in 1968, they received a reprimand from the director of WAVES reminding them that "WAVES are ladies first and always.... Taking off the hat in public is strictly a man's gesture; it is not ladylike" (quoted in Holm 1992, 182).

During the Vietnam War, many Navy women, wanting to be more directly involved in the war effort, requested to be sent to Southeast Asia, but, aside from nurses, only one or two female officers were there at one time on the staff of the Commander, Naval Forces in Saigon, and no enlisted women were allowed to go (Holm 1992, 217).

In 1970, Admiral Elmo Zumwalt became chief of naval operations. Anticipating passage of the Equal Rights Amendment and the inception of the all-volunteer force, in August 1972, Zumwalt issued a directive, known as Z-116, expanding roles for women in the Navy. In the past, the Navy had been content to recruit few women, who were held to much higher standards than male recruits in terms of mental capacity and educational levels, and it wasn't concerned when it failed to retain many of its overqualified female service members. With the end of conscription, however, the Navy would be losing draft-motivated volunteers, and Zumwalt wanted to better utilize and retain women. The Z-116 authorized limited entry of enlisted women into all ratings, allowed a limited number of officer and enlisted women to serve on the noncombatant USS *Sanctuary*, allowed women to serve as commanding officers of shore units, opened the Navy's ROTC program to women, and allowed Navy women to attend the National War College.

Over the course of the 1970s, opportunities for women in the Navy further expanded. In 1973, Navy women become eligible for aviation duty in noncombat aircraft. In 1978, a sex-discrimination lawsuit against the Navy led the courts to rule that the Navy could not use the 1948 Integration Act as the sole basis for excluding women from duty aboard ships. Congress amended the fiscal-year 1979 Defense Authorization Act to allow the assignment of women to ships, but at the Navy's urging, women were still barred from combat ships. In 1979, Navy women became eligible for a number of shipboard duties for the first time (Women's Research and Education Institute 2003).

During the first two decades of the AVF, Navy recruiting ads made occasional references to women as sailors, visually and textually, but the idea that women were a regular part of the Navy was repeatedly undercut. Of course, women *weren't* a regular part of the Navy since they were still restricted from many shipboard duties and entirely absent from combat vessels. Some ads

[86] *Enlisting Masculinity*

refer specifically to men, like one from 1972 that reveals what "new guys" in the Navy earn and informs potential enlistees that the Navy will allow them to grow a beard, or one published in 1973 that shows a picture of a man at a control panel and includes the copy "any man who learns to operate or repair the Navy's sophisticated electronic systems or nuclear power plants guarantees himself a firm foothold in the future." The wording of the advertisements did sometimes make an effort to acknowledge that women could also enlist. For example, an ad from 1972 that features a 1919 recruiting poster states, "The new Navy still gives young men and women the opportunity to visit exotic places," and it promises "the kind of training that helps a man or woman go places inside the Navy or out." Another ad from the same year also mentions women—the copy reads "The new Navy still gives young men (and women, too!) a chance to see the world"—but the use of parentheses and the exclamation point make the presence of women seem like a novelty, and the same paragraph goes on to claim that the Navy offers "the kinds of jobs a man can build a world of his own on" (see figure 4.1). Ten years later, some recruiting materials retained this pattern of referring to the service of men and women but also using language indicating that the generic sailor is a man. For instance, an ad from the Navy Adventure series claims that "today's Navy depends on modern equipment and the men and women who operate and maintain it," but the copy begins by stating "most guys go through job after job," and the picture shows a man with a clipboard in front of a set of controls. The references to women in these advertisements seem like a formality.

Visually, Navy ads from this period sent mixed messages about women. They seem to be trying to reach out to women as possible recruits, but they also offer women as a potential prize for men's service. The subtext in many ads seems to be that joining the Navy will make a man attractive to women. In many ads, men are sailors, and women are their civilian companions. The advertisements that contain several pictures, showing sailors at work and at play, often include one of a man in uniform with a woman in civilian clothes or several men and women together socializing (see figure 4.2). The man may have his arm around the woman. These ads hint at the sexual rewards of being a sailor. The traditional pattern of naval life is long stretches of duty at sea, punctuated by liberty in ports of call around the world, where sailors could indulge themselves with women and alcohol. While the ads don't explicitly mention this aspect of Navy life, the references to travel and the images of civilian women subtly evoke it.

When women are shown dressed as sailors, they are presented differently than the male sailors are. Female sailors are almost always shown with a male sailor or sailors. A single ad in the sample included a picture of a woman by herself—a headshot of a woman in a dress uniform—and that picture was one of several images on the page. Men are pictured in a range of situations. They are shown performing a variety of tasks, from working in the control room of a submarine, to welding, to directing a helicopter landing. Women sailors, on the other hand, are generally not pictured on the deck of a ship, using equipment, or working. Women sailors, like the women pictured in civilian clothes, usually appear in pictures that represent travel or leisure; they are often shown in a glamorous foreign setting, like a pigeon-filled European plaza, near London Bridge, or on a shoreline with ancient ruins. They are travel companions to the male sailors they accompany. In a sense, then, women aren't being shown

Figure 4.2. Navy ad reprinted from *Sports Illustrated*, May 6, 1974. Courtesy of the U.S. Navy.

[88] *Enlisting Masculinity*

as true sailors; even when visually present in naval uniforms, they aren't acting like sailors. The images of them as companions to men and at leisure implicitly feminize them and distance them from the Navy's military functions.

One ad from 1973 reveals just how much trouble the Navy was having in reconciling its desire to use traditional gender roles to attract men and its need to recruit women to fill "manpower" needs in the all-volunteer force. The ad reproduces a 1917 Howard Chandler Christy recruiting poster with a picture of a woman (a "Christy girl") and the phrase "I want you for the Navy." Above this, the headline states, "People used to join us to get away, to get the girl. Today they also join us to get ahead." The copy continues:

> You can still join the Navy and get around; seeing the world is a Navy fact of life. You can still join the Navy and get away from the humdrum and the ordinary to the exciting and the involving. And you can still join the Navy and get the girl (or, if you're a girl, you can join the Navy and get the guy). Girls like the way we've updated our famous bell bottoms with the handsome new uniform (on the sailor below). But the best reason for joining the new Navy is to get ahead.

The claim that girls like the new uniform is a bit confusing, coming on the heels of the preceding sentence about getting the girl and girls getting guys. Are they talking about a new uniform for men that helps them get the girls, or did the Navy design new bell-bottoms for the girls who join and are getting the guys? Are girls sailors, or are they admirers of the sailors who wear the handsome uniforms? To see the uniform modeled on "the sailor below," the viewer looks at a picture of a man and a woman together, *both* of them wearing naval uniforms, but "the sailor" in this picture is the man—the woman is in a skirt. The Navy wants to appeal to (heterosexual) men's sexual desires and offers up women as a reward. It also wants to avoid offending women—though it calls them "girls"—and knows it must reach out to them as well, so the ad makes a token attempt at equality, without addressing whether "getting the girl" and "getting the guy" are equivalent or whether joining the Navy means the same thing for women and men.

The Navy admits that until the early 1990s, it made no serious effort to recruit women into the AVF because its use of women was so limited. At a 1993 conference at the U.S. Naval Academy to commemorate two decades of the all-volunteer force, Rear Admiral Marsha Johnson Evans, who had served as commander of the U.S. Navy Recruiting Command explained:

> What do we know about recruiting women? Frankly, precious little—except that as long as we have needed only a few women in traditional roles, we did not have to prospect. It did not take 31 calls to recruit someone—she walked into the recruiting station ready to sign. And because female demand to join was greater than the number needed, the standards for women could be higher than for men—non high-school graduates and those with Armed Forces Qualification Test scores in lower categories need not apply.

> About a year ago [1992], in anticipation of the expansion of opportunities and in concert with the Navy's desire to begin placing more women in nontraditional career paths, we began an effort to test the market. One year ago, the Navy had no experience in working the female market and no money to undertake research on it.... No advertising money had been spent to create market awareness of opportunities open to women. (Evans 1996, 267)

The Navy didn't believe it needed many women, so it did little to recruit them, and it used women in recruiting materials in token or symbolic ways, often to appeal to male recruits.

Having given some background on women's relationship to the Navy, the focus can now return to the recruiting advertisements during the 1990s, a period when many of the restrictions on women's participation were lifted.

THE RECRUITING ADVERTISEMENTS—PART II: THE 1990s TO THE IRAQ WAR

The Navy began the 1990s with a new advertising slogan, "You and the Navy, Full Speed Ahead," that both emphasized forward motion and progress and harked back to the famed exclamation of Admiral David Farragut during the Civil War battle of Mobile Bay, "Damn the torpedoes, full speed ahead." These ads carry over many of the themes from previous series. All of them make references to advanced technology ("technology so high even our ships fly"), and they link the training in technology to future civilian careers; the caption over a photo of a sailor directing the landing of an F/1-18 Hornet reads: "If you think it looks impressive here, imagine how it looks on a resume." In addition, the campaign also frequently mentions educational benefits and intangibles like challenge, responsibility, and growth. Most of these ads show men performing a task. One features a woman sitting at a control panel, though a man leans over her, turning a knob, as if he is supervising or instructing her (see figure 4.3). The ad also has a small photo of two men and two women in civilian clothes with bicycles; here, again, women are used to represent leisure.

In 1996, the Navy rolled out a new campaign, based on the slogan "Let the Journey Begin." One print ad reads: "It begins with a step away from the known and a step towards the unknown." In the foreground, a serious-looking young man wearing a cap that says "Navy" gazes into the distance. This image is superimposed over a photo of a hilltop covered with tile roofs and a church steeple—it appears to be an old European village or city—overlooking an expanse of ocean with a ship in the background. The bottom of the page reads "Navy. Let the Journey Begin" and gives a phone number to call and the URL (Internet address) for a recruiting Web site. There is no other text on the page, no description of job fields or educational benefits. The other initial ads in the series are similar; they promise adventure by implying that something exciting is on the horizon, and they don't promise anything else. Each shows the face of a young male sailor in the foreground, superimposed on an image of a ship or submarine next to a city that looks foreign. One ad promises "Today is the day when you stop listening to the tales of other lives lived," and another reads "You're born, you go to school, then one day things begin to get interesting."

A FOUR-YEAR EDUCATION THAT PAYS FOR COLLEGE.

Today's high-tech Navy can give you more than just valuable and practical experience. You can also get up to $30,000* toward a college education.

When you sign up for the Navy College Fund, you'll earn up to $30,000 toward your college tuition after only four years of active duty. You can even start using the program's benefits after your first two years.

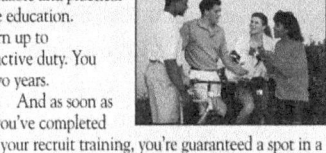

And as soon as you've completed your recruit training, you're guaranteed a spot in a Navy technical training school.

So even before college, you'll be able to get a head start on your career.

Fact is, in just four years in the Navy you can see more, do more and learn more than other people do in an entire lifetime.

Today's high-tech Navy and the Navy College Fund give you the extra edge you need to compete in today's world. And the $30,000 won't hurt either.

For more information, call 1-800-USA-NAVY.

*Up to $30,000 in conjunction with the Montgomery G.I. Bill and four years of active duty.

NAVY
YOU AND THE NAVY.
FULL SPEED AHEAD.

Figure 4.3. Navy ad reprinted from *Sports Illustrated*, October 17, 1994. Courtesy of the U.S. Navy.

A series of television commercials extend the print ads. In each one, Aaron Copland's "Fanfare for the Common Man" rises up in the background. Each begins with a young man—on a farm, riding a bike, studying—who stops what he's doing to look off in the distance, presumably looking for something better or more challenging than his current situation. Each ad continues with a montage of images of Navy life, including dramatic shots of submarines surfacing, small craft skimming the water next to large ships, exotic foreign ports, helicopters flying, an anchor dropping into the sea, and sailors busy at work on deck and in control rooms. The narration in each promises exciting, unexpected new experiences. For instance, one includes the following voice-over:

> It's something you've been waiting for your entire life. It begins with a step away from the known towards the unknown. It will excite you, teach you, move you, and shake you. It will take you to ports halfway around the world and into uncharted waters deep inside yourself. Above all, it will demand your honor, your courage, and your commitment. It's your journey. Start it in the right direction.

These ads go beyond the traditional offer of adventure that a life at sea can bring to promise a transformation. The journey is to a new, better self, possibly even into manhood.

The early 1990s brought both the Tailhook scandal and changes in the law restricting women's shipboard service. The 1991 annual convention of the Tailhook Association of naval aviators led to public revelations of debauchery and accusations of the mistreatment of women, including the groping and abuse of female naval officers in attendance. In 1993, Secretary of Defense Les Aspin ordered the Navy to draft legislation to repeal the exclusion of women from combat ships, and Congress approved the changes (Women's Research and Education Institute 2003). From that point on, women could theoretically be assigned to any Navy billet other than SEALs (because of remaining combat exclusions) and submarine duty (based not on any combat restrictions but on the difficulty of accommodating both male and female submariners in the limited physical space of a submarine). Each of these was a major event for the Navy, and each in its own way challenged constructions of masculinity within the Navy. The opening of combat ships to women, which was fiercely resisted by much of the naval community, threatened the masculinizing function of service on a Navy ship, which stretched back to the days of the romanticized man o'warsman. Tailhook exposed the Navy's tacit encouragement, in relation to naval aviators, of a brand of masculinity that includes risk-taking behavior, sexual aggressiveness, and hard drinking.[6] Although the Navy gave extensive support to *Top Gun*, the 1986 Paramount Studios movie about naval aviators, they withdrew support for a planned sequel because Tailhook "made the drinking and womanizing in *Top Gun* no longer something the navy wanted to brag about" (Robb 2004, 182).

Neither Tailhook nor the opening of roles to women seems to have had much effect on the recruiting materials of the period. The ads revisit themes that have appeared before in Navy ads, which alternate between an emphasis on high-tech career skills and an emphasis on the adventure and challenges of life at sea, in both cases aiming the appeal visually and textually at young men. Despite the new roles for women and the risk that Tailhook may have discouraged women from enlisting, the ads don't reflect an attempt to appeal to women. In the late 1990s, the Army, Air Force, and Marines all began publishing recruiting ads in *Seventeen*, a magazine read by young women, but the Navy didn't. A 1997 *Christian Science Monitor* article on military recruitment of women in the wake of sexual harassment scandals reported that the Navy's recruitment of women was down, not because women were reluctant to enlist but because large numbers of women were choosing to stay in the service, and the Navy had limited spaces on its ships open to women. According to a lieutenant in the Navy Recruiting Command, "We have many, many more women wanting to come into the Navy than we have billets to fill" (quoted in Marks 1997, 3). While in theory many more positions were open to women, the Navy was not rushing to make space for them on ships.

The recruiting problems of the late 1990s affected the Navy as well as the Army. The Navy missed its accession requirements for 1998 by more than 7,000 sailors (Hauk and Parlier 2000) and managed to meet its goals for 1999 only by lowering its target numbers and accepting more recruits with general equivalency diplomas (Myers 1999). In an attempt to reverse the trend, the Navy, while continuing to use the slogan "Let the Journey Begin," introduced a new campaign that focused on the lives of individual sailors.

Each of the print ads pictures a sailor, alone or in a group of sailors, and charts his—or, in one ad in the sample, her—Navy journey. A short timeline lists the sailor's achievements and the age at which each was accomplished. For example, the Navy journey of Aaron Womack, an operations specialist and drummer who is also featured in a television commercial, includes "works in communications dept. on board USS Coronado," "forms band—plays in Singapore," "attends instructor school—develops curriculum for teaching," "certified as master training specialist in anti-sub warfare," "attends naval leadership school," and "earns associates degree in computer science." While Womack's timeline mainly focuses on his naval training, the emphasis of other ads varies. One ad shows a young man out of uniform, who has already left the Navy by age twenty-four for a job with Qualcomm. Others mention travel, education, and buying a "really cool car." The one ad in the sample from this series that features a woman pictures Lieutenant Commander Loree "Rowdy" Hirschmann in her flight suit, flanked by a man and woman in jumpsuits with a plane in the background. Her journey includes, after Navy ROTC and a BA in mathematics, "attends Navy flight school to become a pilot," "lands on aircraft carrier for the first time," "marries fellow Navy pilot," and "debating whether to use GI bill to finance film school or Harvard Business School." Hirschmann is one of the few women to join the elite group of naval aviators—the *Top Gun*, Tailhook guys. She is considering post-Navy careers with some prestige (film school has cultural cachet while Harvard Business School promises corporate success) but with no direct connection to flying, technology, the military, or her naval training. Hers is the only journey that mentions marriage. The ad affirms her femininity, heterosexuality, and desirability, and it removes her from the military even as it offers her as a role model.

These print ads were part of a $20 million campaign developed by the advertising agency BBDO that also included television ads directed by film director Spike Lee (Dill 1999). The five commercials highlight different aspects of Navy life: in "Travel," sailors discuss the exotic ports of call to which the Navy has taken them; in "Homecoming," a young Hispanic man at a welcome-home party is the subject of proud attention from his family and respect and admiration from younger partygoers; in "SEALs," four men discuss the challenges of being a SEAL while the camera shows them in dramatic action; "Education" presents a group of young men and women who have been given the opportunity to go to college, courtesy of the Navy; and in "Band," a group of Hispanic and African American men describe the high-tech jobs they perform on board the ship and the instruments they play in the blues band that they've formed together in their free time. Interestingly, women in the TV commercials are connected with travel and with educational benefits, rather than with shipboard life or Navy jobs.

In the late 1990s, the Navy began using the Internet as a recruiting tool, and advertisements directed potential recruits to its Web site (www.Navyjobs.com). In the "Let the Journey Begin" campaign overall, but especially on the recruiting Web site, the Navy presents itself as an organization that offers experience with cutting-edge technology, opportunity for advancement, equal opportunity, and excellent benefits, including education, travel, and leisure activities. It doesn't try to portray the Navy experience as qualitatively different from civilian life; instead, the Navy puts itself forward as superior to civilian life but not foreign to it. The Navy described itself on the site's "About the Navy" page as follows:

> Today's Navy is a forward-thinking, technologically advanced, worldwide team of highly trained professionals serving their country at sea, under the sea, on land and in the air. Nearly 400,000 active duty men and women proudly serve in today's ethnically diverse Navy, the majority of which, some 336,000 are enlisted Sailors and midshipmen. The opportunities for advancement are equal for all, and with the exception of SEALs and submarines, all assignments are open to women.
>
> In today's Navy you can learn high-tech skills in one of more than 60 job fields, including such dynamic, cutting edge fields as electronics, engineering, computer technology, nuclear propulsion and aviation. The Navy can put you on

the leading edge of technology, and you don't need experience to start. Bring honor, courage, and commitment, and let the journey begin.

By describing itself as "a team of highly-trained professionals," the Navy presents itself as though it were a corporation. It doesn't mention that the service in question is the nation's defense—that this is a *military* organization. Technology and equal opportunity are the two big draws the Navy highlights. The jobs are "dynamic and cutting edge"; they no longer involve physical challenge, "the wind in your teeth." While still showing many more men than women, the Web site features women more prominently and shows them in a wider variety of contexts than the print ad sample.

To high school students and graduates, the Navy specifically offers training, money for college, and the opportunity to travel. The Navy promises: "We can help turn raw talent into polished professionalism and prepare you not just for a career in the Navy, but give you a head start in whatever profession you choose . . . learn how we can tailor a program that best suits your goals." Instead of stressing the differences between Navy jobs and civilian jobs, the adventure and challenge that trumps boring routine, the Navy presents itself as a professional organization, superior to, but not fundamentally different from, the civilian world. It has "better benefits than most civilian employers could hope to match" and recreational programs. In its "Frequently Asked Questions" section, the Navy answers the query "Other than having a good job, what are the benefits of joining the Navy?" with the response:

> Plenty! Here's the short list: Outstanding educational opportunities. Exceptional training in a specialized field. Competitive salary. Excellent promotion prospects. Great sports and leisure programs. Worldwide travel and duty assignment preferences. Plus the Navy offers you non-taxable benefits, and excellent medical and dental care for you and your family.

Nothing here differentiates the Navy from a civilian workplace. None of the benefits have to do with what the Navy actually is and what it does. That the Navy named its Web site Navy*jobs*.com is telling.

The Navy promises college students and graduates: "If you're a college graduate looking to maximize your potential, today's Navy can put you on the fast track to success and personal fulfillment. As a Navy Officer, you'll step into a responsible position that offers you action, adventure and travel opportunities unparalleled in any civilian organization." Navy officers reap many personal rewards: "In addition to traveling and living in exotic locales, you are able to work on personal goals and strive for professional achievement alongside equally driven and talented individuals." The Navy claims that "the standard of living for an officer is excellent," and they bolster that claim with a photo of people playing golf.

This initial version of the Web site can be read as an extension of the trend that began in the 1980s of emphasizing the Navy as a pathway to a career: not a trade, a job, or a good skill, but a professional career. The late 1990s were a period of low unemployment, economic expansion, and the rise of dot-com wealth. Internet-based and technology-intensive start-up firms were celebrated in the media.[7] Instead of emphasizing the differences between Navy and civilian life and the challenges and adventure of life at sea, Navy ships are almost presented as technology-intensive floating corporate campuses, with plenty of perks. A young man may not have the chance to be a part of a high-tech start-up, where long hours are balanced by the excitement and challenge of a new venture, the prestige of working in the economy's hottest sector, and the potential for stock-option wealth, but he can "maximize [his] potential" and be a professional in the technology-intensive Navy. The picture of the Navy presented on the Web site reflects models of masculine achievement that held sway in the civilian world, where jobs in the technology sector carried great prestige. They were framed as strenuous and demanding, requiring technical skill, creative thinking, intelligence, and stamina, and the work done at these high-tech firms was seen as the key to our economic and technological future.[8] The emphasis on equal opportunity also fits with the masculinity of the new dominant corporate culture; despite continuing male privilege and the continuation of practices that help sustain men's dominance of the corporate world,[9] Connell and Wood's (2005) model of transnational business masculinity includes "a self-conscious modernity in relation to nationality, sexuality, and gender" and a "conscious endorsement of gender equity" (359).

This corporate, equal-opportunity view of Navy life did not sit well with many military observers. As was the case with the Army, some commentators blamed Navy recruitment problems on a perceived lack of masculinity in the service's public image and made negative comparisons to the still-virile Marines. To these commentators, the presence of women in some ads, combined with a lack of overt markers of a physical, warrior masculinity, publicly symbolized a feminization of the Navy or an emphasis on gender equality at the expense of the Navy's image as a fighting force.

In an article in U.S. Naval Institute's journal *Proceedings*, former Navy Commander Thomas Strother claims that while young, blue-collar men enlist for a variety of reasons, including economic security or a desire for adventure, "usually the other (albeit rarely admitted) reason was to enjoy the rite of passage: to become a man" (1999). Strother confesses that one of his main reasons for joining the Navy was that "it was different from 'normal society'"; unlike the "feminized culture" of elementary and high school, "it was a bastion of masculinity where young men were encouraged to be a little wild if it contributed to combat readiness." Strother claims that the military's lifting of the ban on gay people serving in 1993[10] and the end of the ban on women serving in combat vessels and aircraft are directly to blame for recruiting problems. According to Strother:

> Since allowing women to serve in combat roles, recruiting slowly has slid in the tank. The Navy has countered this falloff in recruiting with ideas on how to recruit more females. . . . Because of Navy Recruiting "women-in-charge" ads, fewer blue-collar teenaged boys will join. The last thing that many of our prospective male recruits need is another matriarch. Plus, as my 19-year-old nephew told me when I asked him to consider the Navy for the challenge it offered, "How hard can the Navy be if all you have is sissies and girls in it?" . . . The perception in working-class America (in this case New Jersey) is that the Navy is now a haven for gays and women. Their attitude is: What self-respecting teenaged guy would join the Navy? If you believe I am wrong, look at the very macho series of Marine Corps TV commercials. Is the Marine Corps suffering from the horrible recruiting problems that plague the Navy? No. (192)

Strother goes on to ask whether the Navy can "recruit enough gays and women to offset the loss of working-class males who, feeling cheated of that tough Navy boot camp, turn to the still macho Marine Corps or pass up the military entirely" and puts it to the admirals to "decide if it is worth it to toughen the image of the Navy by ending recruiting appeals that deter young men."

Strother conflates the issue of image with the question of the toughness of the Navy as an experience, especially in relation to boot camp. He has been discussing perceptions but seems to take for granted that Navy boot camp must have changed. If the ban on service by gay men and lesbians had indeed been lifted, it was not specifically a Navy policy and would have applied to the "still macho" Marine Corps as well. While the Navy ads of the 1990s and the BBDO "Let the Journey Begin" campaign in particular did show some women, to describe them as "women-in-charge" ads is certainly a stretch, at least as far as the ads in this sample are concerned. Certainly, the Navy wasn't featuring gay sailors in its recruitment materials. The heterosexuality of the most "in-charge" woman shown, Lieutenant Commander Hirschmann, is emphasized in the description of her Navy journey. Clearly, though, it's gay male sailors who concern Strother, as evidenced by his use of the phrase "women and gays," which implies that the two categories are mutually exclusive. This fits with Cohn's (1998) contention that anxiety about lifting the ban on gays in the military has to do with men and masculinity, not with the presence of lesbians. It seems that for Strother, the inclusion of women and the lack of overt machoness in the ads serve to challenge the masculinity of the service overall, making it appear as a "haven for gays," even though Navy policies on homosexuality would not differ from those of the other services. I would argue that the Navy did still deploy a form of masculinity in its late-1990s advertising, but a civilianized, post-masculinity-crisis, transformed masculinity, which, to a traditionalist, does not count as masculinity, certainly not in relation to the military.

The same year, another commentator in *Proceedings*, naval aviator Lieutenant Christian Bonat, negatively compared Navy advertising, and specifically the ad featuring female naval aviator Hirschmann, to Marine Corps advertising. Bonat looks at a Marine ad with a picture of a shaved-headed recruit struggling to climb over an obstacle and the tagline "Pain Is Weakness Leaving the Body." Bonat analyzes the ad as follows:

> The subtext speaks of the mind and body "meeting" a common goal and "winning." Who is the intended audience here? My pop-psychological Madison Avenue analysis is that this service is targeting those in a young, active demographic and offering them a challenge—both physical and mental. No direct benefit or reward is offered, save the anticipated pride and confidence that the recruit soon will have as he succeeds in pulling himself over that obstacle. What does this ad say about the Marine Corps? Is warrior ethos too much to glean out of this ad? Maybe so, but it certainly would reinforce that idea if it already were there. This ad presents a tough and challenging place to be. The Marine Corps shows itself as an organization that the reader would be proud to be a part of—if he could measure up, and if he could get over that obstacle. It also describes an organization that the nation would be proud to have as its premier fighting force. (1999)

Bonat then describes the Hirschmann ad and the features of her timeline, and he asks the same questions about it that he does about the Marine ad:

> Who is the intended audience here? Again, my analysis tells me the service in question is targeting a young, college-bound demographic and offering education benefits, among other things, as reward for going to flight school. At first glance, the cynic in me thinks this is specifically aimed at females, but then again, it could be aimed at young males. What does this ad say about the Navy? First, it certainly must be short of people seeking ROTC scholarships or who want to be aviators. Second, the Navy provides equal opportunity with regard to gender and it provides educational benefits. Any sacrifice for a common goal, reinforcement of a proud heritage, or reference to a warrior ethos? The three service members do connote a team atmosphere. But nothing in this ad even implies any sacrifice—except maybe the late nights spend debating whether to "journey" to Harvard for your MBA. The ad also downplays any challenging training by using the soft verb "attend" when referring to "Navy flight school." Does one "attend" Parris Island? The ad, in an apparent oversight, leaves out "attending" anything else—like a deployment to the Western Pacific or the Persian Gulf in service to the nation's interests, or "attending" a potential foe's hasty departure from the breathing world. Could the national and current service members be proud of the Navy as displayed in this advertisement? With respect to our emphasis on equal opportunity and education, probably so. With respect to the Navy being a challenging organization with a proud heritage and a dedication to remaining a supreme fighting force, however—our recruiting and retention numbers provide the answer.

Bonat sees a great deal in these two ads. He attributes warrior ethos and sacrifice to the Marines and projects that a reader would be proud to be a part of the Marines and the nation would be proud of the Marines as a fighting force, all from an ad that shows someone struggling to meet a physical challenge on an obstacle course. Bonat criticizes the Navy ad for not presenting the Navy's "proud heritage" or status as "a supreme fighting force." As he's described it, the Marine ad doesn't do these things either. Like the Navy ad, the Marine ad doesn't make reference to deployment or killing an enemy. But the Marine ad does have a more overtly masculine subtext, and its physicality, its concern for triumph over pain and weakness, which are traditional components of a warrior masculinity (Goldstein 2001; Morgan 1994), stand in for all of the other values that Bonat reads into the ads. Bonat does not directly connect the Marine ad to manhood, nor does he connect the organizational values he attributes to the Marines to men or masculinity—he seems to be scrupulously avoiding such language—but he does implicitly make those connections. The martial masculinity of the Marines is heightened by contrast with the Navy, which, by merely picturing a woman and tracing out her career, has committed the sin of attempting to appeal to women. ("The cynic" in Bonat thinks the ad is aimed at women, implying that he finds such a strategy objectionable.)

The Navy seemed to take heed of such criticism and began to propagate a more blatantly macho ideal. By 2001, the Internet stock bubble had burst, and high-tech start-ups had lost their venture capital and their allure. This may be one reason that in its next incarnation, Navy advertising shifted away from an emphasis on benefits and career and back toward adventure and challenge—this time with a distinctly martial tenor and a return to a more exclusively male portrayal of Navy life. Around the same time that the Army attempted to revitalize its image with the "Army of One" campaign, the Navy also made major changes in how it presented itself, with a sleek, sharp-edged new campaign. In September 2000, the Navy awarded a contract to the advertising firm Campbell-Ewald, and early in 2001, the Navy adopted the slogan "Accelerate Your Life," rolled out new advertising, and revamped its Web site, changing the URL from www.navyjobs.com to www.navy.com.

A print ad from the new series asks, "If someone wrote a book about your life, would anyone want to read it?" Underneath the picture of a shaved-headed young man in sunglasses carrying gear, the copy reads: "You've got one life. Make it count. Check out the Life Accelerator at navy.com or call 1–800–USA-NAVY." The ads feature a flashy, angular new font and direct the reader to the Navy Web site's new "Life Accelerator," an aptitude test that advises visitors to the site about Navy careers that might suit them. The Life Accelerator has to do with Navy careers, but the pitch that leads potential recruits there evokes excitement, adventure, and a departure from the routine. A television commercial that ran on the hit show *Survivor: Outback* in the spring of 2001 asks the same question as the print ad. As throbbing rock music by the group Godsmack thunders in the background, the viewer sees a quickly shifting series of images, including a face in camouflage makeup, a small craft skimming over the ocean's surface and up into the back of a helicopter, a night-vision scope's view of a man with a rifle, men dropping out of a helicopter into water, and men with rifles dropping over the side of a small boat into water. The imagery is all distinctly martial, the action is fast, and the players are all men.

Bob Garfield, who panned the "Army of One" advertising when it debuted two months earlier, reviewed the initial "Accelerate Your Life" television campaign in *Advertising Age*:

> "Accelerate Your Life" . . . splits the difference between "Be All You Can Be" and "Join the Navy, See the World." It's about ceasing to be a slacker, or a loser in some numbing job, in favor of genuine, heart-pounding adventure. The promise isn't that you'll make yourself into a better person or broaden your vistas via exotic ports of call. It's about the rush, dude. The adrenaline. The experience. Even the danger. The X-Games, basically, only with heat-seeking missiles instead of skateboards. Three very similar spots carve that message into discrete slices. All show rapid pulses of sea-training action, images of warships and dinghies, helicopters and Seals [sic], accompanied by hard-driving percussion and punctuated by black screen. "If someone wrote a book about your life," the voiceover asks, "would anyone want to read it?" And we're, like, ouch. That is sooooo cold . . . but compelling—and, we believe, quite motivating. . . . Not a word here is mentioned about service, or duty, or patriotism or some potential long-term benefit. It's all about the experience right now. (Garfield 2001b)

While Garfield makes fun of the campaign a bit by mimicking the language used by the type of young people he expects will find the ad appealing (and he also later compares the focus on immediate experience with the way illicit drugs are—successfully—sold to the same target market), he highlights the speed, the action, and the distinctly martial tenor of the campaign.

In the summer of 2001, the Navy asked its advertising agency, Campbell-Ewald, to develop a public service announcement "to convey the Navy's core mission of projecting power globally to protect and defend America" ("Life, Liberty" 2004). The Navy was considering several slogans, but after the terrorist attacks of September 11 of that year, one in particular seemed to stand out from the rest and "capture the fresh sense of danger and combine it with the renewed pride and determination felt throughout the fleet." After successful test-marketing, "Life, Liberty, and the Pursuit of All Who Threaten It" debuted on cable TV and in print ads in *Boy's Life* and *Entertainment Weekly* in early 2002. This slogan taps into the remasculinization and militarization of U.S. foreign policy in the wake of the terrorist attacks, reinvigorating and toughening the Navy's image for a post–September 11 audience.[11] (The Army, perhaps because it needed to attract more women to meet its recruiting quotas, did not so wholeheartedly embrace a warrior approach.)

The print ad pictures an aircraft carrier with support ships in the ocean, with a very faint grid pattern superimposed over the page. The headline reads "Life, liberty, and the pursuit of all who threaten it," and small text along the bottom of the page says "For over 200 years, the US Navy has been protecting America's most valuable asset: freedom. If you're ready to answer your country's call, check out the Life Accelerator at navy.com or call 1–800-USA-NAVY." The ad has a sleek, high-tech look thanks to the text fonts and the grid, but it refers to Navy history and tradition and makes an explicit call for patriotic service. The companion television commercial, like previous ones in the "Accelerate Your Life" series, uses thundering rock music and fast-moving, intercut images—including a helicopter rising into the air, a submarine, and a jet taking off from the deck of an aircraft carrier. The voice-over says, "Life, liberty, and the pursuit of all who threaten it. Navy. Accelerate your life."

Another television commercial emphasizes nothing but action and excitement, with a distinctly masculine cast to its appeal. "Minivan" shows a series of very fast-moving images of undersea divers, men with rifles dropping out of helicopters, speeding watercraft, jets flying, and the like. This parade of images is briefly interrupted for a shot of a hapless-looking civilian man, gazing somewhat blankly at a minivan. Over the de rigueur rock music, a voice-over announcer says, "And to think, somewhere, some poor guy is buying a minivan." The Navy, with its fast action and prominent display of weaponry, contrasts militarized excitement and adventure with the undoubtedly dull life of the guy buying the minivan. A minivan is not a fast, sexy car, but an automobile that represents family obligations, meant for hauling kids and groceries—it's a suburban mom's car. The man buying the minivan is implicitly emasculated, highlighting the masculinizing power of the Navy.

A later version of the "Life, Liberty" television commercial and other print ads in the series combine the new emphasis on military action with the kind of appeals the Navy has used over the course of the AVF: adventure and challenge, as well as tangible benefits like access to technology, education, and career advancement. In one ad, for example, a sailor dangles in the air, high above the deck of an aircraft carrier. A to-do list in the corner of the page includes such disparate items as "get airlifted off a carrier," "take psych. Finals in Maui," "run w/bulls in Spain," "decipher code in 6 languages," and "defend freedom." The list draws attention to various benefits of Navy life, like travel, education, and interesting jobs, but the imagery emphasizes the main draw, which is the militarized thrill of the airlift, while the references to Maui and running with the bulls add to the aura of excitement and adventure.

In 2003, the Navy ran a few print ads that departed from the formula, focusing on the Navy as a source of opportunity and a road to professional success, in particular for African American men. Two versions of the same ad feature different pictures—both of black men—with the same text. They read:

> I've never been the type to wait for anything, especially an opportunity. Matter of fact, the only handout that was ever given to me was a Navy brochure. I wanted to see the world . . . I did. I wanted a bright future, and I have one of those, too. I've worked; now I own my own company . . . all, because of the experience I've gained in the Navy. So do what I did. Call 1–800-USA-Navy or log on to navy.com.

In one ad, the top half of the page shows a smiling black man in a sport jacket, sitting at a desk holding a pen and a Navy mug; on the bottom of the page, the desk morphs into water and a jet takes off from the deck of a carrier. These ads seem to assume that for the group targeted, upward mobility is a bigger draw—and perhaps a more coveted marker of masculinity than fast action and adventure.

Overall, the "Accelerate Your Life" campaign was action oriented and militaristic, even before the attacks of September 11, 2001, which only seemed to heighten the trend. Some of the "Accelerate Your Life" TV commercials show a surprising number of guns. The Navy's military role has very little to do with individual sailors carrying rifles—even calling the service members pictured "sailors" seems like a misnomer. All of the ads flaunt Navy vessels, with dramatic shots of technologically advanced ships, submarines, and planes in motion. The Navy personnel engaging in the exciting, martial action all appear to be men. It's possible that some of the individuals obscured by their uniforms and gear are actually women, but the impression is of a male world. The ads don't talk about "the wind in your teeth" or "men [testing] themselves against the sea" as they did in the 1970s, but there is again an emphasis on physicality, toughness, and challenge, this time in the form of a visually expressed technology-tinged warrior masculinity.

CONCLUSIONS: MASCULINITY AND NAVY RECRUITING

Over the course of the all-volunteer force, Navy recruiting appeals have tended to shift back and forth between an emphasis on career and benefits, with the promise of good jobs or high-tech training, and an emphasis on adventure and challenge. Each of these sets of appeals, however, contains a masculine subtext, if not an overt association with manhood. The career and benefits theme was presented first in terms of masculine pride in work that is physically and mentally challenging—"good, hard work"—later shifting to an emphasis on professional careers, personal success, and exposure to cutting-edge technology, more closely aligning the Navy with the high-status careers of the information age. While the latter is less blatantly masculine, the connections to technological prowess, professionalism, and success fit with dominant models of masculinity in the civilian world. The Navy's other main approach is to highlight adventure, offering young men the excitement of life at sea and challenges that allow them to test and prove themselves. In the 2000s, the offer of adventure became more explicitly militaristic, layering a warrior masculinity on top of other kinds of appeals. The fact that the Navy began utilizing what could be considered traditional military masculinity recently in its history shows its lingering appeal and its continuing power to attract some sectors of the wider culture—despite the general displacement of traditional masculinities—when other forms of masculinity may have failed them. The Navy is asserting that its commitment to masculinity hasn't weakened.

The Navy's personnel needs (or at least its understanding of them) are also revealed in its gendering of Navy life. The ads make token references to women as sailors but basically present the Navy as a male world, sometimes using images of women to attract men rather than to recruit women. While almost all Navy ships are theoretically open to women, in practice, space for women is limited, and their marginal status on board ships—the locus of naval power and status—is reflected in their place within the Navy's self-representations. With the creation of the AVF, however, the Navy broke with its racist past—at least representationally—and expanded its offer of masculinity to African American men, tapping into a potential source of manpower that had been underutilized.

CHAPTER 5

The Marine Corps

While military institutions in general are tied to masculinity, the Marine Corps in particular, with its emphasis on combat, has been seen as the force with the most macho and aggressive men. With the end of the draft, the Corps didn't retreat from its association with masculinity but sought to emphasize it. Marine recruiting materials downplay benefits and emphasize challenge, elitism, and martial masculinity. Over the course of the all-volunteer force (AVF), there have been some minor shifts in the Marines' approach, and the look of the ads has changed. Early in the AVF, ads were heavy on text, and some of them showed Marines at work, repairing equipment or working on an airplane's ground crew. Marine Corps ads tried to differentiate the Marines from the other services. In the late 1970s, the work imagery disappeared, and throughout the 1980s, Marines are either on ceremonial display in their dress uniforms, often with a sword, or in a specifically martial context, like dangling out of a helicopter or crawling up a riverbank with their rifles. In a series of ads from the late 1990s and early 2000s, a shaved-headed recruit, his face contorted with pain and determination, engages in an arduous physical task or struggles through some portion of an obstacle course. Despite changes in imagery or shifts in emphasis, overall, Marine Corps advertising has remained remarkably consistent throughout the entire period of the AVF. The dominant message is that the Marines will demand that a recruit prove his worth, but once he's met the challenge, he'll be welcomed into a proud, exclusive warrior brotherhood. The Marines offer a rite of passage into manhood. Marine recruiting advertisements rarely show women and make no attempt to use gender-inclusive language. Marine ads talk specifically to and about men, and they offer them the chance to become warriors.

The analysis in this chapter is based on thirty-nine print advertisements published by the Marine Corps between 1970 and 2003, six television commercials that aired between 1980 and 2003, and two different incarnations of the Marine Corps' recruiting Web site. After briefly discussing Marine Corps culture and providing some historical background on Marine recruiting, this chapter presents an analysis of Marine recruiting materials over the course of the all-volunteer force and how they construct masculinity. It also examines the place of women in the Marine Corps and within Marine recruiting materials and how women fit into the Corps' ideas about gender.

MARINE CULTURE

The culture of the Marine Corps is reflected in its slogans and mottoes: "semper fidelis" (always faithful), "every Marine a rifleman," and "once a Marine, always a Marine." The Marine Corps sees itself as a brotherhood, and according to the Center for Strategic and International Studies, it has "actively discouraged the emergence within the corps of subcultures based on branches or separate war-fighting communities" (CSIS 2000, 13). Or as RAND strategist Carl Builder put it, while each of the other services maintains internal distinctions and hierarchies, "to be a marine is enough" (quoted in Ricks 1997, 189). The focus of the institution is the rifleman, the common enlisted Marine, but that Marine is anonymous and celebrated as one of the group, not as an individual.

In his examination of Marine Corps boot camp, *Making the Corps*, journalist Thomas E. Ricks describes the Corps as "a culture apart" (1997, 19). According to Ricks:

> The Air Force has its planes, the Navy its ships, the Army its obsessively written and obeyed "doctrine" that dictates how to act. Culture—that is, the values and assumptions that shape its members—is all the Marines have. It is what holds them together. They are the smallest of the US military services, and in many ways the most interesting. Theirs is the richest culture: formalistic, insular, elitist, with a deep anchor in their own history and mythology. Much more than the other branches, they place pride and responsibility at the lowest levels of the organization. . . . Alone among the US military services, the Marines have bestowed their name on their enlisted ranks. The Army has Army officers and soldiers, the Navy has naval officers and sailors, the Air Force has Air Force officers and airmen—but the Marines have officers and Marines. (19)

The Marines have a strong sense of who they are and a deep pride in their institution. They celebrate their history and inculcate recruits with the sense that they are the latest in a long line of warriors who have served their country in battles—which are likely to be named aloud at Marine Corps events and celebrations—stretching back to the Revolutionary War.

This strong sense of culture and the greater concern with their identity than with their size, their hardware, or a stratified structure has helped the Corps be an adaptable organization militarily but may make it less flexible in other ways. According to Ricks, because the Corps isn't heavily invested in its number of personnel and its hardware, but rather in preserving its independent culture, the Marines are "less threatened [than the other services] by the post–Cold War cuts in the defense budget—but more worried by social changes, including those relating to gays and women, imposed on the services" (1997, 189). Judith Hicks Stiehm also observes how the presence of women disrupts Marine culture. According to Stiehm, "The Marine slogan 'Every man a rifleman' [sic] glorifies the interchangeability of personnel: the substitutability, the possibility, the equally shared jeopardy of every marine" (1989, 231). This idea of shared risk, which all of the services promote to some degree, is, of course, a myth. Only some men are in positions that make combat or exposure to violence a possibility. Stiehm notes, "Women in uniform make this myth less believable. Their very presence forces recognition that military personnel are *not* 'in this together.' Holding noncombat jobs only, uniformed women are a constant reminder that all those in uniform are not equally jeopardized" (231–232). The presence of women in the Marine Corps upsets the idea of the generic, interchangeable, anonymous, fighting Marine, who sees every other Marine as his brother. Women can't be riflemen, and thus they don't fit into the culture as legitimate Marines. The Marine Corps tends to put women into a special, separate category, both in its institutional practices and in its recruiting materials, which, like Marine culture, celebrate an anonymous warrior.

The strong sense of culture, the insularity, and the concepts of brotherhood and "once a Marine always a Marine" that encourage Marines to privilege their identities as Marines over other aspects of their identities may also contribute to racial problems within the Corps. According to Thomas Ricks:

> The Marine culture also sometimes seems too narrow for some of its own people—the 27,000 Marines who are black. In 1994, for example, the Center for Naval Analyses, a Defense Department–supported think tank, trying to determine why minorities did relatively poorly in joining and rising in the Marine officer corps, pointed to the culture as a problem. "All of the black former Marines present (at a symposium) spoke about the narrowness of Marine Corps culture," the CNA reported. They went on to speak of "the need for blacks to conform to this culture to succeed in the Marine Corps. A particular style of dress was expected: khakis, polo shirts, and deck shoes. Those wearing jeans or silk shirts off duty were subject to ridicule or chastisement from senior officers." (1997, 203)[1]

Ricks believes that though only 6 percent of the officer corps is African American, "the complaints of black Marines about the Corps generally seem to point more to insensitivity, and perhaps an ignorance of how to alter the Corps' culture to make blacks more comfortable, than they do to a deep-seated racism" (1997, 204). The Corps, like the other services, certainly has racism in its history. The Marine Corps, unlike the Army and the Navy, did not recruit any African Americans during World War I. The Corps began, somewhat unwillingly, to recruit black (male) Marines for the first time in 1942, for service in segregated battalions that would occupy Pacific islands that white units had captured from the Japanese (Segal 1989, 106–107). The Corps hadn't intended to continue the black units after the war ended but resumed enlistment of African Americans and then began to integrate them under orders from President Truman (Millet 1991, 468). Full integration was hastened by the manpower and logistical demands of the Korean War. The Marine Corps, like the other services, suffered violent racial incidents during the Vietnam War, most notably in 1969 at Camp Lejeune and Kaneohe Naval Air Station (Segal 1989, 111). As noted earlier, African American men, mainly as a function of socioeconomic status, were overrepresented in the draft and particularly likely to end up in the ground combat forces, which included service in the Marine Corps. The perception that African Americans were bearing an unequal burden in fighting the Vietnam War contributed to the racial unrest.

In dealing with its racial problems, the Corps has promoted the idea that there are no black Marines or white Marines but, as the saying goes, "there are only green Marines" (Millet 1991, 599). Like other aspects of Marine culture, this view of race asks Marines to allow their identities as Marines to subsume other parts of their identities; it also doesn't take into account the ways that this "green Marine" culture has been directed and created by white men or how asking people to make being a Marine the dominant part of their identities may have different meanings and costs for whites and nonwhites. For instance, the off-duty African American Marines Ricks referred to, who were wearing clothes that differed from the white Marine norm, were enacting a different style of masculinity; black masculinities are shaped in relation to a hegemonic masculinity that is not fully accessible to nonwhites (Connell 1995), and in the Marine Corps, as in the larger culture, such masculinities are marginalized. However, in the AVF era, such racial issues seem to be more of a problem for Marine officers than for enlisted Marines, the vast majority of whom don't make a career of service and leave after a few years. Recruiting materials certainly depict African American men, offering them the same warrior masculinity and transformation as white men, though they aren't shown nearly as frequently as white men.

THE RECRUITING BACKGROUND

The Marine Corps is the smallest service, a factor that allows the Marines to claim elitism in their ads in a way that the larger services couldn't do as credibly, and they had the fewest ads, by far, in the sample. In part that may be because they need fewer recruits than the other services, though they need a proportionally large number for their size. The Marines have a smaller leadership structure than the other services; fewer members can stay in the service and be promoted, so turnover is purposefully high, and relatively large numbers of recruits—about 40,000—are needed each year (Freedberg 1999). About 75 percent of enlisted Marines leave the service when their initial term is up (Schmitt 2005a). This structure, along with the high proportion of combat jobs, means that unlike the Navy or the Air Force, the Marine Corps doesn't need recruits with the aptitude for technical training who will stay in the service long enough to justify the costs of that training. The Corps needs short-timers who are looking for a few years of action and excitement before returning to the civilian world. This set of needs helps to drive recruiting strategy; the Marines can use the promise of a warrior masculinity to lure young men who want to spend a few years doing combat-oriented jobs, and they don't need to emphasize benefits or job training, as would probably be necessary to recruit people who would make a longer commitment and do more technical work.

The small number of advertisements may also be attributable to the Corps' skill at forging a distinct public image and its ability to obtain positive media coverage. Throughout its history, the Marine Corps has had to fight off attempts to abolish the service, and it has become adept at justifying its existence and working with the press (McCarthy and Haralson 2003).

During the recruiting crisis of the late 1990s, the Marine Corps, which was able to meet its recruiting goals, was held up as model for the other services to follow. Marine recruiting materials of the period downplayed benefits and highlighted challenge, elitism, and masculinity, and some commentators believed that the other services should emulate the Marines, particularly their appeals to a masculine warrior spirit (Bonat 1999; Keene 1999; Smart 2000; Strother 1999). The Marines were lauded for their recruiting skills, though the Marine Corps attributed its success to the qualities of the service itself, its values and its high standards, rather than its ability to sell itself. Despite the plaudits for the Corps' recruiting skills, it had done poorly at recruiting in the 1970s, as all of the services did, and had trouble again in 1995, missing its goals for the year (Schmitt 2005a). The Marines' problems of the mid-1990s didn't receive as much coverage as the successes of the late 1990s. The Corps has managed to create a mythology about its recruiting practices, and many articles have repeated the claim that the Marines have never used benefits to sell themselves and only offered the chance to become a Marine (Keene 1999; McCarthy and Haralson 2003). One article goes so far as to claim that "the Corps, as it has almost since its inception 223 years ago when legend says recruiting was done out of a Philadelphia tavern, offers little more than a challenge to all comers," taking the word of a public affairs chief for the Marine Corps Recruiting Command that since 1775, "We've really never changed our recruiting approach. . . . We are still offering young men and women only the chance to be Marines" (Keene 1999).

It may be true that in 1775 the Marine Corps offered young men little more than the chance to become Marines, for the simple fact that at the time the Corps didn't have much in the way of benefits to offer. During the Revolutionary War, soldiers and sailors could receive enlistment bounties, but the Marines didn't have that enticement available, and the nascent Corps had trouble recruiting, never meeting its authorized strength. According to Marine historian Allan R. Millet:

> Recruiting officers visited port cities and towns in New England, the Mid-Atlantic states, Virginia, and Charleston, South Carolina, but found few men of "sobriety and fidelity" who would enlist. [The first Marine Corps Commandant, William Ward] Burrows also had to allow his officers to recruit aliens (mostly Irishmen) up to one-quarter of the Corps's strength and reduce the height requirement to 5 feet, 4 inches, although he prohibited the enlistment of blacks, Indians, and mulattoes. Many recruits were physically defective, and Burrows finally had to force his officers to pay for such rejects' expenses from their own pockets. Marine officers often marched their recruits to their camps under armed guard and tried to get them aboard ship as quickly as possible, especially if warm weather was approaching, for desertions increased with temperature and the availability of unskilled jobs. . . . There was little about the new Corps that marked it as an elite military unit. (1991, 31)

Not only was the early Marine Corps not in any way elite but also it served different purposes than the Marines of today. The original functions of Marines were to act as ships' guards (in essence, protecting officers from the crew); provide firepower during battles at sea, mainly from their muskets but in some cases from the ships' guns; and be a part of landing parties for skirmishes on shore. Marines fought on ships but did not sail them. The Marine Corps couldn't find enough men to perform these duties in the War of 1812, despite the introduction of an enlistment bounty (lower than the Army's), and eventually an authorization for advance pay (Millet 1991, 46).

The Corps began to change, in its purposes, its public image, and its ability to recruit, with the expansionist foreign policy of the turn of the twentieth century. The Corps began to perform expeditionary duties, increased in size, and gained prestige, finally becoming the elite and selective force that it claims it always has been. Recruiting posters of the late 1800s made appeals based on benefits (despite the stereotype that the Corps has never done so), namely, pay, job security, food, clothing, and travel, but in the early 1900s, posters began to refer to the Marines' foreign service and to present the Marine as a warrior, with slogans like "The First to Fight" and "If You Want to Fight! Join the Marines" (Millet 1991, 175). Like the Navy, the Marine Corps, playing its part in America's imperialist adventures, was helping to reshape and reinvigorate masculinity in the wake of its late-nineteenth-century crisis (described by Kimmel 1996). During this period, the Corps began to develop its public relations skills. Recruiters wrote articles for newspapers and told stories to reporters about the heroism of Marines in the colonial service and the Spanish-American War. In 1911, the Corps founded a recruiting publicity bureau in New York City. The bureau published *The Recruiters' Bulletin* with adventure stories recruiters could use to entice enlistees, it created pamphlets on the Marine Corps, it worked with major newspapers, and it even produced an early motion picture, *The Peacemakers: An Educational Pictorial Showing the United States Marines in Barracks, at Sea, and on the Field of Battle*, with footage of the Marines fighting in the Caribbean (Millet 1991, 175–176).

From that period on, the Corps cultivated and mainly managed to maintain the image of an elite force of combat-ready warriors. Recruiting posters from both world wars highlight the Corps' connection to combat. During World War I, the Corps could boast that it was a selective, all-volunteer service, as the newly created Selective Service System conscripted men into the Army; as Millet reports, during that war, the Marines' successful recruiting and public relations efforts drew "the cream of the 1917 volunteers," and the Marines accepted only 60,189 of the 239,274 men who tried to enlist (1991, 289). During World War II, the Marines did very well in the rush to enlist after the attack on Pearl Harbor, but as that rush subsided and manpower needs expanded, the Corps had to lower enlistment standards in April 1942 to meet its recruiting quotas. Despite this, and even as President Roosevelt placed all men between the ages of eighteen and thirty-six under selective service and put an end to volunteering, the Marine Corps still managed to maintain its image as an elite, all-volunteer force by identifying the draftees who preferred the Marines and maneuvering them into the Corps and by enlisting seventeen-year-olds (373–374). Despite willingly accepting draftees for the first time during the Korean War (508), within the framework of Cold War conscription, up until the Vietnam War, the Marine Corps generally maintained its reputation and image. The Marine Corps was not perceived as the most prestigious of the armed forces—that distinction belonged to the newer and more technologically advanced Air Force—but it was still the service for warriors; according to surveys conducted during the Cold War, the stereotypes associated with the Marine Corps were "physical toughness and danger" (Moskos 1970, 18).

THE RECRUITING ADVERTISEMENTS

The Marine Corps faced the commencement of the all-volunteer force in dismal condition. While all of the services were suffering a loss of public and self-confidence in the wake of the Vietnam War, Thomas Ricks claims that "the Marines were arguably the most devastated of the services" (1997, 136). Because the Marine Corps is the most combat oriented of all the services, and the war was mainly fought on the ground by combat troops, the Marine Corps was especially damaged and demoralized. The Marine Corps bore more casualties in Vietnam than it did in World War II, and it suffered from high rates of drug abuse and violent racial incidents. As warrior masculinity was under attack in the larger culture by both the antiwar and women's movements, the Marine Corps, as a major purveyor of this type of masculinity, may have felt under siege. Jeffrey Record described the Marines in the early 1970s in the United States Naval Institute's *Proceedings* as follows:

> The Corps registered rates of courts-martial, non-judicial punishments, unauthorized absences, and outright desertions unprecedented in its own history, and, in most cases, three to four times those plaguing the US Army. Violence and crime at recruit depots and other installations escalated; in some cases, officers ventured out only in pairs or groups and only in daylight. (Quoted in Ricks 1997, 136)

The Marine Corps had stopped taking draftees in 1970, and despite its problems, as the draft ended, the Marine Corps believed that its recruits were true volunteers. In fact, only half were (Millet 1991, 611). To meet its personnel needs, the Corps allowed quality to plummet. Half of new male recruits lacked a high school diploma. The poor quality of recruits exacerbated the Corps' problems, and by 1975, the Marines had the worst rates of imprisonment, unauthorized absence, and courts-martial of all of the armed services and high rates of drug and alcohol abuse, second only to the Navy (612). In 1975, incoming Commandant Louis H. Wilson worked to revamp recruiting and raise standards, preferring to increase the proportion of high school graduates and stop accepting recruits from the lowest mental category, even if that meant the Corps ended up below strength, and the Corps slowly began to rebound.

Marine Corps advertising in the early 1970s steadfastly ignored the Corps' woes. While Army and Navy ads from the beginning of the AVF sought to show how the services were changing and improving, which could be seen as an indirect acknowledgment of the military's problems, the Marines began with an emphasis on their elitism—an emphasis that has remained consistent in the decades since—even though, as far as recruit quality in the 1970s went, the elitism was mainly wishful thinking.

In the early and mid-1970s, Marine Corps advertising worked to differentiate the Marines from the other services. The Marines placed themselves in direct competition with the other branches of the armed forces. When the Army began using the slogan "Today's Army wants to join you," the Marines responded with "We're not joining anybody," a slogan that the Defense Department quickly made them drop (Keene 1999). The Marines argued that they were special and a challenge. The ads in this period stressed Marine pride. Several of the ads in my sample from 1974 and 1975 follow the trend of making the Marines stand out from the Army, Navy, and Air Force. Some of them read as follows:

"If you're thinking about the military, you've got three choices or one challenge."

"The Marine Corps gives you as many educational opportunities as the Air Force, Navy or Army. Now, what makes us different: It's as simple as this: we *are* the Marines. A tough team to make."

"The Marine Corps teaches valuable technical skills, just like any other service. Now, what makes us different: We're different because of something we feel: a fierce pride."

"You can earn the same good pay in any branch of the service. So is it worth the sweat to be a Marine? It depends on you. How far do you want to go?"

"You can train to be an aviation professional in any branch of the service. So why start with 3000 pushups and a Marine D.I.? Because it's part of boot camp. And boot camp is part of being a Marine."

These ads serve the double purpose of elevating the Marines above the other services while also reminding or reassuring potential recruits that, like the other services, the Marines, too, have benefits, even if they aren't the reason to join. They subtly highlight the tangible benefits of service, like travel, job training, and education, while emphasizing the intangibles that are specific to the Marines.

From the early 1970s through the present, the Marines have stressed their elitism. They will demand that a recruit prove his worth, but they promise that once he's been accepted, he'll know that he's one of the best—he'll deserve to feel that pride that's a Marine tradition. The two slogans that the Marines have used since the inception of the all-volunteer force—"We're looking for a few good men" and "the Few, the Proud, the Marines"—both emphasize their selectiveness. So does the following ad copy, which appeared between the mid-1970s and the mid-1980s:

"We don't settle for field goals."

"Try out for the varsity."

"The Marine Corps can show you the world. But before you travel in our company, you've got to show us."

"How do you know if you're cut out for the Corps?"

"For over 200 years we've kept our ranks small and our standards high."

"Maybe you can be one of us."
"Quality, not quantity."

One ad that appeared in *Popular Mechanics* in 1976 had an entirely different focus. It presents "the smart way" to join the Marines and talks about guaranteed job training "in exciting fields like aviation technology, aircraft maintenance/ordnance, mechanical/electrical, motor transport, radio communications and more." This ad is striking as a contrast to other Marine recruiting materials from the AVF. The copy begins:

> Be quick. Act fast. Join now. We have good jobs for high school graduates. But remember, there are several million of you, and only a few thousand openings in the Corps. So *now* is the time to act. If you've got the qualifications, you can even sign up for a guaranteed program today, and not begin training for up to six months.

Four pictures show technical work: a man wearing goggles and holding a tool, a pair of hands working on electronic equipment, two Marines surveying, and a ground crew member with a jet. While the ad does emphasize that there are more high school graduates than available spots in the Marines, and the copy also mentions that the Marines are "an elite force" and "it won't be easy," visually and textually the ad stands out; with its emphasis on job training, it could be an ad for one of the other services, and by contrast, it points out the distinctiveness of the Marine Corps' approach to recruiting.

Many ads from the early and mid-1970s were heavy on text, and the pictures that did appear occasionally showed Marines at work on equipment or as part of an airplane's ground crew. In the late 1970s, the ads stopped making references to the other services, they began to be dominated by images, and the text was minimized. From this point on, the ads no longer pictured Marines doing technical or support work. They either display Marines in their formal dress uniforms or show them in an overtly militarized context, with weapons. In addition to a continued emphasis on the elitism and exclusivity of the Marine Corps, as the ads made use of different types of imagery or altered their textual strategies slightly, they continued to target and feature men almost exclusively.

The language and visual imagery of the advertisements reinforce the impression that the Marine Corps is a bastion of masculinity and a place to become a man. While advertising by the other services frequently refers to "men and women," the Marines' print ads virtually always use the word *men* only. Not including the ads the Marine Corps placed in *Seventeen*, which are discussed later, the ad sample contains a single exception to the "men"-only rule: one ad from 1976 makes reference to "a few good men, a few determined women." Other ads from the same year look for "a few good men with ambition" and "men who'll make good Marines." In 1977, the Marines replaced the slogan "We're Looking for a Few Good Men" with "The Few. The Proud. The Marines." Even after the direct reference to men was removed from the slogan, however, the print ads continued to directly address men and describe the Marines in exclusively masculine terms. Marine ads use phrases like "a man's potential is unlimited"; "he's a man who thrives on challenge"; "we take young men, good men, and make them better"; and "men at their best." The expression "a few good men" lingered in the text of recruiting ads. For instance, one from 1990 notes that "pride" can be found in a few good men (see figure 5.1). The ad tells the reader to "take a good look at this man" and to ask whether "you think you see yourself in him." This is not a gender-neutral use of the term *man*, but a clear invitation to young men to imagine themselves as Marines.

Visually, the ads portray a male world. Male Marines pose in the woods in camouflage gear, dangle out of a helicopter, crawl out of a river, or parade in their dress uniforms. The print ad sample, again excluding the ads in *Seventeen*, contained only a single image of a female Marine. In a 1979 ad that asks, "How do you know if you're cut out for the Corps?" a white male Marine in a dress uniform stands in the center of the frame. An African American male Marine stands behind his left shoulder, and that lone female Marine stands behind his right shoulder. She smiles broadly, with her teeth showing. In very few of the ads do Marines ever smile, and when they do their mouths are generally closed. The female Marine sticks out as an anomaly.

This masculine trend continues in a series of ads that debuted in the late 1990s that focus on challenge and self-transformation. They showcase extreme physical challenges as a route to this transformation, a change in self that goes beyond the physical. These ads present individuals, both black and white, struggling to become Marines, and each makes reference to pushing and testing oneself. In every ad, a shaved-headed man, his faced contorted with pain and determination, engages in an arduous physical task, like climbing an obstacle. Each ad also has a small picture of the man in a dress uniform, holding a sword, under the words "The Change Is Forever" (see figure 5.2). The ads proclaim:

"Pain is Weakness leaving the body."
"When quitting is no longer an option, you're halfway there."
"Every day you have to test yourself. If not, it's a wasted day."
"Running won't kill you. You'll pass out first."

Drill instructors exhort their charges with these sayings at boot camp (Ricks 1997), and the ads are making promises about how the process of becoming a Marine will transform the recruit physically and mentally. Neither the ads nor other public pronouncements by the Marines make direct reference to making men out of boys, but the implication is there.

Figure 5.1. Marine ad reprinted from *Sports Illustrated*, September 10, 1990. Courtesy of the U.S. Marine Corps.

Throughout the period of the AVF, in addition to its masculine focus, Marine Corps print advertising has been consistent in its visual portrayals of Marines. Marines are pictured dressed and acting like Marines. The other services tend to show their members in a range of situations—playing sports, socializing with their friends and families, and going to school, as well as

Figure 5.2. Marine ad reprinted from *Popular Mechanics*, April 2001. Courtesy of the U.S. Marine Corps.

working at their jobs or in a specifically martial context. In Army ads, soldiers are often smiling and relaxed and frequently pictured out of uniform. Some Navy ads show ships, and many Air Force ads feature aircraft instead of people. Marine ads feature serious-looking Marines—in uniform—parading, training, engaged in martial action, or posing in their dress blues. They don't appear in civilian clothes or in nonmilitary contexts. Being a Marine is the entirety of their identity. Uniforms not only set warriors apart from other men but also can impart fierceness and discipline, and an impressive ceremonial uniform can convey "the romance of war" (Braudy 2003, 123). Uniforms serve all of these functions in Marine ads. The Marines wear dress uniforms or utility uniforms (fatigues or camouflage battle dress); they don't appear in service uniforms. Dress uniforms are for parades, ceremonial occasions, formal wear, and embassy duty. Utilities are worn for heavy work and in the field. Service uniforms are the everyday uniforms that would be worn in an office environment, and these are the ones that are nowhere to be seen in Marine ads; Marines are either on formal display, engaged in a physical task, or ready for battle, but they are not associated with the day-to-day, routine indoor functions that may be performed by service members.[2]

Not only do Army ads show soldiers smiling and out of uniform, they also tend to present soldiers as individuals; those pictured are often identified by name and military occupational specialty. The potential recruit is offered an accessible model with whom he can identify. Marine Corps advertising, on the other hand, puts forward only an anonymous, generic Marine. Marines aren't identified by name or rank. Some ads picture a shaved-headed recruit, and, of course, one of the main functions of the boot camp haircut is to strip away the recruit's individuality and make him an indistinguishable member of the group. This presentation fits with a Marine culture that glorifies the common Marine, but not as an individual, as a member of the Corps. Being a Marine, a member of the brotherhood, is the core of the Marine's identity. The style of presentation also fits with the culture's elitism; the strong, unsmiling, masculine Marine in his dress uniform or camouflage battle dress (BDUs) is not a figure with whom to identify, but one to which the viewer may aspire. The depictions of Marines in recruiting materials mirrors the archetypal image of the heroic warrior described by Morgan (1994) that appears in a wide variety of cultural representations, from statues to comic books.

The Marine Corps themes of elitism, challenge, and transformation, within a male environment, are also the foundation of the Corps' television and Internet advertising. The Marines are known for their dramatic, memorable television commercials. They produce one major ad every few years and air them during sporting events watched by a young, male demographic and in movie theaters (Minogue 2002). When the Army broadened its commercial airtime purchases to include other kinds of programming to reach a wider audience, the Marines continued to devote their resources to sporting events. The commercials generally show a young man facing a spectacular challenge and then being transformed into a Marine. The TV Marines have conquered an animated monster in a death-trap obstacle course; a labyrinth with quicksand floors, fire-breathing gargoyles, and a hostile knight; and the opposing players in a living chess match. An ad that aired during the 1985 Super Bowl compares making a Marine with forging a sword. In "The Climb," which debuted early in 2002, a man in fatigues scales a sheer rock face with his bare hands. As he struggles up the mountain, images flash over the rock, including Marines raising the flag at Iwo Jima. At the top, a ghostly Marine in battle dress reaches down to help the climber up. Lightning strikes, the climber becomes a Marine in a dress uniform, and he is backed by a row of Marines, including one easily missed woman who can be glimpsed very briefly. The commercial ends with a voice-over: "The passage is intense, but if you complete the journey, you will find your destiny among the world's greatest warriors." The familiar motifs of overcoming an obstacle, transformation, the proud history, and the warrior brotherhood are all on display.

In its various incarnations, the Marine Corps Web site (www.marines.com) has echoed the themes of the print ads and television commercials. In 1999, the Marine Corps Web site welcomed visitors with this introduction:

> They are born in an inferno that tests both mind and body. Those who complete the challenge become beacons of honor, courage, and commitment. What does it take to become one of the few? The answer lies within.

Visitors were asked their gender and their level of education. Male and female potential enlistees (as opposed to officers) were channeled into different pages, each of them animated, interactive sites that featured a drill instructor and a recruit, both of the same sex as the site visitor. The instructor, who informs the visitor, "While you are on my website, I will demand of you and will demonstrate by my own example, the highest standard of personal conduct, morality and professional skill," requires the visitor to address him or her as sir or ma'am and exacts disciplinary virtual sit-ups if the visitor fails to do so. The recruit is led on a challenge—a climb up a mountain—before the visitor reaches the part of the Web site that gives more specific information about enlisting in the Corps.

In 2000, the Marines redesigned the Web site, ratcheting the challenge rhetoric up several notches. The new Web site directed all potential enlistees to the same place, an introduction that portrayed both men and women, though the women appear infrequently and in groups. The introduction to the Marine Corps Web site begins with the same command that drill instructors use to welcome new recruits as they arrive at Parris Island for training: "Get off my bus!" It then continues:

> One must first be stripped clean. Freed of all the false notions of self.
>
> Unhappiness does not arise from the way things are. But rather from a difference in the way things are and the way we believe they should be.
>
> You within yourself. There is no one else to rely on. And when the self is exhausted no one to lift you up.
>
> But finally we wake to realize there is only one way to get through this, and that is together.
>
> Once you've walked through fire and survived, little else can burn.
>
> We came as orphans. We depart as family . . . Do you have what it takes?

The text makes reference to getting through together and to family, because it is during the transforming experience of boot camp that the enlistee becomes a part of the Marine brotherhood, a lifelong bond to all other Marines. And because the Marine identity is all-encompassing, before joining the Corps, the recruit was an "orphan," bereft of his true family, the Marine family.

Each page also contained a hidden message that was revealed when the cursor passed over a particular part of the screen. The text of these messages is as follows:

> It is the Marine Corp that will strip away the façade so easily confused with self. It is the Corps that will offer the pain needed to buy the truth. And at last, each will own the privilege of looking inside himself to discover what truly resides there.
>
> Comfort is an illusion. A false security bred from familiar things and familiar ways. It narrows the mind. Weakens the body. And robs the soul of spirit and determination. Comfort is neither welcomed nor tolerated here.
>
> There you have seen in yourself invincibility. You now confront vulnerability. You have faltered, and the root of your weakness lies painfully exposed with the weight of failure heavy on you. You realize you have been overcome because you walk alone.
>
> There is only determination. There is only single-minded desire. Not one among them is willing to give up. Not one among them would exchange torment for freedom. Finally, they just want to be Marines.
>
> But first, a final test will take everything that is left inside. When this is over, those that stand will reach out with dirty, callused hands to claim the Eagle, Globe, and Anchor. And the title United States Marine.

The Marines are promising nothing short of a total transformation: a full-scale rite of passage, a trial by fire, in which the old self is destroyed and a new, better self emerges. This description of recruit training, which includes rejecting comfort, suffering pain, and overcoming weakness, evokes a ritual passage into manhood, reinforced by the image of "dirty, callused hands." Across many cultures, boys or young men must undergo painful ordeals or pass dangerous, difficult tests to achieve socially recognized manhood, and the lack of such rituals in modern American society has been identified as a cause of social problems or a threat to masculinity (Goldstein 2001). The Marines offer a formal manhood rite for those who feel this lack.

The Web site also includes material aimed at potential officers, and the role of Marine officers as leaders within the Marine "family" shapes how officerhood is presented. Potential officers (those who initially identified themselves as college students or graduates) are offered information about benefits and eligibility, as they would be on the sites of the other military services. These benefits include not only the kind touted by the other services, like promotions and medical care, but also such intangibles as "a lifelong commitment to excellence," "motivation to take the initiative," and "a sense of pride that comes with belonging to the most elite military organization in the world." Unlike the other services' Web pages, the site also provides information about the potential officer's obligations. On the page titled "Resources," potential officer recruits can find links to a discourse on leadership and an explication of the Marine Corps' core values of honor, courage, and commitment. On this same page, General Lejeune compares the relationship between "officers and men" to that between fathers and sons, as officers "are responsible for the physical, mental and moral welfare as well as the discipline and military training of the young men under their command." Here, the family metaphor is extended. All Marines are brothers, and officers are their fathers and strong male role models. Whatever the recruit's experiences in the outside world, the Marine Corps will serve as a nurturing male family.[3] Also, like the Marine Corps' print ads, the language used here doesn't strive for gender inclusiveness.

While the Web sites of the other services sometimes shy away from the central function of each service as a war-fighting institution, particularly in their discussions of jobs and career development, the Marine Web site makes direct reference to combat, just as the print ads often show Marines in a martial context. On the 2000 version of the Web site, the index of career jobs for officers begins with infantry, the "cutting edge of the Corps" where the officer is "trained how to fight." The description of jobs in engineering, tracked vehicles, field artillery, air control, and aviation all make reference to their relationship to combat. The description of "occupations of special support" strains to make them seem as important as the other jobs, sounding almost apologetic: "Every occupational field is vital to the success of the Marine Corps. The following seven support fields are often managerial or administrative in nature; nonetheless, they offer Marine Corps officers an opportunity to lead." Instead of highlighting these jobs for their potential transferability to the civilian marketplace, the support jobs (which are the jobs that women are permitted to fill) are subtly denigrated for not being directly involved in the Corps' combat mission.

The Web site has changed more than once since then, but, as the graphics and interactivity of the site have gotten more complex, each of the iterations has continued to highlight the Marine Corps' exclusivity; to talk about challenge, transformation, and the pride of being a Marine; and to show strong young men (and a very few women) training, parading, and in action as warriors.

WOMEN, THE MARINE CORPS, AND RECRUITING

The Marine Corps is the service most closely associated with masculinity, from its connection to combat, reflected in the saying "every Marine a rifleman," to the well-known slogan, "we're looking for a few good men." Of all the services, the Marines have the fewest women, less than 8 percent of the force. The Navy provides much of its support and medical services, so a greater percentage of jobs in the Marines are closed to women than in the other services. Because of its small size and its focus on combat, the Marine Corps has avoided some of the controversies and pressures over women's participation that the other services faced.[4]

The Marine Corps seems to take a "separate-but-equal" approach to women; it has given lip service to the importance of women to the Marine Corps, while it has tried to keep tight limits on the number of positions women can fill and segregated women in a variety of ways. The Corps has sought to preserve the masculinizing function of the men's training and protect the femininity of women recruits by training male and female recruits separately, the only service to still do so. At Parris Island, women train in their own battalion and have their own barracks, drill deck, mess hall, gymnasium, and beauty shop, only encountering male recruits on Sundays at recruit chapel, where the women sit in their own assigned pews (Ricks 1997, 44). Male recruits are trained by male drill instructors and the women by women. After training, women still aren't always fully integrated. Thomas Ricks notes that in the early 1990s in Somalia, Marine Corps policies caused interservice tensions: "Army women, accustomed to sleeping in areas where their units sleep, usually behind a blanket or poncho draped over a rope, were upset when the Marine commander overseeing the operation got wind of those arrangements and ordered them to move to sexually segregated sleeping areas" (202–203). The separateness of women Marines is also reflected in the continuing references to women who are Marines as "Women Marines." Women in the Army and Navy are no longer known as WACs and WAVES, but women Marines are still "Women Marines." Male Marines are simply Marines, but the femaleness of Women Marines prevents them from being wholly and purely Marines.

In terms of recruiting materials, The Marine Corps has created print ads (described later) that picture women Marines. These materials are clearly aimed at female potential recruits only and are placed in magazines like *Seventeen*, where only young women are likely to see them. Print ads in other kinds of publications, read by a mostly male or a mixed demographic, tend to show men only. The Web pages and the post-2000 television commercials may show one or two women Marines, but they mainly show men, and they don't present mixed groups of men and women working together. The segregation of women, thus, applies to the public face of the Marine Corps, as well as to its internal practices.

The history of women in the Marine Corps is itself contentious. According to Holm (1992), during the War of 1812, Lucy Brewer served as a Marine on the USS *Constitution* for three years as George Baker, and the Marine Corps has acknowledged her as the "first girl marine" (5). But Brian Mitchell, a fierce opponent of women's participation in the armed forces, challenges this story:

Sometimes, however, the revisionists' enthusiasm for a good story overcomes their natural skepticism. Fancy is often mistaken for fact when titillating tales of soft breasts beneath coarse uniform tunics are accepted at face value. Most such tales escape close scrutiny, but one that did not involved a prostitute by the name of Lucy Brewer. Lucy's tale has come down to us in a number of recent "histories" of fighting women, few of which show the slightest inclination to doubt her incredible claim of having passed herself off as a male Marine aboard the USS *Constitution* during the War of 1812. The revisionists seem to accept Lucy's claim on faith alone, without explaining how Lucy managed to conceal her sex for three years aboard the cramped frigate. Conditions on the ship alone would have made her masquerade impossible. The ship had no toilet facilities and no private quarters for enlisted Marines. Fortunately for persons inclined toward greater skepticism, Marine Corps historians have discovered that Lucy was a fraud. Her published accounts of her wartime exploits were lifted "almost verbatim" from official after-action reports filed by the *Constitution*'s commanding officer. Officially, the legend of Lucy Brewer is a "mockery of the bona fide traditions" of the Corps. (1989, 13, quoting from US Marine Corps, History and Museums Division, "The Legend of Lucy Brewer," 1957)

Mitchell sexualizes the "revisionist" view, with his reference to "titillating tales of soft breasts," despite the fact that he cites as revisers Binkin and Bach (1977), who studied women's military roles for the Brookings Institution, and Jeanne Holm, a retired Air Force major general who worked to expand the opportunities for women in the armed forces; neither seems likely to be passing along a tale they found titillating. Mitchell also makes sure to point out that Brewer was a prostitute, echoing the claims made over the years that women in the military are either lesbians or whores. This claim has been explored by various feminist scholars (De Pauw 1998; Enloe 1983; Herbert 1998); the strong association of soldiering with masculinity has encouraged perceptions that women who want to join the military either want to be men (i.e., are lesbians) or want to be around them inordinately (i.e., are whores).

Whatever the status of Lucy Brewer, women were first allowed to enter the Marines during World War I. As a part of the Navy, the Marine Corps was authorized to enlist women in the reserves in March 1917, shortly before the United States entered the war. The Marines waited until August 1918, two months before the war ended, to enroll women, when severe shortages of combat personnel finally led them to replace some of the male Marines performing clerical work at headquarters with women. A survey had indicated that about 40 percent of the clerical work could be done by women as well as by men. The male clerks predicted that it would take three women to replace two men, but the reverse turned out to be true (Holm 1992, 12). Three hundred women, commonly referred to as "marinettes" served as Marines in World War I.

During World War II, the legislation that authorized the creation of the Navy Women's Reserve in July 1942 also authorized the Marine Corps Women's Reserve. Unlike their WAC and WAVE sisters, the women Marines had no official acronym: "according to the commandant, they would be marines" (Holm 1992, 27). Female Marines, however, have never been referred to simply as "Marines"—the term is always modified to indicate their femaleness, and they are known, as previously noted, as "Women Marines" or "WM." Unofficially, Women Marines have been known as BAMS or Bammies, for "Broad-Assed Marines" (Williams 1989, 69).

Despite authorization, the Marine Corps was again reluctant to accept women and, again, only did so once they realized that shortages of combat personnel necessitated that men be freed for combat. The Marine commandant, Lt. Gen. Thomas Holcomb, worried that admitting women would create "untold problems," but in November 1942, he gave in to pressure from his staff and told the secretary of the Navy that "as many women as possible should be used in noncombat billets thus releasing a greater number of the limited manpower available for essential combat duty'" (quoted in Holm 1992, 33). By the summer of 1945, there were 18,000 Women Marines, and 87 percent of the enlisted jobs at Corps headquarters were being performed by women. All of these women were white. Unlike the WAC and the WAVES, which accepted small numbers of black women and segregated them, the Marine Corps did not enlist African American women until 1949 (77).

In the lead-up to the passage of the 1948 Women's Armed Services Integration Act, the Marine Corps took the position that the Marines didn't need women in the peacetime force, since the Navy provided much of the Corps' noncombat support. The Marine Corps conceived of itself, much as it does today, as a combat-ready force available for immediate deployment anywhere in the world, and it did not envision women as a part of this structure, although the Corps saw potential value in a well-trained Women's Reserve that could serve in shore establishments if the Marines were deployed for an emergency (Holm 1992, 117).

During the Cold War, women served in the Marine Corps in small numbers and in limited roles. When the Marine Corps expanded in 1964, the commandant, Gen. Wallace M. Greene Jr., appointed a group of senior officers to study the Women Marines program and plan for a small increase in the use of women. The study group was highly concerned with maintaining quality in the women's program, and it wrote in its report:

> Women Marines must always be the smallest group of women in the military service. In accordance with the Commandant's desire, they must also be the most attractive and useful women in the four lines services. Within a [small] group of . . . enlisted women, there is room for none but the truly elite. (Quoted in Holm 1992, 181)

The Marine Corps decided to raise already-high enlistment standards for women to make sure the Marines' standards were as high as or higher than the standards for the other women's programs, and like the other services at the time, attractiveness and femininity were part of the definition of "quality" for women.[5] However, the commandant also decided to increase the number of women by 70 percent, which would bring the number of women up to 2,750, or 1 percent of the Corps' total strength; to assign women to additional bases; and to open new job categories to women to improve enlistment and retention (Holm 1992, 188). As the number of troops deployed to Vietnam increased, the Marine Corps wanted, as in earlier conflicts, to replace male Marines in noncombat positions with women to release the men for combat duty. During the war, thirty-six Women Marines were sent to Vietnam.

In the 1970s, all of the services except the Marines began the gender integration of officer training. In 1976, the commandant, Gen. Louis H. Wilson, decided to examine the requirement that women be trained separately in a shorter course. The next year, the Marines allowed twenty-two female second lieutenants into the twenty-one-week basic course as part of an all-female platoon within Charlie Company. They were soon referred to as "Charlie's Angels." The next commandant reversed course and partially resegregated the training because the women's successful completion of the course had led to charges that the training had "gone soft" (Holm 1992, 272). The Marines continued to train enlisted male and female recruits separately, while the other services began coeducational training. According to Jeanne Holm, commandant Gen. Robert H. Barrow said more than once of the separate training that "while he wanted his men to be men, he wanted his women marines to remain women" (273).

In 1981, as the Department of Defense undertook a study of accession and retention policies in relation to women, called *Background Review: Women in the Military*, the Marine Corps initiated its own studies on its requirements for female personnel. There were 6,700 women in the Corps at the time, making up less than 4 percent of the service. As a result of these studies, completed in 1984 and 1987, the number of enlisted positions open to women doubled, from 5,000 to 12,000, and the number of officer positions increased from 655 to almost a thousand. With the opening of new positions to women in 1984, the Corps decided to incorporate defensive training that included weapons training into the women's recruit indoctrination program (boot camp). By that time, all of the other services had already begun giving women some form of combat training. While opening new roles, the Marines put a 50 percent ceiling on the number of women who could enter any of the fields open to them—a quota that never applied to men—including those fields that women tend to dominate in civilian employment. By the end of the 1980s, the proportion of women in the Marines had inched up to 5 percent (Holm 1992, 415–418).

While the number of women in the Corps and the roles they could fill were very slowly increasing, attitudes within the Corps about appropriate gender roles weren't changing much. Women were becoming a more regular part of the other services, especially the Army, but in the 1980s, the Marine Corps still worried about the femininity of women Marines. The Marine Corps basic training manual continued to include rules on cosmetics that required women recruits to wear makeup—at minimum eye shadow and lipstick (Williams 1989, 63). In interviews with female Marines conducted in 1985, sociologist Christine Williams found a general belief that the Marine Corps is more concerned with the femininity of its female personnel than any of the other branches. She notes:

> Several women told me they had chosen the marines over the other services because it emphasizes the femininity of its female recruits more than other branches: "One thing I liked about the Marine Corps is that it's the only service that requires that you wear makeup during training. . . . I like that because it kind of symbolizes that they really want you to be feminine." But femininity means more to them than dress and grooming. The women I interviewed understand the difference between the rough-and-tough marine and the expression of femininity the corps expects from them: "You are in the marines, but they don't want you to lose the fact that you are female. They don't want you to act macho. . . . It's one thing they always want you to remember—you're a lady." (Williams 1989, 75)

In the era of the all-volunteer force, the Marines have continued to insist on strict gender divisions. The enforced femininity of female Marines differentiates them from and reinforces the masculinity of male Marines.

The legal and policy changes of the early 1990s opened thousands of new positions on ships, in aviation, and in ground units to women in the Marine Corps. The rescinding of the "risk rule" made women eligible to fill 48,000 new positions in the Marines (Women's Research and Education Institute 2003). In a 1994 hearing of the House Armed Services Committee Military Forces and Personnel Subcommittee, Assignment of Army and Marine Corps Women under the New Definition of Ground Combat, Lt. Gen. George R. Christmas testified that at that time (October 1994), the Marine Corps included 7,713 women—613 officers and 7,100 enlisted—among 174,000 Marines. While the policy changes would lead to new assignments for women, the Marines would proceed slowly and deliberately. General Christmas expected that the number would rise to 10,400 women, or about 6 percent of enlisted Marines and 7 percent of officers, over the next fifteen to twenty years. Women were a small part of the Marine Corps, and the Marines expected that to remain unchanged, even as new roles were opened to women.

During that same hearing, the Marine Corps stated its intent to devote resources to the recruitment of women. According to the written testimony of General Christmas:

> An additional investment will be made in our advertising program to inform women of expanding opportunities; by FY 1997, we will spend $1.8 million more than we did in FY 1994, with additional funds channeled to print and television advertisements that target high-quality women candidates. We also will begin a direct mailout program to potential female applicants. (1994)

Though they allocated only a small budget to the recruitment of women—for comparison, the television commercial "The Climb" cost $23 million to make in 2001 (Minogue 2002)—the Marine Corps did create print ads aimed at women.

Six different ads appeared in *Seventeen*, each running several times, with the first appearing in 1995 and the last in 2001. The first two use the same text but with different pictures of the head and shoulders of a noncommissioned officer in a dress uniform holding up her sword. The headline states: "You can look at models, or you can be one." The ads continue:

> Do you have what it takes to be a role model? A model of integrity, intelligence, and courage? If you're an individual who thrives on challenge and never gives less than your best, you could be doing things most people only read about. You could become a leader, an inspiration. You could become a United States Marine. Do more than look at models, be one.

Another ad reads, "You can go anywhere if you've got the right make-up," and a fourth says, "Get a make-over that's more than skin deep." These two ads that refer to cosmetics both picture a woman wearing camouflage utilities and camouflage face-paint, and both talk about the internal qualities that are part of being a woman in the Marines. All the ads make reference to conventions of femininity and fashion that are a foundation of the magazine in which they appear. In one sense, these ads implicitly point to the superficiality of a feminine concern for appearance, contrasting a concern with makeup and models with the inner strengths developed by the Marines (despite the fact that the Corps has insisted upon its female members appearing sufficiently feminine). However, these ads also seem fully accepting of the tropes of femininity they refer to—the line "you can go anywhere if you've got the right make-up" is more playful than satirical or critical. In addition, the women in these ads are noticeably attractive and even feminized. The woman in camouflage seems put-together and pretty, with her long hair neatly tied back in a braid, and the women in the "models" ads are clearly wearing cosmetics.

These ads fit with one of the general conventions of Marine advertising, in that they offer intangibles rather than benefits. They also differ from the ads aimed at men in one way that is particularly striking. These ads present the only exceptions in my sample to the anonymity of the individual Marine. In 1998, the "you can look at models" ad began identifying the Marine pictured as Master Sergeant Marialena Bridges, and this same ad also appeared in a later issue with the picture of another woman, identified as Sergeant Eborah Lawson. The other two ads both picture and name the same woman, Captain Roma Sharpe. Perhaps within the context of *Seventeen*, the Marine Corps wanted to let readers know that these women aren't, in fact, models and that women Marines not only actually exist but also are attractive and appropriately feminine, not a female version of the masculine male Marine. The whole idea of the anonymous Marine may not apply as easily to women; the female Marine is an exception, not a member of the brotherhood. The mere fact that female recruits don't have their heads shaven means that they don't become one of an anonymous mass but retain their individuality along with their femininity.

From 1999 to 2001, the Marine Corps ran a second, very different set of ads in *Seventeen*. These ads were part of the "The Change Is Forever" campaign the Marines were running in other magazines but with women in place of the men. One has the headline "Pain is weakness leaving the body," and the other "Every day you have to test yourself. If not, it's a wasted day." The rest of the text, about challenge and transformation, is the same as in the male versions of the ads, and in both a female recruit struggles with an obstacle, her mouth grimacing with determination. In these ads, the women aren't overtly feminized—though unlike the men, their heads aren't shaved—and they are shown in a moment of physical exertion. In what seems to be a major shift for the Marines, women are being offered the same things as men and being put in the same situation.

It's not clear why the Marine Corps altered its approach to women in this second set of ads. The Marines may have decided that the women who would respond to the transformation ads would best fit the Marine culture. Either they were becoming less concerned with drawing sharp distinctions between male and female Marines, or they decided that society has changed such that women who are tough and up for a challenge can still be what the Marines consider appropriately feminine. It's also quite possible that the Marines weren't that concerned with recruiting women—after all, they had been meeting recruiting goals when the other services hadn't and weren't under the same pressure or scrutiny—so they didn't go through the effort or expense of creating a separate advertising concept to appeal to women. This view would seem to be supported by a recent admission by the Marine Corps' advertising agency that the print ads aimed at women in the 1990s weren't very sophisticated and didn't involve much research (Quenqua 2008). It certainly didn't presage a new approach to recruiting women, since Marine recruiting in the subsequent period and in television commercials continued to present male and mixed audiences with visions of men who prove themselves and achieve the status of Marine warriors.

Whatever way the Marines attempt to reach women, the Corps is careful to limit the audience for its representations of female Marines. In the chapter on the Navy, I discuss an article by naval aviator Lieutenant Christian Bonat (1999), who favorably compares the male version of the "Pain is weakness leaving the body" ad, with its "warrior ethos," to a Navy ad that followed the career of a female naval aviator. Bonat seems critical of the Navy for the very attempt to appeal to women. It did not seem to occur to Bonat that the Marine Corps might also be making a pitch specifically to women—and with the very ad he praised. One key difference in strategy between the two services is that the Navy placed its ad featuring a woman in *Sports Illustrated*, where men like Bonat and young men in general might see it, while the Marine Corps made the decision to place the ad picturing a woman in a magazine where only young women would be likely to see it, leaving its masculine image intact in front of a male audience.

CONCLUSIONS

The Marine Corps has faced the challenge of recruiting an all-volunteer force by reinforcing the ties between masculinity and military service, offering young men the chance to test themselves and, if they prove worthy, join an elite brotherhood. Women are almost completely absent from Marine Corps advertising, except in the few ads aimed at women in magazines read by young women. The Corps recruits very small numbers of women and segregates them in various ways. The public face of the Marine Corps is fully male and fully masculinized.

The culture of the Marine Corps is reflected in its recruiting materials, which portray anonymous, generic Marines, strong, hard young men who are shown only as Marines, not in any other contexts and not as individuals. The connections to combat are reflected and highlighted by martial images of Marines, fighting or training in camouflage fatigues or perfectly turned out in dress blues and brandishing a rifle or a sword with rigid military bearing. The Marines have the strongest culture of any of the services, and they are concerned with finding recruits who are attracted to that culture (and not just to military life in general) and want to be a part of it.

Marine Corps advertising isn't just masculine; it specifically presents a warrior masculinity. Marine recruiting materials generally downplay benefits and economic incentives, so their appeals don't draw on models of masculinity tied to economic independence or technological prowess and mastery of machines. The structure and personnel needs of the Marines (which are connected to the culture) also drive the recruiting approach. Marines use only one version of masculinity because they are looking for a particular type of recruit—short-timers who are interested in combat jobs—who responds to that appeal. According to Richard H. Kohn, a military historian at the University of North Carolina, "The Marines tend to attract people who are the most macho, seek the most danger and are attracted by the service most likely to put them into combat" (quoted in Schmitt 2005a).

The brand of masculinity portrayed in Marine advertising is often held up as a model, and, in fact, many commentators see the Marines as the only service that utilizes masculinity it its appeals (e.g., Smart 2000; Strother 1999). Warrior masculinity seems to be the only form of masculinity recognized in these cases. There are some who believe that the military should remain the last bastion of a strong form of masculinity, of fixed and certain male roles and privileges, even and especially if that form is no longer dominant outside the military. The Marine Corps taps into those desires and offers itself as that bastion.

CHAPTER 6

The Air Force

In the period before conscription ended, the Air Force was considered the most glamorous of the services, and for many draft-eligible young men, it was a more desirable option than the Navy, Marines, or, especially, the Army. Since the end of the draft, the Air Force has developed appeals, based on the Air Force's technological and career-related strengths, that draw on conceptions of masculinity that are not particularly martial or militaristic. In the early 1970s, for many young men, militarized ideals of manhood had been discredited by the Vietnam War, and during those years, military recruiting across the branches did not emphasize the martial aspects of service or show a lot of militaristic imagery, like weapons and combat uniforms. Over the course of the next several decades, though, the other branches made intermittent use of specifically martial forms of masculinity in their imagery and appeals; the Air Force, for the most part, has not.

Air Force recruiting has emphasized job training and has specifically offered respect and advancement to blue-collar, mechanically inclined young men, reinforcing a working-class masculinity that values skilled labor and economic independence. This was especially true of recruiting advertisements in the 1970s but continued as a theme in later ads as well. For a brief period in the early 1980s, Air Force advertising highlighted the intangible benefits of service, but it soon returned to an emphasis on job training, education, and benefits. One lasting theme that began during this period was the evocation of pride and awe in the Air Force's sleek aircraft and advanced technology. The Air Force had always showcased its technology in relation to job training and skills that would be valuable in the civilian world, but from the 1980s on, the Air Force has used imagery of aircraft to lend glamour and appeal to the service as a whole.[1] Technology is "widely acknowledged as [a] powerful [motif] of hegemonic masculinity" (Lohan and Faulkner 2004, 319), so the deployment of technology in recruiting materials implicitly masculinizes service in the force. The Air Force has offered, by association with the world's most advanced technology, the masculine advantages of mastery, dominance, and control. In recent years, the Air Force has offered recruits not direct physical excitement, as the other services tend to do, but the vicarious thrills of video games, which provide extreme experiences through the mediation of technology. The picture of manhood painted by the Air Force also in many ways coincides with the "tough and tender" new world order masculinity postulated by Steve Niva (1998) (and described in chapter 2), in which aggression is tempered by compassion and technological might and power are used for benign dominance and humanitarian ends.

After a brief discussion of Air Force culture, this chapter presents an analysis of Air Force recruiting materials over the course of the all-volunteer force, and it also examines the place of women within the Air Force and its recruiting materials to trace out the service's constructions of gender and specifically of masculinity in its representations of military service. The source materials include fifty-two different advertisements published by the Air Force between 1970 and 2003, ten television commercials that aired between 1980 and 2003, and two different incarnations of the Air Force's recruiting Web site.

AIR FORCE CULTURE

The Air Force is the youngest of the armed forces, and it emerged out of a specific military concept, that of air power, and a specific technology, the airplane. The culture of the Air Force is built around the airplane and those who fly it. According to RAND analyst Carl Builder (1989), the Air Force worships "at the altar of technology" (19) and measures itself by its aircraft, favoring technological advancement and performance over quantity. The Air Force is anxious to always be at the cutting edge of aircraft technology.

Just as in the Army, there is a crucial distinction in power and status between the combat arms and the supporting roles. In the Air Force, there is a strict hierarchy that places pilots—who make up a much smaller group than combat specialists do within the Army—above all others. These pilots, who are in the dominant position in the service, identify themselves with the planes they fly more than with the Air Force itself. According to Builder, "The pride of association is with a machine, even before the institution" (1989, 23). Builder explains that the pilot's fundamental concern is with flying, not with war fighting or issues of security and defense:

> Air Force pilots delight in showing visitors their toys. It is not hard to get an invitation to sit in the cockpit, to share its owner's excitement with the power

and freedom of flight. The cockpit visitor will probably find it easier to engage the owner in a discussion of the difficulties and restrictions associated with weather and airspace in peacetime than the relationship of the man and machine to war. This is not to denigrate the great skill and courage of those who are prepared to fly and fight but simply to note that flying and flying machines are nearest to their hearts. The prospect of combat is not the essential draw; it is simply the justification for having and flying these splendid machines. (23)

This emphasis on the machines and technologies more than on the service itself is quite different from the cultures of the other services. In the Navy and in the Marine Corps, the pride and loyalty of service members is firmly lodged in the institution itself. Army culture doesn't glorify equipment and technology, but rather the skills of service members (Builder 1989, 24), and a firm focus on combat grounds the cultures of both the Army and Marine Corps.

Although the Air Force inherited concepts and customs from its parent service, the Army, the Air Force is the least tradition-bound of the services, and it is also the one that most resembles large, bureaucratic, civilian organizations. In terms of the ratio of tooth to tail, the Air Force's combat components—its pilots, aircraft, and missiles—require a vast support apparatus. According to military sociologist Charles Moskos, characterizations of the U.S. military tend to run along two lines: "on the one hand, there is the view, documented in many scholarly studies, that the contemporary military establishment is increasingly sharing the attributes common to all large-scale bureaucracies in a modern complex society," and "on the other hand, there is the continuing portrayal, especially in the popular culture, of the military as a quasi-feudal organization with features quite unlike those found in the community at large" (1970, 37). Moskos finds that the "organizational characteristics tending toward convergence with civilian structures have been most apparent in the Air Force" (37), and he goes on to describe the Air Force as having a "maintenance-shop and office atmosphere" (61).

As the youngest and least tradition-bound of the services, the Air Force has been relatively free of racial strife and fairly willing to integrate African American men into the service almost from its inception. When President Truman's Committee on Equality of Treatment and Opportunity, commonly known as the Fahy Committee, began working in 1949 to implement the executive order mandating racial equality in the armed forces, it found that the Air Force favored integration and was ending racial quotas and making personnel assignments and promotions on merit, not race (Binkin and Eitelberg 1982, 27). When the Air Force was first established, about 6 percent of the total force was African American, a figure that had risen to about 10 percent by the time the draft ended (Gropman 1998, 165–166). African Americans were somewhat underrepresented in the draft-era Air Force, which was able to attract the highest quality recruits (in terms of test scores and education level), but the service suffered few racial problems. The Air Force could not escape turbulence during the Vietnam War, however. Like the other services, it experienced racial unrest in the form of a riot in May 1971 at Travis Air Force Base, even though it "had been virtually free of racial problems" (Binkin and Eitelberg 1982, 36). During the AVF, the Air Force has been 12 to 16 percent black, with African Americans serving in numbers roughly proportional to or slightly higher than their numbers in the general population. African American men have been a regular presence in Air Force recruitment advertising, though a minority in relation to the representation of white men. African American airmen are presented in the same manner and context as white airmen, although one ad in the sample, from 2002, specifically celebrates the Tuskegee Airmen of World War II, who "escorted bombers into Europe and equality into America."

Another distinct aspect of the Air Force is that while it wields awesome destructive power, including the nation's arsenal of nuclear-armed intercontinental ballistic missiles, the Air Force is, in a sense, the least militaristic of the military services in terms of its culture. In the other services, those who serve at the lowest levels may be warriors—the common soldier, sailor, or Marine may be in combat. In the Air Force, however, it is officers, and an elite few at that, who fly the fighters and bombers that can destroy an enemy. The institution as a whole has less of a warrior culture than the other military branches. This tendency may be heightened as the Air Force increases the use of unmanned drone airplanes (a difficult and controversial transition for a force dominated by pilots) and further develops space-based weaponry. According to the Center for Strategic and International Studies, "Some observers also perceive a shift from an air and space force to a space and air force, with the future dominated by nonaircraft systems in space" (CSIS 2000, 11). These new weapons systems may increase the Air Force's ability to deliver lethal force but will also further distance those who inflict violence from the violence itself. Even with increased destructiveness, the Air Force may become more like a highly technological civilian organization and less traditionally militaristic, as many of its warriors "fight" from computer consoles on U.S. bases.

THE RECRUITING ADVERTISEMENTS

Before the advent of the all-volunteer force, the Air Force had little experience with recruiting. The Air Force came into being as a separate branch from the Army on September 18, 1947, and Congress authorized a peacetime renewal of the selective service system in 1948. Throughout the period of the Cold War draft, the Air Force attracted all of the qualified personnel it needed. The Air Force had the most glamorous reputation of all the services (Moskos 1970, 18), and enough young men preferred it to the other services or sought out its technical training that it never needed conscripts, nor did it need independent recruiting campaigns. According to Army historian Robert K. Griffith Jr., as the draft wound down and the Department of Defense (DOD) thought about how to build a force without conscripts, in spite of its success at bringing in volunteers, the Air Force focused on trying to claim a large portion of recruiting resources, much to the chagrin of the Army. When the Army requested funds for proficiency pay for recruits who went into the combat arms after basic training, the Air Force tried to get a share of the money. The Air Force also argued that the Army should not be allowed to experiment with paid advertising on its own but must work with the other services, and it tried to demand a share of the Army's barracks rehabilitation funds, even though the Air Force had the most modern facilities and the Army some of the oldest (Griffith 1996, 56). Despite its posturing at neediness, the Air Force entered the era of the all-volunteer force in arguably the best position of any of the four service branches.

With a few exceptions, most Air Force recruiting materials have offered a masculinity tied to technology, mostly in connection with an economic appeal—either a good technical skill for a blue-collar worker or, in later ads, the promise of a high-tech career—but also as a vehicle for dominance and mastery, the projection of benign power, and vicarious experiences of adventure and excitement, as in a video game. Technology itself, and not just the economic benefits that accrue from proficiency in its use, has long been associated with masculinity.[2] Technology is a "medium of power" that is a "historical aspect of male power," based on a technological division of labor between men and women, in which jobs that require technical knowledge, from creating and designing to repairing technological goods, have been heavily dominated by men, while women have historically been limited to jobs in which they may use technology, but they don't need to understand it (Cockburn 1985, 8). Advanced technology is coupled with masculinity through masculine-marked categories like rationality, logic, science, history, progress, and transcendence (Massey 1995). While the Army and Navy also make appeals based on technology, it is more central to the Air Force's self-representations.

In the early period of the AVF, Air Force recruiting embraced a marketplace philosophy, showcasing the service as a route to economic advancement. Ads from the early 1970s focus almost exclusively on the economic benefits to enlistees. While the Army and Navy also pushed benefits and job training during this period, the Air Force emphasized them even more emphatically. The Air Force's chief selling point was that it would give airmen skills that are highly valued in the civilian work world. The headlines of three ads from 1972—when the services began advertising in earnest in anticipation of the draft's end—demonstrate this clearly: "The Air Force skill. You can take it with you"; "The job we guarantee you today, can guarantee your future tomorrow"; and "I learned my job in the US Air Force." The service bragged that the "re-usable skill" is an "Air Force specialty." One of these ads makes a reference to national defense, but the Air Force's role in defense is not what it seems to be proudest of:

> But let's not kid ourselves. The Air Force trains men and women with the idea of keeping them as valuable contributors to its ultimate mission . . . the defense of our nation. But, inevitably perhaps, each year some choose to leave us. Yet, even then, the Air Force can take pride in knowing that of all the military services, *we* are the foremost producer and provider of this nation's most precious resource: its skilled workers. (Emphasis in original)

Instead of expressing pride in its traditions or history, the Air Force claims pride in its production of skilled workers. The reference to defense is an anomaly during this period. The ads are devoted almost entirely to the issue of job training, and they assume that most enlistees won't make a career of the Air Force but will spend some time learning a skill and return to civilian life. Many of the ads feature double images of the same task being performed, once by an airman and once by a civilian (see figure 6.1). In some cases, like the ad just quoted, ad copy that promotes skills training also frames that training as a contribution to the nation as a whole. Another example of this reads as follows:

> Art Edwardson fell in love at the age of 6½. In his mind he still sees her. A vision of metallic beauty, poised on the runway, waiting to take off. Art held on to his young love through high school, until the Air Force made his boyhood dream a reality. A dream he lived out as a pilot in the Air Force. Today Art is a pilot for one of the world's largest airlines. His story is the perfect example of an Air Force specialty . . . the re-usable skill. . . . The product of the Air Force's training programs are skilled technicians. They represent a substantial natural resource for the whole nation. The jobs we train America's youth for are needed not only by the Air Force, but also by the civilian job market. In fact, each year over $300 million worth of Air Force investment in trained manpower is returned to the civilian economy. Remember. The re-usable skill . . . it's an Air Force Specialty.

This ad promotes the Air Force as a positive economic force for the country, not a drain on its resources, and it promises young men a bright economic future, as well as making reference to the lure and beauty of airplanes, a theme that would become more prominent in the visuals of later Air Force ads.

Throughout the 1970s, the word that is used most frequently in Air Force advertising copy seems to be *skill*, though the ads also highlight other tangible benefits like vacation time, medical care, job security, and educational opportunities. During this period, the Air Force used the slogan, "Find Yourself in the US Air Force." Contrary to the colloquial meaning of the expression "find

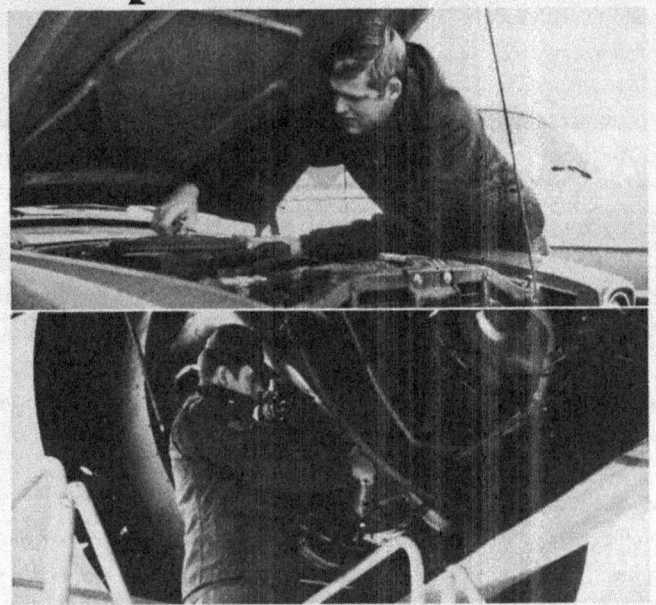

Figure 6.1. Air Force ad reprinted from *Popular Mechanics*, April 1972. Courtesy of the U.S. Air Force.

[136]   *Enlisting Masculinity*

yourself," the ads say nothing about self-discovery or personal emotional growth; they're talking about finding oneself by figuring out how to turn an interest into a good, solid skill. An ad from 1973 begins, "If all your job pays is money you should read this," but instead of alluding to intangibles that a job might theoretically "pay," such as satisfaction or pride, the headline refers to other concrete benefits like thirty days of paid vacation in the first year. Similarly, the slogan the Air Force began using in 1976, "A Great Way of Life," seems to refer to a good job, benefits, and the chance at an education, not to a life of adventure, challenge, or service.

Overall, Air Force recruiting ads of the 1970s aren't at all militaristic in tone or in their imagery—in the early 1970s they tended to picture jet engines rather than jet fighters. The Air Force doesn't offer recruits a traditionally martial masculinity, but it does put forward a working-class version of masculinity grounded in skilled physical labor. The Air Force presents itself as a place for a man to learn a trade and advance himself; for instance, the service claims that "Air Force training gives a man a skill he can always carry with him." This kind of blue-collar manhood is further exemplified in the following ad copy, with its references to "craftsman's hands" and "a master at his skill" (see figure 6.1):

> Start with an inquiring mind. Add a passion for making things work. Then combine these qualities with a love of machines and a craftsman's hands, and you've got a natural born mechanic. When the Air Force gets hold of a guy like that, they'll spend thousands of dollars to train him to be a master at his skill.

The Air Force offers young, blue-collar men a recognition of their worth and promises them respect, development, and economic security and self-sufficiency. Several ads from the 1970s published in *Popular Mechanics* specifically look for potential recruits with "inborn" or "inherent" mechanical abilities. Some of them challenge the reader with a spatial reasoning quiz as they validate his technical skills and interests. While many young women in the early 1970s may have had mechanical skills, these skills were more likely to be recognized and encouraged in boys, and the references to such abilities being natural or inborn evokes a masculine skill to be treasured.

In the late 1970s, Air Force ads made a visual shift and began to associate service in the Air Force with sleek, sophisticated aircraft. Even as the ads continued to emphasize benefits and job training, the imagery began to include fewer pictures of men repairing machinery and more pictures of planes in flight. Soon, the dramatic images of aircraft began to dominate the ads entirely; many ads from the early 1980s include little text, allowing the images to speak more loudly. This change would seem to indicate a broadening of the attempted appeal from a blue-collar, mechanically inclined (presumably male) audience to a somewhat wider public. The ads provide a different idea of technology, moving from a narrow emphasis on mechanics and specific jobs to a more expansive vision, in which the excitement the most cutting-edge technology can generate lends glamour to the service as a whole.

Ads from the early 1980s make reference to "serving your country" and "a proud spirit," and the Air Force began to use the slogan "Aim High." One ad that appeared occasionally between 1982 and 1985 sounds an inspirational tone and barely mentions concrete benefits. Over a dramatic shot of an F-15 Eagle (or an F-104 Starfighter in a second version of the ad), the text reads:

> Reach for new horizons. It's never easy. But reaching for new horizons is what aiming high is all about. Because to reach for new horizons you must have the vision to see things not only as they are, but as they could be. You must have the dedication to give the best you have. And you must have the courage to accept new challenges. The history of the Air Force is a history of men and women reaching for new horizons, dedicating their vision and courage to make our nation great. You can join us in our quest for new horizons. Our pay and benefits are better than ever, with opportunities for growth and challenge. Aim High! Find out more. See your Air Force Recruiter....

The ad combines national pride and patriotism with the offer of a challenge, and it's a far cry from the ads touting the reusable skill.

The Air Force's emphasis on intangibles didn't last, however, and for the rest of the 1980s and into the 1990s, recruiting ads offer job training and experience, while the striking imagery of graceful aircraft in flight, futuristic-looking planes, and even the occasional shot of the space shuttle allows the technical work described to bask in reflected glory. After the calls for service and the promise of challenge, the Air Force ad that ended up appearing the most frequently in the ad sample, running more than a dozen times between 1985 and 1987, sounds a lot like the ads from the 1970s:

> We'll pay you to take the most exciting classes anywhere.
>
> You'll learn electronics, avionics, aircraft maintenance, health care sciences, management or logistics—the Air Force will train you in one of more than 200 technical specialties America needs today. You'll get hands-on experience with the latest equipment, and we'll pay 75 percent of your tuition for off-duty college courses, to get you even further. Whatever your goals, the Air Force will equip you with the skills to get where you want to be. If you're looking seriously into your future, Aim High to a future in the Air Force.

The Air Force needs good, technically inclined workers who want a skill, maybe with the associated glamour of airplanes. The Air Force presents itself as a workplace, not a way of life or a calling. Despite the phrase "most exciting classes anywhere," it promises none of the adventure or excitement of the

Navy, nor the rite of passage or warriorhood of the Marines. This impression is reinforced by a 1986 ad aimed at potential officers that reads: "As an Air Force second lieutenant, you'll manage people, projects and offices; you'll be in charge, making decisions, shouldering the responsibility. You'll belong to an organization dedicated to achievement, innovation and high technology." The Air Force could be a large manufacturing concern, with a sizable technical workforce managed by a professional staff.

The sample contains few advertisements from the 1990s. In the post–Cold War period, the Air Force faced personnel cuts that, proportionally, were almost as large as those faced by the Army (McCormick 1998, 29). The small number of ads that were published talk about career opportunities and cutting-edge technology. The Air Force lightly spoofs the Navy's customary offer to see the world in a 1990 ad that promises: "Join the Air Force and See the World's Most Exotic Terminals" (see figure 6.2). Technology, not exotic ports of call, provides the thrill. The Air Force has computer terminals "where dogfights are played out with sweaty realism" and "where futuristic aircraft designs are modified in just seconds." Working at a computer terminal can be a passive experience, but here it is framed in active terms. Images of colorful computer graphics stand in for "the most sophisticated computer technology in the world," and the reader is invited to "become a part of it." An ad from 1992 pictures an F-117A Stealth fighter and calls it the "hero of Desert Storm and America's most famous disappearing act." Any of the other services would certainly talk about *people* as the heroes of Desert Storm, but the Air Force is touting itself as "the high technology world of tomorrow" and offering its machinery as a reason to enlist.

In 1997, the Air Force published an ad in *Popular Mechanics* that, like earlier ads, explicitly looks for potential recruits who are "mechanically inclined." This one reads:

> Your dad thinks you oughtta get a job out at the airport. Your buddies think you oughtta come work at the garage so you can hang out with them. Your brother thinks you oughtta come work at the plant. Anybody ever ask you what you want to do?
>
> If you're mechanically inclined, the Air Force could be the perfect place for you. Where else could you learn about Tactical Aircraft Maintenance, Aerospace Propulsion, and everything in between while earning a good salary and learning to be a leader? If a mechanically oriented career is what you want, think about the Air Force. It's one road that can take you anywhere.

In this ad, the references to a father, brother, and buddies, along with a picture of a young man, make it clear that the ad is talking to men, while the list of potential job sites—the airport, the garage, and the plant—place the targets of the ad in a working-class milieu. The Air Force wasn't advertising broadly or

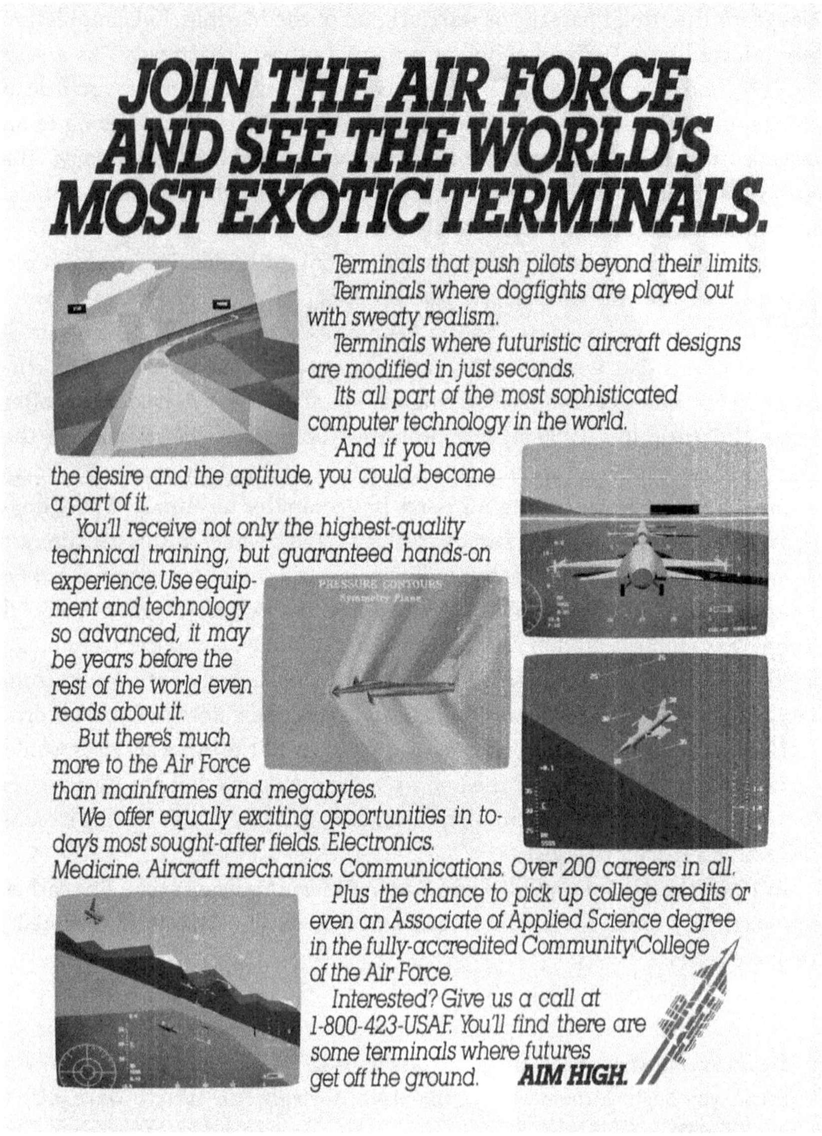

Figure 6.2. Air Force ad reprinted from *Sports Illustrated*, February 19, 1990. Courtesy of the U.S. Air Force.

trying to sell itself to a wide population. It wanted people with specialized skills, who would, presumably, be young men from a blue-collar background. This is reflected in the fact that throughout the period of the all-volunteer force, the Air Force placed more ads in *Popular Mechanics*, a magazine aimed at men who like to build things and are interested in mechanics, technology, and machines, than it did in *Life* or *Sports Illustrated*.[3] In the late 1990s, the Air Force, among the other strands of its appeals, was still offering itself as a place

[140] *Enlisting Masculinity*

where mechanically inclined young men could earn respect and appreciation and develop a career.

Although the Air Force had always had a relatively easy time recruiting and been able to keep its standards high, like the Army and Navy, it faced recruiting problems in the late 1990s. While the strong economy clearly had an impact on the general recruiting environment, the Air Force in particular may have been the service most affected by the boom in the technology sector, since the Air Force specifically targets the young people who are interested in and qualified to work with advanced technology, the same demographic that was most in demand in the civilian economy.[4] In fiscal year 1999, the Air Force missed its goal of 32,673 by 1,727, or 5 percent (Myers, 2000). The Air Force had been spending relatively little to market itself—$12 million to the Army's $100 million in fiscal year 1998 (Chura and Snyder 1999)—and its recruiters were outnumbered by those of the other services by a margin of thirteen to one (Peterson 2000). In 1999, though, for the first time ever, the Air Force paid for television advertising in an attempt to boost its ranks. The TV commercials and a corresponding set of print ads provide the "flight plans" of three recent high school graduates who have joined the Air Force, and their reasons for joining. The plans feature a Hispanic young man who hopes to someday become a doctor and joined to gain independence, serve his country, get an education, and see the world; a young white woman who joined for the challenge the Air Force provides and to gain skills, earn money for college, and see the world; and a young black man who's a track and field athlete with an interest in mechanics, a fascination with airplanes, and a father who served in the military. The print ad sample contained two flight plans—those of the two young men—both of which appeared in my sample a number of times.

Each of these ads shows the young man's face, looking off into the distance, as well as a row of small pictures along the bottom of the page. The small pictures include images of aircraft, leisure activities, travel (the coliseum in Rome, Asian architecture), and airmen and officers (including a couple of women) in dress uniforms and in camouflage. The elements of each flight plan include such markers of personal fulfillment as earning respect, leaving behind small-town life, and making one's family proud, as well as references to travel, education, and personal skills. One of the flight plans includes the goal "Be better with the computer than my girlfriend is." With this statement, the Air Force at once acknowledges that women can be good with computers, which makes the Air Force seem forward-thinking and may appeal to women, but it's still focused on the young man and puts him in a position to surpass his girlfriend, even as it shows that a young man associated with the Air Force can attract women. In the other plan, Kevin Collins, the African American athlete, wants to "be a hero to someone," "show people [he] can fix anything," "see places [his] dad told [him] about," and "ride [his] motorcycle across the desert." Being a hero, being competent to fix things, following in one's father's footsteps, and riding a motorcycle across the desert all hint at masculinity, though not in a particularly militaristic way.

In 1999, the Air Force also commissioned a study by the "corporate identity firm" Siegel & Gale to help it develop a symbol and a theme to represent the Air Force. The firm interviewed members of the Air Force, the Air National Guard, the Air Force Reserve, and civilians about how they view the Air Force and its identity. The researchers found, according to an article in *Airman*, that "instead of one unifying theme, the Air Force has many different ways of expressing its identity" and that "there was little consistency in the visual representation of the Air Force." Siegel & Gale found four dominant themes: "individual achievement, intelligence and technology, core values, and mission," and they recommended that "mission" be the main focus of the Air Force's identity, with the other three themes playing support roles. The firm "concluded the Air Force is a world-class, mission-ready organization" and "recommended the theme 'World Ready,'" along with a new visual symbol that updates the Hap Arnold wings and star (Bosker 2000). In addition to their findings on the Air Force's visual messaging, the corporate researchers concluded that the service's overall image needed to be harder: "the USAF was seen as an organization of nine-to-fivers, not warriors. They had the corner on speed, not courage. They were seen as professional, but soft" (Cooke 2002).

Siegel & Gale produced a series of television commercials meant to portray "the dedication and professionalism of Air Force people." According to the assistant director of the ads, while they show off Air Force hardware, the main intention was to show what it means to be an Air Force member, "the team spirit and sense of adventure in what the rest of the Air Force does." The commercials also tried out a new slogan for the Air Force, "America's Air Force—No One Comes Close." According to Brig. Gen. Ron Rand, Air Force director of public affairs, "'No One Comes Close' really describes our Air Force. . . . People in the focus groups interpreted this to mean no other country in the world comes close to the United States; no other Air Force in the world comes close to doing what we do; and no other endeavor comes close to the high-tech opportunities available to people in the Air Force" (Getsy and Johnson 2000). The commercials were intended to send different messages to different audiences: for current Air Force personnel, "We understand the sacrifices you and your family make every day to protect America"; for recruits, "Join the best air force in the world and learn the best technology"; and for influencers like parents and community members, "This is an air force of integrity, excellence, and service before self" (Cooke 2002). The commercials were broadcast in movie theaters, on the cable networks MTV and ESPN, during the Olympics, and on the show *Who Wants to Be a Millionaire* (Winter 2000).

Perhaps to counter the impression that the Air Force is soft, the commercials include some patriotic and militaristic imagery, like airmen wearing combat gear or saluting in front of a giant flag. The commercials call Air Force personnel "remarkable individuals serving their country" while stirring music plays in the background. Advanced technology is also showcased. One commercial portrays a midair refueling of stealth aircraft, and another shows off the F-22 Raptor, "a plane so advanced it dominates everything in the air" but appears on radar no larger than a bird, "the meanest, baddest bird on the planet." Familial imagery plays a role as well. The scenes of Air Force personnel include an airman in camouflage fatigues carrying a small child. One commercial, "Lullaby," begins with shots of small blond children playing as a woman's voice sings a lullaby: "Sleep my love and peace will send thee all through the night; guardian angels will attend thee all through the night." A woman reads to the children, and the scene freezes. That freeze-frame becomes a photograph on the instrument panel of a jet fighter, an F-117 Nighthawk, flown at night by a male pilot. There is more use in these commercials of militaristic imagery than in previous Air Force self-presentations, but the emphasis is still more strongly on the powerful technology of the aircraft than on a militarism that inheres in an individual airman or his personal use of weaponry. The portraits of airmen as fathers-protectors calls on the traditional theme of the masculine protector that has historically motivated men to fight (Elshtain 1987; Goldstein 2001); the idea of airman as protector also leads the way toward the compassionate, hybrid masculinity that is more pronounced on the Web site and is further discussed later.

In the summer of 2000, the Air Force's Web site (www.airforce.com) expressed the themes that Siegel & Gale identified (individual achievement, intelligence and technology, core values, and mission). The site is a far cry from the skill-focused early ads of the all-volunteer force. It emphasizes the history of the force, its technology, and its missions. The main part of the site is divided into three sections: past, present, and future. "Past" presents a history of the Air Force, starting from well before the Air Force existed, back in 1903, up through the present, along with a timeline noting missions, new technologies, events, and historical firsts. The history of the 1990s describes both military operations, such as Desert Storm and Operation Allied Force, the 1999 NATO-led air strikes on the former Yugoslavia, and humanitarian and relief missions in Somalia, Bangladesh, and the Philippines. The Air Force ends this history with the promise that "as the new century begins, the Air Force will maintain this constant readiness to respond with humanitarian help, wherever it's needed, and to keep its resources honed and ready to defeat any threat from any quarter that jeopardizes the security of the United States at home and abroad." This section on the past also includes "the boneyard," which describes retired aircraft, and "flight plans," which gives brief biographies of three members of the Air Force: the actor Jimmy Stewart, Major General Dick Catledge, and pro-football player Chad Hennings.

"Present" is divided into six sections: Air Force life, the Hangar, technology, flight plans, Air Force arcade, and media gallery. "Air Force life" includes discussions of basic training, officer candidate school, base life, and similar kinds of information. "Air Force life" also presents the Air Force's core values of integrity, service before self, and excellence and describes the "Air Force spirit," which is an "unrelenting passion for personal growth—for pushing yourself further than you ever thought possible." "The Hangar" describes itself as "home of the most sophisticated aircraft in the world today," aircraft that "protect and defend . . . train and explore, and they're piloted by an elite few." This section shows off pictures of and facts about a wide range of aircraft.

Even beyond aircraft, technology is a key component of the Air Force's image. The pages on technology specifically describe communications, flight systems, weaponry, and aerospace systems. The "weaponry" page strives to show off the technological advances of Air Force weapons, while at the same time down-playing their actual purpose and the devastation of war. The page states:

> While the obvious purpose of military weapons is a destructive one, the technology behind their power is actually designed to preserve lives—those of civilians as well as our military personnel. Today's advanced weapons guidance technologies allow us to be so extremely precise in our targeting that the loss of innocent lives during battle situations may be virtually eliminated.

The Air Force also promises that Air Force personnel will avoid the risks of combat. They claim that the same technology that protects innocent civilians "also protects our warfighters by enabling them to guide weapons like the AGM-88 HARM to a specific ground location from outside the target area—and safe from harm." This section goes on to claim that the Air Force, in cooperation with civilian researchers, is developing methods to "destroy the nitrogen oxides that cause smog and acid rain—essentially 'zapping' pollution from the sky" and that "computer innovations developed to help smart weapons find their targets will soon be used to help radiologists detect breast cancer earlier in mammograms." The Web site's section on the future is mostly concerned with future technology and the potential of outer space. The Air Force envisions itself in the future as a space-based force, "instantly aware, globally dominant, selectively lethal, and virtually present . . . a smaller, leaner service totally focused on accomplishing its mission anywhere at a moment's notice."

On this Web site, the Air Force is proud of its history and even prouder of its technology. It touts benefits like travel, training, and money for college, but it doesn't push them hard. The Air Force cultivates a warrior spirit that is mediated by technology to appeal to kids who spent their adolescence blowing things up and battling in space in video games, kids who prize mastery of technology. By stressing the anticipated extreme precision of Air Force weaponry and by actually providing video games on the Web site, some of which include instructions to "eliminate ground targets" ("F-15 Eagle Clean Sweep"), the Air Force is advancing an antiseptic, high-tech vision of warfare from a distance that is efficient, carries minimal risk, and punishes only the guilty. The Air Force is presenting an image of itself as a benign force that provides aid and assistance to those in need, vanquishes threats with the most advanced intelligent technology in the world, and is creating technology not just for fighting, but to better the world, to fight pollution and breast cancer. The recruit who joins this service is participating in this benevolent dominance and can make claims to mastery. This vision of service put forward by the Air Force reflects the set of characteristics that Niva (1998) ascribes to new world order masculinity, with the references to humanitarian work, devastating technological power put to benign ends, and strength leavened with compassion.

As the Army and Navy launched major new campaigns in 2001, the Air Force also developed a new slogan, "Cross into the Blue," and rolled out new ads. The Air Force seems to have decided not to focus on the force's mission, as had been recommended, but instead created a more individualistic campaign. This campaign, which has a slick, cutting-edge look, tries to imbue the potential recruit with a specialness that the Air Force is able to recognize, using the line "We've been waiting for you," and it links technology with excitement and adventure.

In one TV commercial, scenes of a snowboarder whipping along a snowy mountain morph into shots of an FA-22 Raptor racing through the sky. Physical adventurousness and excitement are linked with the technological and militaristic excitement and prowess of Air Force aircraft. The Air Force also wants recruits whose adventurousness is limited to virtual realms. In another ad, a video game player turns into a fighter pilot, overtly linking war fighting with video game playing. This connection at once assures the recruit that he has the necessary abilities and that his "skills," which may have been denigrated by the authority figures in his life (parents, teachers), are actually valuable and necessary—the Air Force claims to have been "waiting for" just such a young person, while also promising him that he'll have access to a "game system" that is much cooler and more exciting than whatever he's playing on at home. In making connections between video game playing and the Air Force, on the Web site as well as in television commercials, the Air Force can draw on the masculine identification and feelings of bodily power that many young men achieve through gaming (see the discussion of Piot 2003 in chapter 3). Most video games present a world structured by values associated with masculinity: "they are about conquest, winning, scoring points, assertion, and domination" (Brunner, Bennett, and Honey 1998, 81). Video games may be a way for boys to construct a masculine identity. Jenkins (1998) argues that through such elements as exploration, the repudiation of maternal culture, the inculcation of mastery and self-control, fantasy role-playing, scatology, and violence, video game culture mimics the nineteenth-century "boy culture" in which boys acquired masculine skills and values. Through frequent references to video games, the Air Force allies itself with a cultural realm where technology and masculinity are deeply interconnected.

In addition to the television commercials, three different "We've Been Waiting for You" print ads ran in *Sports Illustrated* in 2002 and 2003. One states, "Fastball—90 MPH, Slap Shot—120 MPH, Human—1,500 MPH" and pictures a pilot's oxygen-masked and helmeted head in the dome of a cockpit. In the second ad, a trio of sleek F-15 Eagles and an A-10 Thunderbolt fly above a forested mountain topped by a picturesque old city; the caption reads: "Some people backpack across Europe. Some don't." The third ad asks, "Ever wish science fiction wasn't?" above a shadowy picture of a futuristic-looking plane. All three also include a blank Air Force identity card with the outline of a young man's head and the phrase "We've been waiting for you." These ads offer the potential recruit the chance to stand apart from others in cool, high-tech ways—getting to go superfast, flying across Europe in fighter jets instead of backpacking, and working with "science fiction" technology.

After a redesign, in early 2002, the Air Force's Web site focused on five central "missions" that might appeal to a potential recruit: humanitarian, health care, flight, aerospace, and research. The reference to humanitarian missions is notable. None of the other services highlight humanitarian missions in this way. The earlier version of the Web site noted the specific humanitarian and peacekeeping missions of the 1990s as part of the Air Force's history, and while the Air Force removed the historical timeline, the emphasis on humanitarian action increased with its framing as a major career area. The "Humanitarian Outreach" mission page says, "Expect more from your peers. Expect more from yourself. Sometimes the enemy is an earthquake, hurricane or flood. Air Force humanitarian missions save lives and bring aid and comfort to those in need. Do you expect more from yourself?" The text is illustrated with a picture of three men next to a gurney with a helicopter hovering behind them. They are in camouflage: one wears a flight helmet, another sports dark sunglasses, and the third talks into field telephone. The look is distinctly military—no one would confuse these airmen with the Red Cross. Interestingly, of the pictures that accompany the five missions, this is the only one that doesn't include a woman. Humanitarianism is sometimes associated with women or with femininity; some commentators who want to keep the military focused on combat tasks and traditional war fighting try to minimize the importance of both relief work and peacekeeping or denigrate them by casting them in feminine terms, as social work or caring for children.[5] The Air Force, however, is gendering humanitarian missions as masculine. The Web site allowed visitors to sign up for a monthly e-mail newsletter, "News from Inside the Blue," and this bulletin often featured a dramatic account of a humanitarian mission, including natural disaster relief, medical assistance, humanitarian support in war zones, and instances when advanced technology helped to save lives.[6] Again, this picture of masculinity evokes Niva's new world order masculinity.

[146] *Enlisting Masculinity*

The descriptions of the other missions—excluding health care—include references to cutting-edge technology, a recurrent Air Force selling point, and, in a newer move, to power and dominance. The "Aerospace" mission page reads: "Be ready to go above and beyond. The future of aerospace power transcends the skies into outer space. And we command the entire aerospace column from aircraft to spacecraft. Are you up for the challenge?" The page on "Scientific Research" states: "Be on the cutting edge. We've got the latest technology and the sharpest minds—because today the military mind is as important as military might. We stay in front by utilizing new technologies to ensure air dominance. Do you have what it takes to be on the cutting edge of technology?" And finally, the "Flight" mission page challenges a potential recruit to "Embrace a future in the Air Force. Things are constantly changing in this fast paced world. And no one can match our speed, global range, precision and power. We can be anywhere, anytime in a moment of crisis. Think you can keep up?"

Commanding the aerospace column, ensuring air dominance, and maintaining unmatchable speed, range, precision, and power are all assertions of might. The Air Force presents itself in these descriptions in a distinctly more militaristic fashion than it had in the past, although to nowhere near the degree that the Navy was militarizing its recruiting image at around the same time. This change goes along with the depiction of a pilot, previously discussed, in the "Cross into the Blue" print ad, whose face is obscured by his helmet and mask. It is a more warrior-like portrayal of a pilot than had been customary in Air Force advertising—the image implies impersonality and impenetrability, a powerful force with the ability to be destructive. The assertions of dominance and the militarism on the Web site are clearly linked with technology. While the other services may highlight advanced technology to varying degrees, no service makes the connection so direct; certainly the military prowess of a Marine does not depend on the Corps' hardware (let alone its software).

Most of the Web site, however, explores the career opportunities and the benefits of an Air Force life. The Web site profiles five people with careers in flight, with brief entries under the categories "my career," "my life," "my education," and "my technology." They include Captain Tim Baggerly of airborne communications, who has learned in the Air Force "to live [his] life to the fullest and do [his] job with integrity" but who also has "a life on the other side of that gate," one that, according to the accompanying images, includes golf; Technical Sergeant Tom Parker, a crew chief who trains mechanics, enjoys the chance to travel, and spend his free time at fishing tournaments; Major Fritz Heck, a fighter pilot who graduated from the Air Force Academy, has flown a number of combat operations, and now has friends all of the world; Senior Airman Genis Timmerman of security forces, who joined the Air Force so that she could start a career in law enforcement at the age of eighteen, feels that the Air Force has given her "the chance to mature and take responsibility," and who likes "to play sports, work out, dance and cheer" in her free time; and

Senior Airman Marilyn Pool, an air traffic controller who discusses the importance and excitement of her career. Pool's profile is particularly interesting. In the section on her life, Pool, who is African American, talks about her personal growth and becoming a "more articulate, disciplined and well-rounded individual," as well as about her financial security and stability. She goes on to note: "I've learned how to balance a full-time job and be the mother of a two-year-old girl. Motherhood is great and the benefits have been wonderful. One of the things I enjoy most is traveling and spending time with my boyfriend and daughter." This page is buried fairly deep in the Web site, but it's advertising the Air Force as a place where women can have both a career and a family. Not only that, but the reference to the boyfriend shows that this airman is clearly a single mother.

Photo galleries portray world travel (England, Alaska, Venice) and leisure activities (boating, surfing, windsurfing, golf, white-water rafting, camping), as well as on-base amenities like sports facilities, base exchange stores, and nicely decorated dormitory rooms. The various pages describe a fulfilling life that includes career advancement, travel, adventure, personal growth, and friendship. There are also several references to family life. The Air Force promises: "You'll have time to advance your career, bond with your peers, spend time with your family and grow as an individual." Air Force bases "are designed to be functional and family-friendly, with lots of opportunities for fun family get-togethers" and "in addition to recreation centers, pools and playgrounds, Air Force bases offer a variety of youth programs like t-ball." While the Web site certainly devotes most of its attention to the Air Force's technology and the careers and benefits available to potential recruits, the recurrent references to family are notable. The Air Force may be attempting to appeal to women but also, perhaps, to men who may want a more well-rounded life than they might imagine possible in the other services. The Air Force needs to find people who are suited to working with technology and who will stay in the Air Force long enough for the service to get a return on its investment in their expensive training, but who may not have perceived themselves as military types or as suited to military life. These potential recruits are offered the chance to be a part of an institution whose technology gives it power and dominance, that engages in exciting and demanding humanitarian work, and that offers a good career, all while allowing for a normal family life.

WOMEN, THE AIR FORCE, AND RECRUITING

The Air Force has had the most complex relationship with women of any of the services. The Air Force faces the fewest legal restrictions on women's participation, and from its inception as an independent service after World War II, women were integrated into the organizational structures. However, while the

Air Force was in the best position of any of the services to utilize women, it had the least incentive to recruit them because the Air Force could always attract the highest quality male recruits. The other services all had higher standards for women recruits than for men and could therefore make a choice between recruiting higher quality women or lower quality men, but the Air Force could attract enough men to hold them to higher standards as well. The Air Force has frequently taken the lead in opening opportunities to women—it was the first service to train male and female officers together, the first to open ROTC to women, and the first to allow women with children to enlist—but it also kept women off airplanes, limiting the aviation positions in which they could serve, well beyond what the law against women in combat required. The Air Force has the largest percentage of women, and, unlike the other services, its advertising hasn't promoted overtly militaristic forms of masculinity, but the small amount of advertising the Air Force has done over the course of the all-volunteer force has mainly been aimed at technically inclined young men, and women have been only a token presence.

During World War II, before the Air Force was an independent military branch, the aviation components of each of the services were the most enthusiastic about the participation of women. The aviation components didn't have long-standing institutional practices or traditions, and they were working with new technologies that weren't firmly tied to gender roles. The Navy's Bureau of Aeronautics was staffed with young officers figuring out how to work with the new technologies. In the months before WWII, they encouraged the Navy to draft legislation to allow the recruitment of women, and they identified a wide range of skilled and technical jobs related to aviation that they thought women could perform (Ebbert and Hall 1993, 28). Nearly half of the women in the Army during WWII served with the Army Air Force (AAF) as Air-WACs. About a thousand women served as WASPs—Women's Airforce Service Pilots. These women had civil rather than military status, but they ferried military aircraft, towed gunnery targets, and taught flying. They didn't fly combat missions, but they performed other kinds of military flying to free male pilots for combat (Holm 1992, 64).

When women became a permanent part of the regular armed forces in 1948, they were integrated directly into the Air Force, even as the Air Force's parent service, the Army, kept women in a separate corps. The Air Force's decision not to segregate women into a separate corps had less to do with ideas about gender than it did with a concern that the Air Force not have any separate organizations. The new Air Force rejected the Army's structure, with its myriad units like the Signal Corps, the Quartermaster Corps, and the Women's Corps (Holm 1992, 122). As part of that integrated structure, Air Force women officers were incorporated into the male promotion lists—up until a woman hit the legal ceiling at lieutenant colonel, when her male contemporaries and subordinates would begin to pass her by—and while the direct competition might be seen as a sign of equality, it had the practical effect of putting women at a disadvantage, because they weren't eligible for career-enhancing pilot and navigator jobs, but they competed for promotion against men who were (123).

While there was no separate women's corps, up until the 1970s, Air Force women were called WAF, just as Army women were called WACs and Navy Women were WAVES. Women were also placed in a separate category from men in that they could not be pilots. The 1948 legislation barred women from serving on "combat aircraft engaged in combat missions." All of the services took that prohibition further than the law required and, as a matter of policy, closed all pilot jobs to women on the grounds that any pilot should be available for any kind of mission at any time. On the same basis, they did not allow women to serve as navigators or in most flight crew positions (Holm 1992, 126). Flying is the Air Force's core mission, and women were excluded from that core, just as they were kept off Navy ships and out of the combat arms in the Army and Marine Corps. Despite its reputation as the most forward-thinking and gender-integrated force, the Air Force was as resolved as the other services to exclude women from its central military function.

Air Force leaders envisioned the WAF as a small, elite group of women. In deciding how to utilize women, the Air Force used four criteria: physical demands, psychological and environmental suitability, career opportunities (women would be barred from any field if positions up the career ladder were closed to them), and, in unclear cases, a poll of professional opinion. According to these criteria, the Air Force decided to close to women 158 of 349 enlisted specialties, although more might be opened during a mobilization for war (Holm 1992, 139).

During the initial two years of women's integration, the Air Force didn't meet its goals of 300 officers and 4,000 enlisted women, falling short by about 100 officers and 200 WAF airmen. According to Holm, the Air Force was surprised by the shortfall: "After the success of the wartime AAF in recruiting Air-WACs, it had simply not occurred to Air Force leaders that women would not flock to the new, glamorous service" (1992, 139). In response, in 1950, Air Force Chief of Staff General Vandenberg asked Jacqueline Cochran, director of women pilots for the WASPs during WWII, to examine the WAF program, passing over the female WAF director, Colonel Geraldine May. Cochran, who during World War II had fought to keep the WASP pilots as a separate female corps under female leadership (her own), was highly critical of many aspects of the program. Her biggest criticism was that the Air Force was not recruiting women of a high enough quality, and her main criteria seemed to be attractive physical appearance and grooming (142–143).

More than once during the Cold War, the existence of the women's program was threatened. In 1951, the Pentagon pushed to rapidly expand the number of women in each of the services to keep down Korean War draft calls. The recruiting drive was a failure, especially for the Army and the Air Force, which had set unrealistically high goals. If the point of a peacetime women's service was to provide the basis for wartime mobilization, but the expansion plan failed in the Korean War, then Air Force planners wondered why they needed a women's program. Developments in defense strategy further threatened the WAF. President Eisenhower's "New Look" defense policy of massive retaliation envisioned an air war decided by forces in being. There would be no time in a future conflict to expand the forces, according to this strategy, because early use of air power would be decisive, so, again, having a small group of women as the nucleus for an expanded wartime force couldn't be the rationale for the program (Holm 1992, 166).

In the late 1950s, overall manpower reductions led the Air Force to shrink the already-small WAF program. (Of course, increases in Air Force end strength had never led to increases in the number of WAF.) There had been about 7,200 women on active duty in a force of 734,000 in 1958, with a ceiling on women's participation set at 8,000. The Air Force decided to reduce that ceiling to 5,000 by 1960 and to remove women from nontraditional fields and place them only in jobs that "women do better than men" (Holm 1992, 172–173). In 1961, the Office of the Director of Personnel Plans put forward a study that recommended phasing out the WAF program entirely, but resistance from Capitol Hill and the Pentagon, which was unwilling to cut a volunteer program at a time when reservists were being recalled to deal with international crises, saved the women's program (174).

In the 1960s, the WAF was a token program in which women served only in traditionally female occupations. Women recruits had to meet high standards for education and mental capacity, and they were also expected to meet a high standard of personal attractiveness (the desire for military women to personify respectable femininity, as identified by Enloe 2000, at work again). In 1966, according to Holm:

> The Air Force Chief of Staff admonished the commander of the Recruiting Service to get "better looking WAF." Physical appearance became the chief criterion in the selection process; each applicant was required to pose for four photographs: front, side, back, and full-face. Civil rights leaders assumed the photographs' purpose was to determine race, but this was not the case—it was a beauty contest, and the commander of the Recruiting Service was the final judge. (1992, 181)

In the late 1960s, as in the other services, the trends slowly began to shift under the pressures of the Vietnam War and the growing women's movement. The secretary of the Air Force ordered a study of the possibility of expanding the WAF program to keep down draft calls. The Air Force, unconcerned about the other services or the larger manpower issues raised by the Vietnam War, resisted, since it was having no trouble recruiting high-quality men, many of whom enlisted in the Air Force to avoid being drafted into the Army (Holm 1992, 189). The Air Force eventually agreed to a small expansion.

After some early resistance, the Air Force eventually sent more than 500 women, more than half of them officers, to Southeast Asia, mainly to serve with the Thirteenth Air Force in Thailand (Holm 1992, 223–224). In 1969, the Air Force became the first service to open ROTC to women on a test basis. The AFROTC test was successful. The few women who had been allowed in performed well, and the air science professors reported that the presence of women helped to make AFROTC a more acceptable presence on campus (269), which would have been a significant concern in the face of antiwar activity on university campuses during that period.

As noted before, in the early years of the all-volunteer force, Air Force recruiting advertisements emphasized job skills and training, underpinned by a working-class version of masculinity. Some of the ads from this period do make rhetorical reference to women as well as to men, such as a 1972 ad on "The Air Force skill," which notes that each year "thousands of young men and women enlist," or another ad from the same year, with the headline "I learned my job in the US Air Force," which states that "one of the best reasons to join the Air Force is to take advantage of the training they offer young men and women." Despite the references to women, the ads all seem to target men, and only men are pictured.

The image of a woman appears in the sample for the first time in 1976. The ad contains a large picture of an F-16 Fighting Falcon, as well as three smaller pictures of Air Force personnel: two white men crouched under a jet, an African American man working on piece of equipment, and a white woman with a clipboard standing in front of two reel-tape computers. From that point on, in ads that picture people—as opposed to just aircraft or text—if several people or several different photos are included, there may be a woman among the men. It is usually, however, just a single woman who is shown, while several men will also be pictured. Most of the pictures of women are small and not the main visual focus of the ad. In some cases, the women are pictured in tiny photos that run along the bottom of the ads. Many of the ads in the sample feature a single man or a group of men, but only one shows a woman without any men. This ad, discussed later, only ran in *Seventeen*. The only other exception is a drawing of a dejected-looking cheerleader in a 1977 ad about the Community College of the Air Force that states: "Now our college has almost everything but a football team. And cheerleaders." Of the thirty-three ads in the sample that include a picture of a person or people, women appear in nine of them, including the drawing of the cheerleader. The few pictures of women do tend to feature them working, as airmen or officers, rather than at leisure or as civilians, as is common in the Navy ads.

In 1977, Air Force women became eligible for aviation duty in noncombat aircraft. The Air Force waited longer to let women compete for these positions than the Army or Navy, which opened them in 1974 and 1973, respectively (Women's Research and Education Institute 2003). The supposedly more gender-neutral Air Force had held out longer than the other services, perhaps because flying is the Air Force's central mission, and Air Force men resisted allowing women into the heart of the Air Force. The recruitment advertisements don't reflect this change in any way, probably not just because women played such a small role in Air Force recruiting ads but more likely because the ads from the 1970s don't tend to show pilots or air crew; they focus on enlisted airmen and technical and mechanical skills.

The ads from the early 1980s seem more gender neutral than the earlier ads aimed at blue-collar young men, mainly because they are dominated by images of aircraft and most of them don't show any people (though some include a small, inset picture of a man at a control panel). The visual emphasis is on the beauty and grandeur of the aircraft, not on the people who fly or maintain them. While the ads from this period don't seem either to reach out to or to exclude women, in practice, the Air Force was attempting to hold the line on female enlistments. In 1981, the Air Force joined the Army in an attempt to limit the number of women in the military while evaluating their effect on combat readiness. While the Army seems to have been attempting to force a return to the draft, Holm, who had served as WAF director, believes that the Air Staff feared that if the Army held down female enlistments, the secretary of Defense might look to the Air Force to take up the slack and recruit additional women to leave more men for the Army (Holm 1992, 391). While the Air Staff attempted to put limits on the recruiting objectives for women, in 1985, Congress, faced with the pressure to allocate more recruiting funds to the services to improve the quality of men recruited, told the Air Force that in 1987, 19 percent of new recruits should be women, and in 1988, the number should be 22 percent. After 1989, Congress mandated that the Air Force no longer set separate accession and strength ceilings for women, even as the other services, more restricted by combat exclusion law, could do so. The DOD's 1988 "risk rule" on combat exclusions opened 2,700 more positions to women in the Air Force, although the Air Force resisted actually assigning women to some of the new jobs until 1990, when DACOWITS[7] made an issue of it. By the end of the 1980s, 97 percent of Air Force jobs were theoretically open to women, and 77,000 of them made up 14 percent of the service (Holm 1992, 421).

The National Defense Authorization Act for Fiscal Year 1992–1993 removed legislative restrictions on the assignment of women to combat aviation. In April 1993, the Clinton administration, under Secretary of Defense Les Aspin, decided to allow women to compete for assignment to combat aircraft. For the Air Force, this meant that virtually all jobs could be filled by women, with the exception of combat control, special operations forces, and TAC Pararescue positions. In 1998, female aviators flew operational combat missions for the first time, enforcing the no-fly zone in Iraq. The next year, they participated in combat operations in the air war in Kosovo (Women's Research and Education Institute 2003).

Since the late 1980s, when Air Force recruiting ads returned to an emphasis on job training, women have been occasionally included in the imagery of Air Force advertising. Women are a recurring presence in Air Force recruiting materials, but a minor one. In 2000, the Air Force began running an ad in *Seventeen*, a magazine aimed at adolescent girls, specifically for its officer training programs. The ad shows a rural landscape—fields and forests—from an upside-down and tilted view, presumably out of an airplane, with the caption "From up here your career takes on a whole new perspective." Small text along the bottom of the page reads, in part:

> Get the kind of training that prepares you for anything life can throw at you. And it starts with a scholarship through the ROTC program, or enrollment into the Air Force Academy. Either way, you'll get the responsibilities, challenges and training to prepare you for a career in life.

The upside-down view lends some excitement, but it's basically a career-based appeal. The ad isn't offering job training in a good skill but the college-bound equivalent. There is nothing in this ad that seems to be aimed specifically at women. It seems like an ad that could have appeared in *Sports Illustrated* or another magazine aimed at young men, though I came across it only in *Seventeen*. The Air Force did not place any ads in *Seventeen* before this, and then it ran this one ad for five months in 2000. The Air Force may have felt pressure to aim more directly at a female market when other forces were doing so during a period of recruiting difficulty, or the Air Force may have felt some pressure to increase the number of women at the Air Force Academy at this particular period.

In early 2003, a series of reports by a Colorado television station and complaints to the office of a U.S. senator from Colorado led to congressional and Pentagon investigations of sexual assaults at the Air Force Academy, located in Colorado Springs. Military inquiries found that more than fifty young women said they had been raped or sexually assaulted by fellow cadets during the previous ten years and that the academy had dissuaded them from reporting the attacks and punished some of those who did.[8] In June 2003, a few months after this scandal broke, in what may be a coincidence, the Air Force once again began running a recruiting ad in *Seventeen*. This ad is a part of the "We've Been Waiting for You Campaign," and it specifically targets young women. In this ad, the blank Air Force ID card shows the outline of a distinctly female head, as indicated by the haircut (which serves to point out the maleness of the heads drawn in the other ads in this series, some of which might otherwise seem gender neutral). The ad shows the head of an aviator in a cockpit, turning around to look at something, with another fighter jet in the distance behind. Not much of the face is showing between the helmet and the oxygen mask, but it appears to be a woman. The text along the top of the picture says, "The best man for the job came in second." It's a direct offer of equal opportunity, and an equal opportunity to do something challenging and exciting that has traditionally been in the domain of men.

Two different ads in one young women's magazine, each running four times during the period studied, aren't much from which to generalize. On its Web site, the Air Force has certainly made some effort to include women and to show them in a variety of contexts. Over the course of the all-volunteer force as a whole, however, despite the putative gender neutrality of Air Force practices and the breadth of jobs open to women, women are a token presence in Air Force recruiting ads, which seem mainly aimed at young men, either mechanically inclined blue-collar types or, more recently, technology-savvy video gamers looking for a cool career.

CONCLUSIONS: MASCULINITY AND AIR FORCE RECRUITING

The Air Force, in its recruiting materials, has not based its appeals for service on a warrior masculinity, nor has it offered recruits a chance to test their manhood through physical challenges. Air Force advertising, as fits with Air Force culture, is rarely militaristic. Airmen and officers are usually pictured in their work uniforms, not in fatigues, which imply combat, nor in the dress uniforms meant for ceremonial military displays. There are no references to or images of missiles—a key element of U.S. defense strategy and a major element of the Air Force's arsenal—anywhere in the ad sample. This may be because missiles don't imply daring and glory in the same way that the airplane does and because missiles mainly sit in their silos, awaiting potential threats; they also carry immense destructive power. Airplanes, which have both military and civilian functions, get all of the adoration. Air Force aircraft are instruments of war, but their flight doesn't evoke violence, and though Air Force fighter jets and bombers are clearly a different breed from nonmilitary planes, it is the sleekness, power, and beauty of these planes that is highlighted, more than their lethal potential.

Air Force advertising has focused on skills training, offering mechanically inclined young men the chance to acquire valuable skills that will help them advance in the civilian economy and that are a source of respect. Despite very occasional references to women, the job-training ads concentrate on blue-collar men, making the Air Force seen like a haven for them, and while not offering them a Marine Corps–style warrior masculinity, the Air Force is basing its appeal on a working-class version of masculinity founded on economic independence and mastery of a skill.

The Air Force has also made advanced technology a central draw, showing off sleek aircraft and, on its Web site, describing communications, flight, weaponry, and aerospace systems that are the most advanced in the world. These technologies offer potential recruits the chance to be associated with power and dominance, even if their particular Air Force jobs won't directly involve the deployment of these advanced systems. The Air Force even seems sometimes to be promising that war and military force can be experienced as an exciting, bloodless video game. The recruiting Web site emphasizes the Air Force's humanitarian role as well, painting humanitarian missions as dramatic and important. Thrill-seeking video game players and snowboarders (both of which were pictured in Air Force TV commercials) will find excitement in the Air Force, whether through amazing technology or humanitarian work that is like an extreme sport.

The glamour and exhilaration of Air Force technology are also theoretically accessible to women as well as men. Almost all Air Force jobs are open to women, and though women are a very minor presence in Air Force advertising, when they are portrayed, it is generally in ways that are similar to how men are pictured. The Air Force has also made some small recent attempts to target women in print ads placed in *Seventeen*, making offers of equality. Over the course of the all-volunteer force as a whole, though, the Air Force has generally attracted a large number of high-quality recruits, and much of the recruiting the Air Force has done has been specifically aimed at people with technical and mechanical skills—who the Air Force presumes are more likely to be young men—rather than at the general population of high school graduates.

The appeals to and portrayals of men, which make up the bulk of Air Force recruiting materials, can be thought of in terms of the new world order masculinity described by Steve Niva (1998). As I described in chapter 2, Niva argues that the 1991 Gulf War ushered in a new paradigm for masculinity that retained some of the markers of previous forms of hegemonic masculinity, like toughness and aggressiveness, but also included compassion. The Vietnam War discredited military masculinity, and cultural productions of the early 1980s, like the Rambo movies, attempted to heal the wounds of Vietnam with violent displays of hypermasculinity, but the Gulf War allowed a redemption of masculinity by highlighting a form that better fit with American gender relations after the women's movement and with America's conception of itself as the benevolent and responsible leader of the post–Cold War world. The tough and tender model of manhood is also embedded in America's advanced technology, the superiority of which reveals the superiority of Western men. In addition, this model of masculinity, instead of posing itself in stark contrast to femininity, involves a new, somewhat more progressive set of gender relations: "Whereas both the pre- and the post-Vietnam War man sharply differentiated himself from women and their activities, the Gulf War's new man sought to include women in his world, even if restricting them to strictly noncombatant roles" (Niva 1998, 120).

The Air Force's portrayal of itself to some degree reflects Niva's conception of new world order masculinity. The Air Force doesn't emphasize toughness or aggressiveness, but it does assert its power and dominance. It also claims that its technology makes war less deadly, and it highlights its humanitarian mission as an important function, one that is both demanding and rewarding (and it masculinizes humanitarian work as well). This balance fits with the tough and tender paradigm. The links between technology and warfare are stronger in the Air Force than in any other service, and the Air Force gives primacy to the technologist, validating and conferring respect on his skills. The Air Force, in the period since the Gulf War, has given women access to most roles, including formerly restricted combat roles (or, rather, it was directed to do so by its civilian overseers). In actual practice, women haven't achieved full equality in the Air Force, but the Air Force can wear its putative gender neutrality and inclusiveness as a badge of its progressiveness.

Throughout the course of the all-volunteer force, the Air Force has focused on tangible benefits available to recruits, whether skills training, a good career, or, as portrayed on the Web site, a comfortable lifestyle with a balance between work and other aspects of life, like leisure or family. Air Force advertising is highly individualistic. There are a few perfunctory references to teamwork, but the emphasis is either on the airman and his skills or on the Air Force's technology—the airplanes, not on the Air Force as a collective. The other services, particularly the Marines, offer recruits the chance to become a part of something larger than themselves; the Marines focus on the group and celebrate their group identity and culture. The Air Force is at the other end of the spectrum. For most airmen and officers, it offers a work environment that is similar to that of a civilian bureaucratic organization, albeit one that uses a lot of sophisticated technology, with both offices and technical work areas. The Air Force does not promise to transform the recruit and give him a whole new identity that will subsume his old self. This fits with the Air Force's culture, which valorizes technology, does not have a particularly strong warrior culture, and allows its most elite members to identify more strongly with aircraft than with the institution itself. The Air Force offers technology-related forms of masculinity that don't demand a complete transformation or a new identity and will allow the airman or officer to pass comfortably between and find status and opportunity in both the Air Force and civilian worlds.

CHAPTER 7

Recruiting a Volunteer Force in Wartime

The preceding chapters have examined the gendered constructions of service developed by each branch over the course of the all-volunteer force (AVF) and, more specifically, their deployment of various forms of masculinity. This chapter takes up the question of how these constructions and the branches' attempts to recruit are altered by the context of war fighting. While the U.S. armed forces have been sent into combat many times during the AVF era, until Operation Enduring Freedom (in Afghanistan) and Operation Iraqi Freedom, they were not called on to engage in sustained conflicts. The Iraq and Afghanistan Wars are the U.S. military's first attempts to fight protracted wars without relying on conscription to fill the ranks. From the American Revolution through the Vietnam conflict, men were drafted when a war couldn't be successfully waged by volunteers alone. The current[1] wars are being fought by a recruited force, and gender is a key component of military recruiting. The rigors of combat supposedly justify warrior masculinity, and war can alter gender roles both in the military and in society at large. The AVF is much more reliant on women's labor than the military ever was during periods of conscription. Not only do women make up a historically high percentage of the U.S. military but also these wars, like other wars, have expanded women's roles and, in particular, women's exposure to and participation in combat. If combat is no longer recognized as the exclusive province of men, the military's ability to make use of masculinity may be compromised. The questions, then, are how the military branches gender service in wartime recruiting appeals and how their recruiting strategies have or haven't changed in response to the Iraq and Afghanistan conflicts.

The terrorist attacks of September 11, 2001, and the invasion of Afghanistan did not have a perceptible effect on the print advertisements of any of the branches. The Army and Navy had instituted major new advertising campaigns shortly before the terrorist attacks, and they continued with them. The Navy had already begun its sharp-edged "Accelerate Your Life" campaign and commissioned the "Life, Liberty, and Pursuit of All Who Threaten It" slogan before the September 11 attacks, and it believed this tougher image was appropriate for the times. The Air Force had been in the process of rolling out the "Cross into the Blue" campaign at the time of the attacks. Like the Navy campaign, the Air Force's was created before September 11, but according to the advertising agency account director, the campaign's message did not need to change because "a patriotic mind-set already exists—we don't need advertising to create that" (Lauro 2001). According to the *New York Times*, "In all of the armed services, recruiters have been pretty much sticking to their scripts in trying to persuade young men and women to join the military, not in order to fight the current war, but to make a career choice" (Chen 2001). In December 2001 and in 2002, the Army published an ad that shows a face in profile, wearing camouflage face-paint and a combat helmet, with the caption: "Every generation has its heroes. This one is no different." With the evocation of combat and the reference to heroes, the ad seems to be a response to the terrorist attacks. However, the ad appeared in the sample only twice, and the bulk of the Army's advertising was a continuation of the "Army of One" campaign, with similar imagery and appeals and, indeed, many of exactly the same ads as before the attacks or the commencement of war in Afghanistan.

Initially, the Iraq War did not have much of an effect, either, mainly because military recruiting generally went well at the start of the war, aided by a slowing economy. According to press officers for the service branches, the war in Iraq did "not [cause] them to alter significantly the messages at the heart of their marketing campaign[s]" (O'Brien 2005). Early on, the recruiting commands may have been hoping that significant troop deployments to the Iraq and Afghanistan theaters of operations would be short-term, and so they should continue to focus on attracting recruits who were committing to the services themselves and who would stay in the armed forces as the international situation changed. The end of the draft may have made the Army, in particular, skittish about referring directly to war. (The other service that engages in ground combat—the Marine Corps—has different recruiting needs, as discussed, and embraces its combat role in recruiting materials.) Even after the clear, quick victory of the 1991 Gulf War, the Army was wary of mentioning Iraq or showing too much combat footage because it might scare off potential recruits by reminding them of the realities of warfare. Colonel John Myers, director of advertising and public affairs for the Army Recruiting Command, said at the time: "You've got to be careful how combat, or the potential for combat, is displayed in your commercials. . . . We don't want to be misleading, but too much combat footage interferes with the long-term attributes of Army service that we want to portray: money for college, skills training and relevance to a civilian career" ("The War in Military Ads?" 1991). In any case, once the Iraq War began to affect enlistments in 2005, the Army and Marine Corps were the services that had to decide how or whether to make use of the wars in recruiting materials because they were the ones struggling to fill their ranks. As one Navy recruiter put it, "Basically you have two branches at war, the Army and the Marines, and two branches more or less at peace, the Navy and the Air Force" (Jensen 2005). The Air Force and Navy were flooded with recruits looking to get the benefits of military service without facing the risk of being wounded or killed in Iraq or Afghanistan (Moniz 2005).

Before examining how each branch has reacted to the Iraq and Afghanistan conflicts as they project images of themselves and constructions of service in recruiting materials, an important contextual factor to highlight is how the conflicts have expanded women's military roles. About 11 percent of troops who have been deployed in Iraq and Afghanistan are women (Alvarez 2009b). Women are officially barred from direct ground combat (infantry, armor, and some field artillery units) and from units that "co-locate" with combat troops, accompanying them to provide support. According to Cynthia Enloe, military guidelines on women's participation are created "with one eye on the personnel needs dictated by military doctrine and the other eye on the preservation of the ideological bond between masculinity and military service" (1993, 85); definitions of combat are meant to allow the use of women's labor but maintain distinctions between men and women. According to the formal policy, women don't engage in ground combat, but this doesn't mean that military women in Iraq and Afghanistan aren't participating in combat activities or are shielded from the fighting. While women aren't serving in the infantry or driving tanks, the lack of a clear front and rear has exposed them to hostile fire. According to the *New York Times*, in Iraq, "They are driving huge rigs down treacherous roads, frisking Iraqi women at dangerous checkpoints, handling gun turrets and personnel carriers and providing cover for other soldiers" (Alvarez 2006). Although women are technically forbidden from serving in any support unit that accompanies and remains with a combat unit on the front lines, "In reality . . . this so-called co-location is taking place . . . [and] the Pentagon has stretched the language of the policy, mostly because there are not enough troops, men or women" (Alvarez 2006). Women have been sent to work with all-male combat units in Iraq and Afghanistan both because they have been trained in skills that the unit needs (such as communications, medical care, or vehicle repair) and are available and because those units may want women on hand to interact with and search local women (Tyson 2008). Army commanders have not only pushed the limits of the combat ban, in some cases they have simply violated it and sent women on raids where they've directly engaged with the enemy (Alvarez 2009b).

The expansion of women's military roles has met some resistance. In 2005, Representative Duncan Hunter (R-CA), then chairman of the House Armed Services Committee, introduced proposals to make sure women weren't co-locating with combat units and ending up in combat in violation of official policy. The committee passed amendments that would remove women from combat support units in the war zone (which, due to the lack of a clear front line, was almost the entire Iraqi theater of operations at the time), closing them out of 22,000 jobs, and that would require Congress to give its approval before the Defense Department placed women with combat units. The Pentagon protested the measures, which were ultimately defeated, arguing that women, who made up about 20 percent of combat support units in Iraq, were needed in these roles and that pulling them out would hurt morale and endanger operations (Bender 2005; Tyson 2005). However, the military still occasionally shows public deference to the combat ban, even as it violates it in practice. Private First Class Monica Brown earned a Silver Star, the nation's third-highest combat medal, for "repeatedly risking her life . . . to shield and treat her wounded comrades, displaying bravery and grit." Shortly after her acts of bravery, the Army removed her from the camp in Afghanistan where she had been serving as medic for a cavalry unit because the unit had been taking her out on combat missions—including the one when her actions earned a medal—in violation of regulations (Tyson 2008).

THE ARMY

Army recruiting went well early in the Iraq War, helped along by the slowing economy. (A rise in unemployment generally makes the military a more attractive option and increases enlistments.) Army officials were worried, however, about the demands the war would make on that branch, and in preparation, they raised signing bonuses for hard-to-fill positions, increased college aid, increased their advertising budget (to $227 million), and began offering a fifteen-month enlistment option, instead of the usual minimum two years, in the hopes of attracting more college students (Schmitt 2003b). By the time the fiscal recruiting year 2004 ended on September 30, 2004, the Army was beginning to feel the strain of the war. It had managed to meet recruiting goals, but with a smaller than usual cushion of delayed-entry volunteers pledged to come in the next year. It also needed to call up former soldiers using the Individual Ready Reserves program. The Army decided to lower enlistment standards, allowing in more recruits who lacked high school diplomas or who scored in the lowest acceptable categories of the military's aptitude test (Schmitt 2004).

In 2005, recruiting problems worsened, and the Army failed to meet its annual recruiting goal. Army recruiters were under such pressure that some of them began to bend the rules, ignoring disqualifying medical or criminal records or helping applicants cheat on aptitude tests (Cave 2005). The war was making young people more hesitant to join up and making parents, who often play a role in enlistment decisions, more resistant to their children enlisting. The Army responded by pushing even more money into recruitment marketing—$320 million for the next fiscal year—with a portion of that to be spent on ads aimed at parents (Kiley 2005). While recruiting overall was becoming more difficult, African Americans, in particular, began to shy away from the Army, concerned that they would wind up in combat, fighting a war that, for the most part, they didn't support. African American enlistments dropped not only below recent historic levels but also below their proportion of the qualified population (Arndorfer 2005). This is of special concern to the military, because African Americans have been important to the success of the all-volunteer Army. While racial relations certainly aren't perfect in the Army, many African Americans have found it to be more of a meritocracy and better integrated than civilian society, and African Americans serve in the Army in disproportionately high numbers (Moskos and Butler 1996).[2]

In 2006, despite a fairly strong economy, the Army managed to meet its targets. The Army had further relaxed standards, raising the maximum age for enlistment and giving waivers to some recruits with felony criminal convictions, and it increased enlistment bonuses, as high as $40,000 for particularly dangerous job categories (Shanker 2006). The Army missed some monthly recruiting quotas in 2007 but rebounded from the shortfalls by offering a $20,000 "quick ship" bonus to recruits who could report to basic training by the end of the fiscal year, September 30 (Shanker 2007). In 2007, the Army also had a new advertising theme, "Army Strong" (discussed later), and a new set of recruiting messages to get the attention of potential recruits. In 2008, the Army met its recruiting goals for the year, helped once again by a sluggish economy, as well as by expanded education benefits and a drop in violence in Iraq (Alvarez 2009a).

From 2004 to 2007, the Army published ten different print ads in the sample's source magazines. The "Army of One" print ads mainly highlight the development of leadership skills and character (often illustrated with a young man in combat gear), with mentions of job experience and the excitement of weaponized technology (for instance: "What's so cool about working on computers in the Army? Some of them can do sixty"). Several of the ads are aimed at parents—and these *don't* include weapons—addressing their hopes for their children and tying the Army to a parent's values ("You taught him about respect, honor and courage").

I also viewed thirty-eight television commercials that the Army produced between 2004 and 2007, and the ten I viewed from 2003, which were counted in chapter 3, are also relevant.[3] These commercials compose various campaigns aimed at a variety of audiences. While most are meant to sell the Army to young people, many are aimed specifically at "influencers"—mainly parents but also other adults in the community who might influence a young person's decisions. A sizable portion of the ads—more than 10 percent—are designed for the "Hispanic Market," as the Army puts it, some of them in English and some in Spanish. (Many ads feature and seem to be aimed specifically at African Americans, but the Army Accessions Command doesn't categorize them separately.) Several different types of approaches are used in Army recruiting commercials. Character development is a common theme. The concepts of service and patriotism make a very occasional appearance. Many ads include combat imagery; a few of these make veiled references to the wars, mainly through visual clues, but a lot of them don't acknowledge them. Some focus entirely on job training, benefits, and civilian career prospects. A few of the ads aimed at influencers are entirely lacking in visual or verbal references to the martial aspects of the Army; they give no hint that the Army ever wages war, let alone that they were in the process of fighting two. Women appear occasionally in the Army commercials, though rarely as an ad's protagonist. In addition to being included in groups of soldiers standing in formation, women are likely to be shown in a work context (at a computer or providing medical care). Women may be shown doing physical training, like climbing an obstacle course, and female soldiers are sometimes militarized to the degree that they are pictured in the Army combat uniform, but they are absent from the scenes of combat action, of men riding tanks and aiming weapons and dropping out of helicopters. Female soldiers don't pose with their rifles; scenes of combat help to masculinize the Army's image.

In the months after the invasion of Iraq and in 2004, the Army produced several commercials that allude to the war (though they don't mention it directly), calling on themes of patriotism and service and offering recruits the traditionally masculine roles of defender-protector and hero. One ad says of the American soldier: "He is a selfless defender of our rights and freedoms." Another ad warns that "an uncertain world is upon us" but promises that "our Army will always be there" and that "one soldier can make a difference." A third declares that "every generation has its heroes. This one is no different." All of these commercials portray young male combat soldiers and show desert-like landscapes or urban areas that seem meant to evoke Iraq.[4] Some of them use still photos that have a documentary quality, giving the impression that they are footage from the conflict in progress. The still photos and moving images show combat footage, like soldiers riding in helicopters and tanks, patrolling a street, and rappeling down a building, but also include a few shots of them interacting peacefully with civilians, smiling with young boys, and shaking a woman's hand.

Two spots from 2004, "The Right Thing" and "Cut from the Same Cloth," both use historical footage to draw comparisons between the soldiers of the past and the soldiers of today and, by implication, place the Iraq War into American history alongside earlier wars, though neither ad names Iraq or even uses the word *war*. Both ads juxtapose recent footage of combat soldiers in the desert with footage from World War II, Korea, and Vietnam; we see soldiers in combat situations—riding a landing craft on D-Day or traveling down a jungle river in a small boat with rifles raised—as well as in other contexts: reading letters from home, eating, posing for pictures next to a 38th-parallel sign in Korea, celebrating the liberation of France. One ad begins, "What we did was the same thing American soldiers have been doing for generations. Soldiers now and soldiers then, there's the same courage, determination, willingness to serve." The other one mentions both the hardships and the glories but says that service has always been about "doing the right thing." Both end with a reference to the chance to make history. The ads include men of various races and ethnicities. No women are shown, apart from a French woman in the World War II footage who runs up to a soldier in a Jeep and kisses him on the cheek. Her presence is a small hint that women are a potential reward for the victorious soldier or a reminder of what soldiers presumably fight to protect (see Elshtain 1987 and Goldstein 2001 on these feminine war roles). Young men are being given the chance to follow in the footsteps of the men who've come before them and take their place in history as part of the brotherhood of war.

In the same time period that the Army was running these rather serious ads that evoke the war and make a call for service, they also aired other commercials that talk about what soldiers get out of the Army—both tangible benefits like job training, experience, and money for college and intangibles like discipline and learning "what you're made of." A whole series of commercials from late 2003 and 2004 attempts to draw viewers to the Army's Web site, www.goarmy.com, to watch a set of videos called "A Day in the Life of an Army of One," each of which explores the life and job of an individual soldier. The ads are teasers meant to drum up some suspense about what will happen, and they portray the Web videos as though they are a reality show. All of the soldiers featured in these ads are men. The stories portrayed in the ads include soldiers in Hawaii who have to dynamite rock out of a volcano to make a road; a soldier in Alabama training to be a helicopter pilot (he tempts the audience to the Web site with the line "If you think that's cool, wait till you see what I'm going to do next"); A Fort Irwin, California, soldier who was born in the Soviet Union and now drives a Stryker armored combat vehicle; the Camp Rudder, Florida, ranger school (viewers are invited to "see if James makes the grade, only at goarmy.com"); and training for Operation Iraqi Freedom at Fort Irwin. One of these commercials makes a direct reference to the conflict in Iraq. The rest don't, and all of the videos take place in the United States, making it seem as though most soldiers are serving far from the battlefield, but they still get to do exciting things that may involve "cool" military equipment.

Also in 2004, the Army began airing several commercials aimed at parents rather than at potential recruits themselves in an effort to counter parental resistance to their children's enlistment. Ten different spots of this type were broadcast over the course of the next few years, including one that aired on Spanish-language channels. Two feature young women who want to join the Army; the rest feature young men who either want to or have already joined. Most of these ads take the form of a conversation in which a child approaches a parent about joining the Army. In a couple of them, parents talk about being impressed by the changes in their children since they've joined up. Many of the ads are oblique—the kids are talking about something important that they want to do, but the Army isn't mentioned until the end title card. For example, in "Responsible Choice," a young woman talks to her father as he sits at the table drinking a soda:

DAUGHTER: "Dad, did you hear what I said?"
FATHER: "Yeah. Tell me again how you came to this conclusion?"
DAUGHTER: "OK. Number one, it's a challenge. Number two, it's not what everybody else does."
FATHER: "I'll give you that one."
DAUGHTER: "It's important. And as far as careers go, I'll do more and I'll have more choices later."
FATHER: "So, when did you start talking like me?"

The words "Become a Soldier" flash on-screen, accompanied by the Army's star logo and the www.goarmy.com URL. Other commercials end with a direct message to the parents: "Help them find their strength."

In these ads, the kids are likely to make reference to something the parent has said about life, and they imply that the Army will help them find their way and let them do the constructive, responsible things their parents want them to do. One young man says to his father, "It's about what you said the other day, about doing something for myself, maybe something important." Another young man makes reference to an earlier conversation about "careers and stuff" and the father's comment that "the trick is to find something that fits who you are and what's important to you." All of the ads show young people taking decisions about their future seriously, putting thought into it and being mature. The Army is a potential way for young people to achieve their life goals. But while joining the Army is clearly presented as a big deal and something that children and parents should discuss, one issue in particular is glaringly absent from the conversation. All of these ads entirely avoid the subject of war. Even though the risk of combat in Iraq or Afghanistan is likely to be a parent's biggest concern and source of resistance, the ads don't even make the faintest reference to it.

While none of the ads mentions war or combat, some of them do contain a masculine subtext, a subtle suggestion that the Army will make a boy into a man. In "Dinner Conversation," a young black man tells his mother that he's found someone to pay for college and slides out an Army brochure. She looks a bit skeptical. He mentions job training but ends with the argument, "It's time for me to be the man." In "Interview," two parents on a farm discuss how proud they are of their son in the Army, a handsome young man wearing his dress uniform; not only is he "a stronger, more driven individual" but also the father admits that the son can outrun him now. A third ad shows a man addressing a son who is apparently home on leave after his Army training. He tells him: "You got off that train back there, you did two things you've never done before, at least not at the same time. You shook my hand, and you looked me square in the eye." The underlying message is that the Army will help a boy grow into a man his parents can be proud of, the kind who can shake his father's hand and look him square in the eye.

In 2005, as the influencer ads continued to run, the Army debuted several commercials that present young men in civilian contexts, showing how life in the Army prepared them for the work world while also allowing them to have intense, exciting, character-building experiences. (A few ads from this period also focus on the intense experiences and excitement without making the connections to civilian jobs.) In one, a former soldier is introduced to a group of coworkers at a new job in a hangar full of helicopters. The boss gives everyone some instructions, and the group chats with the new guy a little. One asks him, "You ever been around anything this fast before?" The viewer sees a series of action shots from the protagonist's life in the Army, working with AH-64 Apache helicopters that zoom overhead. He responds with an understated, "Yeah, in my last job," and the voice-over announcer says, "See how Army training gives you strength for now, strength for later at goarmy.com." In another ad that uses this "new guy on the job" theme, a young firefighter is told by an older one, "We're a pretty tight group here. That doesn't happen overnight. People have to learn that they can count on you." The viewer then sees the firefighter as a soldier, among a large group that is climbing up and rappeling down walls, helping each other up and holding each others' ropes, cheering each other on and congratulating each other in a happy roar when they are done. It is a scene of physical challenge, teamwork, and male camaraderie. Ads like these imply that the Army provides challenge and adventure but also offers skills that lead to job success, a claim that the Army has been making throughout the all-volunteer force era.

In the fall of 2006, the Army retired the tagline "An Army of One" and introduced a new slogan and a new campaign, "Army Strong." The Army planned to spend $1.35 billion over five years on the "Army Strong" campaign, placing ads not only on TV but also on blogs, social networking sites, and other new media outlets. Lieutenant General Robert L. Van Antwerp, head of the Army Accessions Command, said of the new theme: "There's a strength built into you through training, teamwork . . . and this kind of service makes a difference in your life" (Elliott 2006). In the lead television commercial, the voice-over announces:

There's strong, and then there's Army strong. It is more than physical strength—it is emotional strength. Not just strength in numbers, but the strength of brothers. Not just the strength to get yourself over, the strength to get over yourself. There's nothing stronger than the US Army, because there's nothing stronger than a US Army soldier. There's strong, and then there's Army strong.

Meanwhile, on-screen the viewer sees images of soldiers jogging in formation, saluting, running to a helicopter, climbing an obstacle course and helping each other through it, jumping out of planes, and posing in a field with their rifles, among others. In one shot, a soldier walks down a street past civilians, and a boy turns to look at him as he passes. A few women are included in the montage, standing with other soldiers in formation and climbing a rope net. The vast majority of the soldiers, and all of those pictured in combat contexts or with their rifles, are men. While there are scenes of military action, like paratroopers jumping out of the back of a plane and helicopters patrolling the skies above combat soldiers, none of them specifically suggests the Iraqi or Afghan battlefields. A sixty-second version of the initial commercial, which the Army made available on YouTube, included a few brief shots of what seemed to be a desert setting, but the thirty-second version that would air on TV didn't contain them. As the *New York Times* reported, "The new campaign, at least initially, will not address the war." An ad agency executive told the *Times*:

> We certainly didn't want to avoid the subject.... There's absolutely no avoiding it. But we wanted to focus on the timeless qualities of the Army... the strengths you take away from being a soldier, which help us in the present conflict and help you live your life.

General Van Antwerp also claimed, according to the *Times*, "that additional parts of the campaign might reflect... 'the likelihood you're going to deploy' if you join the Army" (Elliott 2006). Nevertheless, the "Army Strong" ad doesn't reference the Iraq War, and subsequent ads did not reflect the likelihood of deployment.

None of the ads that followed in 2006 or 2007 directly acknowledge the war, but they do take a variety of approaches and offer a range of rewards for service. These include honor, a strong character, and finding out "what you're really made of"; job training, educational benefits, and cash incentives; experience as a leader; the development of personal qualities that will lead to career success in the civilian world and personal fulfillment; and adventure and excitement. The Army Accessions Web site published the eight initial print ads of the "Army Strong" campaign, three of which appeared in this study's ad sample. The copy reiterates the incentives just mentioned. All eight present young men in the Army combat uniform, either posing with family or in a militarized context (holding a rifle, using a touch-screen monitor's navigational tool in a combat vehicle, preparing to drop out of a Chinook helicopter). Several of them feature or include African American or Hispanic men, and one is in Spanish. The only women pictured are family members—two soldiers' mothers and a little girl embracing her uniformed father, over the caption "Being Proud is Strong. Making Others Proud is Army Strong." Although the visuals include militarized elements, nothing in the imagery suggests the battlefields of Iraq or Afghanistan—green grass is the most common landscape feature, and none of the language refers to combat or deployment.

Overall, Army recruiting during the Iraq and Afghanistan wars has downplayed the wars themselves, occasionally making oblique references to create the image of a protector and defender. More often, combat imagery, disconnected from the actual conflicts, has been used to indicate adventure and challenge, an exciting masculine world. Aside from references to fighting, Army commercials occasionally contain a traditionally masculine subtext, subtle suggestions that the Army can help a boy grow into a man. However, Army recruiting uses a whole host of appeals, including tangible benefits like job training, money for college, and signing bonuses, rehearsing pitches they have used throughout the period of the AVF. Women are included in the appeals, but their presence tends to be secondary to the men's. They are excluded from all combat imagery, just as they are officially barred from ground combat, but the exclusions in the advertisements go even further than the actual restrictions faced by military women—female soldiers aren't shown with their M16 rifles or in the field performing combat support functions. Women aren't explicitly feminized, but they aren't fully militarized either, perhaps to keep the masculine appeal of combat intact for young men and to avoid the whole sticky question of women's roles in the ongoing conflicts.

THE MARINE CORPS

Despite the plaudits for the Marine Corps' culture and recruiting tactics, context is clearly important to recruitment. In January 2005, the Marines missed a monthly recruiting goal for the first time in a decade (Schmitt 2005a) and continued to have intermittent recruiting problems in the years that followed. The Iraq War dampened Marine Corps recruiting, warriorhood, evidently, being a less attractive proposition when there is an actual war to fight. By early 2005, the Marines were suffering 31 percent of military deaths in Iraq but made up only 21 percent of U.S. forces. Recruiters complained of a "Falluja effect"—televised images of combat and news of military casualties influenced the public's view of service in the Marines (Schmitt 2005b). Marine recruiting rebounded in 2007 and 2008. The Marines credit a fine-tuning of their recruiting strategies, including the use of social networking sites like www.myspace.com, as well as their continued emphasis on the

Marine Corps' ethos rather than on benefits, while other likely factors include the slowing of the economy, large bonuses and special benefits for new recruits, the addition of new recruiters, and an increase in waivers for recruits with criminal histories ("Marines Far Surpass" 2008; "Marines Smash" 2008).

From 2004 to 2007, the Marine Corps did not publish any print advertisements in the sample's source magazines, but it increased its output of television commercials, airing four different ads in that same period, and releasing three in 2008, the year after the sample period ends. Like earlier Marine Corps advertising, the commercials emphasize transformation, personal challenge, and elitism, and they evoke a masculine realm, almost entirely devoid of women, where men of all races and ethnicities become warriors, part of the proud Marine brotherhood.

At the very beginning of the Iraq War, in late March 2003, the Marine Corps introduced a new ad with training and combat footage, meant to take advantage of the nation's patriotism and interest in the unfolding conflict. A press release from the Marine Corps' ad agency, J. Walter Thompson, described the commercial as "a moving, documentary-style look at Marines' preparedness to go into battle reflective of the mood of the country" ("New Marine Corps" 2003). "For Country" includes combat footage shot by Marines in Afghanistan during Operation Enduring Freedom, as well as in other parts of the world (McCarthy and Haralson 2003). The minute-long ad follows Marines in training and in action, interspersed with titles that flash on screen; they read "For Country," "For Courage," and "For Honor," before the familiar slogan "The Few/The Proud/The Marines" appears. The commercial clearly shows Marines in a combat context, though nothing in the ad directly indicates that some of the footage was shot by real Marines in Afghanistan, making the connection to the ongoing wars more implicit than direct. A Marine spokesman told the *New York Times*, "It's a much more serious commercial, appropriate to run at this time, when there are actual operations." He said, "All our commercials have an element of combat in them . . . we make it clear that when you join the Marine Corps, there's always a chance you'll have to serve" (Elliott 2003). The commercial uses stirring classical music and lacks both a voice-over and the quick jump cuts that are a common feature of recruiting commercials. It offers a statelier, more majestic vision of war, meant to inspire pride and patriotism, as well as to glorify combat. It also says something about the place of women in the Marines. About halfway through the minute-long spot, there is a single, brief shot of women jumping hurdles on an obstacle course. The scores of other Marines pictured—preparing for and participating in combat, carrying weapons and jumping out of airplanes and riding tanks, drilling proudly in their dress blues—are all men. Women are such a small part of the ad as to be easily missed, their brief presence clearly a token.

Another commercial from the Iraq War period made direct reference to the Marines' combat role and evoked the ongoing conflicts. The 2007 public service announcement "Devil Dogs," which is similar to the two ads with historical footage the Army created in 2004, tries to burnish current Marine Corps activities by showing them as part of the larger whole of Marine history of defending the country and making the world safer. An announcer says:

> They've stormed beaches and freed countries; protected the weak and defeated the strong; shown courage and compassion. They've raised our flag and our hope. They've been called leathernecks. They've been called devil dogs. But above all, they're called Marines.

On-screen, historical film of Marines from World War II is interspersed with more recent footage: there are shots of Marines riding landing craft and storming the beach on D-Day, surrounded by foreign children, riding tanks, aiming rifles, celebrating V-J day and participating in victory parades, dropping out of helicopters, feeding children, raising the flag at Iwo Jima, and shaking hands with civilians. The Marines are shown in martial action, in peaceful interactions with appreciative civilians, and in celebration of victory. There is a single shot of the head of a woman Marine in combat gear, but as in "For Country," it is a token inclusion set off from the groups of male Marines working together. This ad offers recruits the chance to be heroes and to see themselves as part of a warrior brotherhood of protectors stretching back through American history.

After "For Country," the Marine Corps returned to the transformation script in October 2005 with a new ad, "Diamond," that debuted during NCAA college football broadcasts ("Marines Present New Facet" 2005). The ad begins with a shot of Earth from space, zooms in on the planet, closer and closer, down to a young African American man[5] standing on a lawn, then past him down below the earth's surface through layers of fiery rock. A piece of carbon lights up, and in its surface we see the young man training to become a Marine (running an obstacle course, shooting a rifle, drilling, etc.). The carbon is transformed into a diamond, and within it, the young man into a Marine in a dress uniform with a sword. A voice-over intones: "In all the world, there are a select few who at their very core are capable of incredible transformation. Under the most grueling conditions they are shaped, hardened, sharpened, ready to stand with the most elite of all warriors, the few, the proud, the Marines." This ad fairly overtly offers a male initiation ritual and makes direct references to elitism and warriorhood.

In 2007's "Applications," which debuted during the NCAA's Final Four basketball tournament, a drill team beats out a rhythmic tattoo, with rows of Marines in dress blues moving in unison, spinning rifles, and performing precision drill maneuvers. Shots of the drill team alternate with quick cuts of action footage—a jet taking off from a carrier deck, helicopters skimming over the desert, tanks firing, and Marines saluting the flag, raiding a building (which looks like it might be in an Iraqi city), rising out of water, crouching in foliage with rifles, training, and marching alongside a drill sergeant. Titles flash on screen: "We don't accept applications," "Only commitments," and the voice-over says, "The few, the proud, the Marines." The spot is meant to point out "the fundamental difference between applying for a school, job or other position and committing yourself to becoming a Marine" ("A Heart-Pumping" 2008). Twenty-two seconds into the thirty-second spot, a single quick shot of a woman doing a sit-up flashes on-screen.

In January 2008, just past the end of the print-ad sample period, the Marines released a commercial that departs from the established Marine Corps strategy by showing neither combat nor the transformation of a young man into a Marine. "America's Marines" features the Silent Drill Team in a line that stretches across sections of America. Classical music plays, and the commercial moves at a stately pace as Marines in dress blues present and twirl their rifles. A Marine in profile raises his sword against a cloudy sky, and a line of Marines runs across a series of American scenes, including a light house, New York's Times Square, farm fields, old brick buildings, main streets, marble edifices, a skyscraper, the St. Louis Arch, the Rocky Mountains, the Grand Canyon, the Hoover Dam, and the Golden Gate Bridge. An announcer says:

> There are those who dedicate themselves to a sense of honor, to a life of courage, and a commitment to something greater than themselves. They have always defended this nation and each other. They still do. The few, the proud, the Marines.

According to Lt. Col. Mike Zeliff, assistant chief of staff for marketing and advertising, the Marine strategy "has evolved beyond transformation"; the Marines are aiming at a generation of young people who are "concerned about the greater good," and so they are trying to emphasize "the intangible benefits of service to country" (Tilghman 2008).[6] The ad doesn't feature combat, but its language and visuals do evoke the idea of Marines as patriotic protectors.

In the spring of 2008, this commercial was noted in press coverage of a new Marine Corps initiative to recruit more women. The pressures of the Iraq War were finally forcing the Marine Corps to approach the recruitment of women more seriously, in part by running print ads featuring women in magazines like *Shape*, *Self*, and *Fitness*, specifically to reach athletic young women. Media coverage has pointed to one ad in the campaign in particular that pictures a female Marine demonstrating a martial arts maneuver for a group of male Marines sitting at her feet—an ad that has no connections to combat or the current conflicts. According to an executive at the agency that created the ad:

> The ad featuring a woman commander is intended to appeal to young women who are weary of being separated from boys and men in sports and are eager to

prove themselves on a larger stage. . . . The message is that the Marine Corps offers a unique opportunity to earn that title and be shoulder to shoulder with your male counterparts. . . . That's an important aspect for the young women seeking that challenge, women seeking an opportunity for a great and selfless endeavor. (Quenqua 2008)

The headline on the ad reads: "Wanted: Leadership that inspires Marines under your command, and Americans everywhere." The smaller text on the page begins, "There are no female Marines only Marines" and goes on to talk about unity in the Corps and "what it takes to complete the journey and earn your place among an elite few." It's an egalitarian message, but one that is in many ways false. The ad executive talks about women who don't want to be separated in sports and being shoulder-to-shoulder with male counterparts, but the Marine Corps, alone among the services, separates men and women recruits during basic training and has also been more insistent than the other services on keeping men and women in separate quarters in the field, separating women from the rest of their units.

The Marine Corps also frames the "America's Marines" commercial as part of their effort to reach women. As the *New York Times* put it, "The message is a unisex one of patriotism rather than macho swagger" in contrast with the ads aimed at men that "often [show] male recruits parachuting from airplanes, wielding big guns, driving heavy tanks and stampeding across the ground" (Quenqua 2008). Because the ad was first broadcast on *American Idol* and not during a sporting event, the Marines hoped they would attract women's attention; according to a partner at the media agency that placed the ad, *American Idol* "helped us get that female audience that we're looking for" (Quenqua 2008). The Marines claimed to expect that this ad would appeal to women for the two simple reasons that the ad was broadcast during a show that women watch and that it didn't feature combat and "macho swagger," despite the fact that not a single woman is pictured as a role model for potential female recruits.

While the Marine Corps has been willing to publish ads featuring women in magazines read by women, they continue to resist making women a significant part of their broader public image. The egalitarian print ads showing a woman as a leader are being published only in women's magazines and will be seen mainly by women, not by men. Merely the briefest glimpses of women ever appear in Marine Corps TV commercials, when they appear at all. Even the commercial that was intended to appeal to women as well as men doesn't include any women. In front of a male audience, the Corps keeps its masculine image intact.

In general, the Marines' advertisements during the Iraq and Afghanistan wars present a masculine world of combat, with occasional indirect references to the conflicts and more overtly patriotic appeals. The Marines' basic pitch and constructions of gender remain unchanged. The Marines promise young men the chance to challenge and prove themselves, to be protectors and heroes, and to be a part of a brotherhood. More mundane inducements like job training and benefits are scrupulously avoided. It's a chance for men to have access to a strong, traditional form of masculinity that is no longer dominant or readily achievable in the civilian world; of course, one of the costs of access to that version of masculinity is the risk of actually having to go to war.

THE AIR FORCE

The Iraq and Afghanistan conflicts increased the popularity of the Air Force with military recruits. Despite generating a backlog of enlistees, the service continued to sell itself, not placing many print advertisements in the sample's source magazines, but airing commercials and developing a major new TV and Internet campaign. Between 2004 and 2007, two Air Force ads appear in the print ad sample, both in 2005. One follows the trend of flaunting the Air Force's powerful advanced technology. The silhouette of a Predator drone and an airman bears the headline, "You can run. But that's about it." According to the copy, the Air Force's applied technology isn't just the highest on the planet, but on "earth, in the air and throughout the solar system." Thanks to the Air Force's aircraft, spacecraft, and satellites, "There's no place to hide when you're being tracked by the United States Air Force," which is "bad news for an enemy, good news for a talented young person seeking a career in intelligence gathering." As in earlier materials, the Air Force provides power by association, vicarious dominance and control.

The other ad appeared in *Seventeen*, the third in the sample published there by the Air Force. The headline reads, "Girls often dream about the day they'll change their name." A sheet of loose-leaf notebook paper, with doodles of hearts, flowers, and little boxes in the margins, is covered with the signature of "Sarah Lassiter." Each time her name is written, an Air Force rank is written in front of it, from "Airman Basic Sarah Lassiter" all the way up through "General Sarah Lassiter." The text at the bottom of the page begins, "As a woman in the United States Air Force, you'll change what people call you every time you grow through the ranks. There are over 150 career fields in the USAF, providing limitless possibilities to lead." As in the earlier "Best Man for the Job Came in Second" ad, the Air Force is again trying to appeal to a desire for equality and to career ambitions, this time by playing on the stereotype that girls dream about getting married and becoming "Mrs." Somebody. Here, they are offered the chance to improve their status on their own, though the feminine doodles of hearts and flowers serve both to be humorous and to keep "Sarah Lassiter" recognizably feminine, even though she's looking to a career in the military to better herself. The Air Force has done little to appeal specifically to women, but when they do so, they make equality and advancement the bases of their appeals.

In 2005, the Air Force also unveiled a new arcade-style video game, "USAF: Air Dominance," for use on mobile recruiting center trailers that the Air Force brings to events like NASCAR races. The game involves piloting three aircraft: an F-22 fighter coming to the assistance of an aircraft under attack, an unmanned Predator doing photo-reconnaissance, and a C-17 transport on a humanitarian relief mission. The Air Force wanted to draw the public's attention to humanitarian missions and unmanned aerial vehicles, and to do so in an enjoyable, easy-to-use format. Instead of trying to make the game highly realistic, the Air Force wanted to ensure that, unlike many difficult-to-learn flight simulator games, it would be, in the words of one of the game's developers, "more fun and playable" (Peck 2005). When players are done enjoying "Air Dominance," recruiters are on hand to complete the link between the game and the service.

Like the print ads, the television advertising during this period avoids any references to the ongoing wars. The Air Force continued its "we've been waiting for you" campaign, in which the qualities displayed by kids—usually some type of technical savvy or daring—demonstrate their potential for success in the Air Force. For instance, a group of snowboarders passes a "trail out" sign. One of them whips out a GPS device and points them in the right direction. Then we see that young man in an airplane cockpit as a bomber pilot. In another commercial, a man in the passenger seat of a police car directs the driver to a group of teens on a street corner and then picks out a young man who is waved over to the car. The passenger asks the young man, who seems to be his son, for help fixing his laptop. He becomes an "Airborne Ops Tech." The use of the police officer gives the young man a slight air of danger, though he is clearly smart, skilled, and not actually in trouble. Brash physicality is displayed by a shifting set of sporting young men, from a group of boys riding bikes through a construction site, to a troop of skateboarders, to homemade car racers, to a surfboarder, to a snowboarder, culminating with an Air Force FA-22 Raptor pilot. Two other "we've been waiting for you" TV spots show a young man collecting food from his school cafeteria and giving it to a homeless man, before he is presented in his Air Force persona as a loadmaster directing a food drop out the back of a cargo plane, and a young woman transfixed by a tornado becomes a crew member on the space shuttle.

In the fall of 2006, the Air Force launched a new, video-centric Web site built around the slogan "Do Something Amazing," introduced by commercials that use portions of the video clips to highlight the concept that Air Force personnel get to do amazing things. The page of videos is introduced by the following copy:

> This site is dedicated to the amazing things the Airmen of the United States Air Force accomplish around the world. Every day we are fighting on battlefields overseas, operating space satellites, defending cyberspace and keeping our skies safe for all. These amazing clips provide a personal, never-before-seen look at our awesome skill and fighting power.

At the end of 2006, the featured videos included "Security Forces," showing how airmen work with canines to detect drugs and bombs; "Thunderbirds," the Air Demonstration Squadron that performs acrobatic aerial maneuvers; "Bomb Squad"; "The Raptor," a stealth tactical fighter; "In-flight Refueling"; "Air Drop"; "Special Ops"; and "Boom," in which stuff gets blown up. The phrase "our awesome skill and fighting power" seems to be using the term *awesome* in the double sense of both awe-inspiring and, as it is more colloquially used, totally cool.

Some of the "Do Something Amazing" commercials and videos from 2007 focus on the Predator drone (the "eye in the sky" that's "protecting the good guys"), a HALO (high-altitude, low-opening) parachute jump, and a cybersecurity network warfare officer who says, "You could say that being cyber warriors, we're always at war, we don't have to go to the desert." The predator and cybersecurity spots just barely hint at the ongoing conflicts, and in a later video that again features the Predator, an airman describes being overseas and having Army personnel approach him in the hangar to ask if he's part of the Predator program and to thank him because on combat patrol their lives were saved by intelligence gathered by a Predator.

During the Iraq-Afghanistan war period, Air Force recruiting pitches became sharper edged and more militarized, but in a highly technologized way. The Air Force has continued to occasionally showcase its humanitarian role as an exciting opportunity and as a facet of the Air Force's identity as a powerful and dominating but benevolent force. Piloted fighters and bombers have receded somewhat in the Air Force's self-presentations, as unmanned aircraft, cyberspace security, and satellites and control of space come to the fore. While soldiers and Marines continued to fight in Iraq and Afghanistan, the Air Force has implied that its technology and the personnel who control and maintain it are key to American security. The Air Force intimates that its recruits can claim the mantle of warrior, that they will defend America and protect American lives, without getting anywhere near a battlefield. The Air Force has begun to more explicitly offer warriorhood—mainly to young men, but without completely excluding women—but an indirect, vicarious warriorhood that is totally mediated by technology.

THE NAVY

Navy advertising from 2004 to 2007 didn't depart in look or tone from the "Accelerate Your Life" materials that were published and aired from 2001 to 2003. The single print ad in the sample from this period, published in 2005, bears the headline "Studying rocket science is more fun when you actually have rockets" and is illustrated with several pictures of missiles firing from fighter jets and ships. The rest of the copy touts "hands-on training with the most advanced technology in the world" and invites readers to visit the Navy's Web site and use the "Life Accelerator" if they're "up to the challenge." Television commercials are also characterized by militarized action and excitement, sometimes including a pitch for some benefit like high-tech training or education. They continue in the vein of the "Life, Liberty, and the Pursuit of All Who Threaten It" spot with quick cuts; exhilarating martial imagery, like armed SEALs skimming over the water in small, fast-moving boats or dangling from helicopters; and thundering rock music, usually by the hard rock-metal band Godsmack. The script of one commercial is connected to the print ad, with sailors firing rockets and the line about rocket science. Another one asks, "Why should you consider getting an education in the Navy?" The camera zooms over the deck of an aircraft carrier as the answer is provided: "Because *this* is one of your classrooms." Navy spots tend to show special operations forces, like SEALs, carrying weapons and wearing camouflage face-paint, despite the fact that only a tiny minority of naval personnel serve in such positions, and the oceanic context of their actions visually distances it from the Iraq and Afghanistan wars.

The Navy's Web site at this time also exploits the draw of intense action and excitement. The homepage featured the faces of six different sailors with a dateline and a brief account of their naval roles. They include a man parachuting out of a plane: "1930 Coupeville Washington; Plunge to the ground. At 140 MPH. For Self. For Country. For Freedom. No Experience Required"; a man on an aircraft carrier: "1900 South Pacific Ocean; Guide F-18 pilots onto carrier decks. Launch sophisticated weaponry. Change the world. Welcome to your day job"; a firefighter: "1330 Manama Bahrain; Somehow 'superhero' doesn't do them justice. Don't just change the rules. Change the game. Faint of character need not apply"; and a pilot: "0800 Iraq; Pilot the fight for freedom. At twice the speed of sound. They call us adrenaline junkies. Like that's a bad thing." These men are doing important, exciting, technologically advanced or physically daring work. They are superheroes and adrenaline junkies. Two women are also included in the gallery, but instead of defending freedom or changing the world, they are taking care of other sailors, serving in traditionally feminine roles: one is a nurse, the other a dentist.

The portrait of the pilot is the one direct reference to the Iraq War in the Navy's recruiting materials, and the focus is on the adrenaline rush of the experience.

CONCLUSIONS

Military recruiting during the Iraq and Afghanistan wars departs from the practices of earlier wartime periods by continuing to offer the same range of inducements used throughout the course of the all-volunteer force and making only limited, mostly indirect references to the conflicts at hand. The military, and in particular the Army, which is bearing the brunt of the two wars, along with the Marines, implies that military service is about many things—war fighting being only one among them—and that it can provide various types of tangible and intangible benefits. Combat imagery, disconnected from the conflicts, is used to denote a masculine realm of challenge, excitement, and brotherhood, and some ads suggest that the military is a place where young men can grow fully into manhood. Women continue to be a peripheral presence for all of the services, rather than an integral part of the military's image. The wars have expanded women's military roles, but in the recruitment materials, their position has actually retracted. Women are out in the field with combat troops, but in recruitment ads, they are visually restricted from dangerous tasks, perhaps to appeal to young men by making sure combat retains its masculinizing function or to avoid scaring off young women and their parents. While in reality women in the services are performing combatlike roles, military recruiting helps to keep combat male in the public imagination.

CHAPTER 8

Conclusion

While some military watchers have claimed that all of the services, aside from the Marines, have abandoned masculinity in their recruiting appeals, this study clearly shows that this is not the case. At the inception of the all-volunteer force (AVF), the military's ability to deploy masculinity as a recruiting tool was constrained because dominant conceptions of masculinity were being disrupted by various social, economic, and political changes in American culture; because traditional military forms of masculinity were discredited by both the Vietnam War and the women's movement; and because women were becoming a more important source of military manpower. However, while these challenges to masculinity made the links between military service and masculinity more complex, the result was not the neutering of military service in recruiting appeals but the alteration of military masculinities. The military branches reacted to the changes in the larger culture and presented several versions of masculinity, including both transformed models that are gaining dominance in the civilian sector and traditional warrior forms that can appeal to those who are threatened by the changes and looking for a refuge.

The Marine Corps is the branch that fully depends on a traditional masculine form. It has consistently depicted a warrior masculinity, with hard young men portrayed in martial contexts, either in a combat situation or on ceremonial display. The Marines inform potential recruits that they'll need to prove their worth before being accepted into the brotherhood, in effect offering them a rite of passage into manhood. Based on their structure and personnel needs, the Marines need to use only one version of masculinity in their appeals. The Marines can use the promise of a warrior masculinity to lure young men who want to spend a few years doing combat-oriented jobs, and they don't need to emphasize benefits or job training as would probably be necessary to recruit people who would make a longer commitment and do more technical jobs. The type of young man who responds to the call of a traditional masculinity will also best fit into the strong warrior culture of the Marines.

All of the other services, however, must use various inducements, some of which are economic in nature. Although some commentators refuse to recognize such appeals as masculine, they do offer the earning potential and economic independence that are prerequisites for manhood in American culture. Many of the ads touting the material benefits of service either frame earning in masculine terms (e.g., "the kinds of jobs a man can build a world of his own on") or contain other visual or textual elements that reinforce the masculinity of recruits. In addition, the Army, Navy, and Air Force have all used more than one form of economic appeal, shifting from the promise of a good job or a blue-collar skill to the language of professionalism and career, often in connection with cutting-edge technology. This change in the way that economic benefits are framed taps into the evolving masculine forms of the economic sphere. As chapter 3 argued, in the larger culture, well-paid, status-granting manufacturing jobs disappeared, and knowledge-society, information-based careers became the main route to a comfortable lifestyle, social prestige, and, with them, masculine achievement. Linking military service to careers and professionalism allows the services to exploit the masculine model that has gained dominance in the economic realm. In addition, as technology plays a larger role in the projection of military force, diminishing the need for physical strength in many military jobs but requiring technical training that may be transferable to the business world, convergence between civilian and some military forms of masculinity becomes more likely.

The Army, in addition to using economic appeals, has offered character development and personal transformation, developing a soldiering masculinity that makes reference to traditional warrior traits like strength and courage and involves displays of weaponry and other martial visual markers. This version of soldiering masculinity, however, is accessible and unaggressive, personified by regular guys. The branch that needs to find the largest number of recruits puts its martial form of masculinity within reach of the average young man, unlike the Marine Corps. The Army also created ads that combine martial imagery with the language of business, creating a bridge between the older forms of masculinity with which Army service had been associated and forms that are becoming hegemonic in the civilian world. This serves both to revitalize Army masculinity, making it seem more up-to-date, and to validate the business world as a source of status and prestige for young men.

The Navy's main noneconomic approach is to highlight adventure, offering young men the excitement of life at sea and challenges that allow them to test and prove themselves. In the 2000s, the offer of adventure became more explicitly militaristic, layering a warrior masculinity on top of other kinds of appeals and reaffirming the Navy's commitment to a strong form of masculinity. The Navy has also bolstered the image of the sailor's life with references to tradition and patriotic calls to service that evoke a romantic idea of the Navy and a glorious past with which the potential recruit can associate himself.

Unlike the other services, the Air Force has not drawn as directly on martial forms of masculinity. Aside from economic appeals that specifically target mechanically inclined young men, the Air Force has offered, by association with the world's most advanced technology, the masculine advantages of mastery, dominance, and control. In recent years, the Air Force has promised recruits not direct physical excitement, as the other services tend to do, but the vicarious thrills of video games, which provide extreme experiences through the mediation of technology. The picture of manhood painted by the Air Force also in many ways coincides with the tough and tender new world order masculinity (Niva 1998) in which aggression is tempered by compassion and technological might and power are used for benign dominance and humanitarian ends.

The choices made by each branch about how to portray service in recruiting materials seem to be driven by their individual personnel needs and their cultures. The branches develop campaigns that they believe (using research and in consultation with their advertising agencies) will attract the type of recruit they want in a given period, with its particular economic, social, and cultural context. According to the advertising sample, the services tend not to respond to international events or military missions in deciding how to portray themselves, making at best oblique references to real-world events and missions.[1] Historically, the military branches have needed to recruit small numbers for a standing force or engage in major recruiting efforts for a specific conflict; recruiting posters from World Wars I and II are familiar icons in American history. Since 1973, the military branches have had to recruit fairly large numbers for a standing force (nowhere near as large as the mass armies of World Wars I and II, but vastly larger than pre–World War II standing forces, which numbered in the thousands, not the millions), rather than for participation in a particular conflict. They need to attract young men to service, not to participation in a particular mission or even a particular type of mission. As discussed in the previous chapter, the Iraq and Afghanistan wars have played mainly indirect roles in military recruiting, rather than serving as the centerpiece of recruiting appeals. In fact, the recruiting materials aimed at parents, who have become a focus of concern and attention in recent years, scrupulously avoid any mention of the wars.

Overall then, while an appeal to serving one's country may make an occasional appearance in a recruiting advertisement, military service is not tied to a concept of duty or to citizenship. With the end of conscription, at bottom, all of the various appeals are based on the individual getting something out of service, whether tangible, material rewards, like job training or benefits, or a set of experiences or characteristics, like personal fulfillment, adventure, the feeling of being a part of something larger than oneself, or even the Marine

Corps' rite of passage into manhood. This emphasis on individualistic reasons to serve may, because of the military's association with masculinity and status as one of its standard-bearers, have its own effect on ideas about masculinity: the disconnection between service and duty or obligation may help to reinforce the rational, individualistic aspects of masculinity over those tied to collective values.

The branches make choices about how to recruit based on their particular cultures and personnel requirements, and they draw on conceptions of masculinity or specific masculine characteristics and models that are circulating in the larger culture that they believe will best meet their needs. Though it may not be their explicit intention, the models that the branches choose to draw on are thus reinforced and recirculated, possibly in an altered form, bolstered by their connection to institutions with such strong historical ties to masculinity. While each branch generates its own prototypes of service, there are similarities and overlaps, as the branches mine a few key masculine models that are becoming dominant in the larger culture—professional and managerial forms, masculinity tied to mastery of technology, hybrid masculinity that combines toughness and aggression with compassion and egalitarianism—as well as the more traditional warrior form that still retains some salience. In this way, the military helps to cement particular understandings of masculinity in American society, at least until the next major set of social, economic, and political changes destabilizes them.[2]

One clear trend in military recruiting is the increasing role of technology in the services' appeals. Advanced technology, and information technology in particular, plays a key role in the American economy, it has transformed many military jobs, and it is becoming central to the armed forces' self-presentations. Service members are constructed as professionals who work with the most cutting-edge technology. The deployment of technologized masculinity, however, goes beyond an economic framework that connects service to high-status civilian careers. In addition to high-tech jobs, technology is important to military constructions of masculinity in other ways. Through the manipulation of technology, which is visually represented by elements such as control panels, screens with data, computer consoles, and complicated electronic arrays, servicemen get to exercise mastery and wield power, controlling some small part of American military might and feeling connected to American technological superiority and dominance, even if they don't participate directly in combat. The Air Force is particularly dependent on the glamour and mystique of technology in its recruiting materials, even going so far in a few cases as to portray the use of military force as an exciting, bloodless video game (though with "America's Army," the Army quite literally offers war in the form of an exciting, bloodless video game). While the Marine Corps continues to offer the direct, physical experience of combat, the other services, and especially the Air Force, play into a fantasy of video game war and imply that the recruit may experience the vicarious thrill of brandishing American military power by working with advanced military technology. The increasing military importance of unmanned aerial vehicles, as well as the expansion of the Air Force's mission into the realm of cyberspace security, heightens the direct connections between information technology and military might. The pilots of drone aircraft can, in fact, wage war with a joystick in front of a computer monitor, thousands of miles away from the site of physical destruction and death. How the military branches choose to frame and present these roles, as well as how far they go in constructing the protection of computer networks as "cyberwar" fought by "cyberwarriors," will have ramifications for the gendering of these roles and our ideas about masculinity.

Another finding is that adventure and excitement are still part of the attraction of military service in recruiting materials. All of the armed forces make this offer in some form. This implies that however hegemonic masculinity has changed, some men still want to prove themselves through adventure and challenge. The military takes advantage of that desire by showcasing its ability to provide those experiences. Earlier in American history, young men could test themselves by conquering nature or settling the frontier; today's outlets include extreme sports like snowboarding, skateboarding, and mountain biking (and even extreme stunts) that young men can participate in or experience indirectly through the consumption of media like the X Games or the TV show and subsequent movie series *Jackass*, in which participants perform dangerous and ridiculous stunts. Video games themselves are a way to virtually indulge in extreme experiences and engage in competition. Recruiting ads regularly use the words *adventure*, *challenge*, and *exciting*, and they present dramatic images of action. Once recruits join one of the services, they may never directly experience the forms of action and adventure portrayed in the ads, but each of the branches has at one time or another tried to communicate that it is a place to escape the constraints of the civilian world and experience life more intensely.

In examining the various forms of masculinity that the services construct, one question that arises is how women fit into these masculine appeals. Men make up the bulk of each service, from a low of about 80 percent of the Air Force to a high of just over 92 percent of the Marine Corps, but the services have depended on women to meet their personnel needs and make the AVF a success, and they have faced political pressure to expand the participation of women. The draft tied men as a group to the military. The end of male conscription made the connection between masculinity and soldiering less automatic, and the services could theoretically have attempted to degender service in recruiting materials, but instead they reforged the link, constructing masculinity both in ways traditionally linked to warriorhood and in alternative forms. In the recruiting ads, women have been offered some limited access to characteristics and experiences that have generally been associated with men, like testing themselves, having adventures, and developing careers, and the inclusion of a few token women in recruiting materials has become routine. However, the representations of service, which feature women so much less frequently than men, make it clear that men are the primary audience and the desired target. The approach to representing women taken by each service differs, but in every case, combat and warriorhood are still associated exclusively with men; women aren't shown with weapons or engaging in overtly martial action. (Women are, of course, still officially barred from direct ground combat.) The image of the service member as a professional who works with technology is in principle an idea of service that is more accessible to women than a physical strength, direct combat idea of service. Women are, in fact, given some representational access to this version of service life. However, technology has preexisting connections to masculinity, and many aspects of the armed forces' deployment of technology in recruiting materials do not downplay but rather reinforce the connections to masculinity. Thus far, the expansion of women's military roles in Iraq and Afghanistan has not led to a concomitant expansion of the roles they play in recruiting materials. If women's combat roles in the current conflicts lead to changes in official military policy, then representations of gender in military recruiting may evolve. For now, the military branches, which are utilizing women's labor in combatlike tasks, are careful to distance them from the imagery of combat in recruiting advertisements.[3]

In terms of the particular approach of each service, women are most marginal to the combat-intensive Marine Corps, both in practice and in recruiting materials. Women are presented most frequently and most like ordinary, unexceptional members of the service by the Army. The Air Force, which is in the best position of any of the services to utilize women's labor power, might be expected to take the lead in the portrayal of women in its recruiting materials. However, the Air Force, which has had a relatively easy time recruiting qualified personnel, has tended to target technically inclined young men. Women were initially barred from serving on ships, and even after the restrictions were lifted, the Navy had difficulty integrating women. Women's limited access to ships is reflected in Navy recruiting materials, which tend to present women in token ways or as an inducement for men to serve. To find enough recruits, early in the AVF the Navy turned to African American men, making special attempts to reach out to a formerly underrepresented and discriminated-against group, presumably under the assumption that greater racial integration would be less disruptive to the Navy's culture and less problematic than greater gender integration.

When it comes to intersections of race and gender in recruitment materials, there are similarities across the branches. Each branch has its own racial history, and the success of racial integration has not been even across the armed forces—though the military as a whole surpasses civilian society on measures of racial equality—but the representations of service created by the different branches share commonalities. African Americans have found better opportunity and more of a meritocracy in the military than in the civilian world and have entered the volunteer force in disproportionate numbers. While both African American men and women serve at disproportionately high rates, and both have helped to make the AVF a success, only African American men are a significant part of the idealized picture of the military presented in recruiting materials. African American women are largely excluded from the imagery of recruitment. Recruiting ads for each of the four branches regularly depict African American men; in some cases, they are the central figure. Each branch also includes some images of women, but almost all of them are white. Twenty-seven different Army print ads in the sample picture women as military personnel or potential recruits. Only four of the more than thirty women pictured are African American. Four Navy advertisements include images of African American women, a quarter of the number of white women shown. Seven Marine Corps ads show women (not including a few proud moms of male Marines); one is African American. Of the nine Air Force ads that contain women, only a single African American woman is pictured, and she is merely one of a group of graduating students. Some recruiting advertisements include a black man and a white woman, as though this meets a set of diversity requirements.

African American women are underrepresented in recruiting ads and overrepresented in the military, especially the Army. In the 1990s and early 2000s, they made up between 45 percent and 48 percent of female active duty enlisted forces in the Army and between 22 percent and 32 percent in the other branches.[4] In many years, African American women outnumber white women in the Army's enlisted forces. High rates of enlistment on the part of African American women are reinforced by low rates of attrition. African American women in the Army are twice as likely as white women to complete their enlistments. Moskos and Butler speculate that a major reason for this may be that, for African Americans, "the grass is not greener in civilian life" (1996, 42). Military planners may rely on the discrimination that African American women face in American society to steer them to military service, even if they are neglected in recruiting appeals. The model image of women's service created by the armed forces is by and large white. To the larger (white) culture, a white woman may more generically represent "women" and be seen as more feminine, and thus it is less threatening to underlying gender ideologies when she takes on military roles.

The picture of service drawn by recruiting materials that I've been describing contributes to the overall image of the U.S. military, as well as to paradigmatic conceptions of masculinity. I have argued that the military is not just another institution in America, but one that has special ties to the nation and to concepts of citizenship, even though service is no longer an obligation. It also serves as a standard-bearer of masculinity, which both reflects and shapes socially dominant ideas about gender. The military in many ways serves as a representative of the nation, to both domestic and foreign audiences. The general image of the U.S. military that is created by the combined effect of the recruiting materials of the various branches is of a technologically advanced fighting force that is progressive on racial and gender issues, while still maintaining gender divisions and keeping women away from direct combat. This vision of the military combines transformed versions of masculinity that are civilianized or that can include both strength and a softness or compassion (possibly suitable for humanitarian missions) with pockets of a more traditional warrior masculinity associated with the Marines and with ground combat, and it promotes and circulates these masculine forms. This book is about the imagery projected by the armed forces, and it can't make claims about how those representations are consumed and thus how they contribute to American identity. However, I suspect that the limited inclusion of women, the idea that the military is a showcase of racial integration, and the focus on advanced technology help the United States to envision itself as a mighty but modern, forward-thinking nation that represents social equality and democratic values, with corresponding ideals of manhood.

In addition to the specific findings about how each of the U.S. military branches genders service in recruiting materials and how the masculine models they deploy relate to the larger culture, this study serves as a reminder that the military's links to gender go beyond what happens within military institutions themselves. Not only do the armed forces create and implement policies that are gendered, in relation to such matters as training, job eligibility, uniforms and appearance, and personal relationships among military personnel, but also they create and propagate images of service members for public consumption that attempt to legitimate and normalize particular understandings of soldiering and related ideas about gender. The gendering of military service begins long before a recruit reports for basic training. Many Americans feel distant from their military because they lack a direct, personal connection to it. The lack of a draft has allowed most Americans to disregard the military, but that doesn't mean that they aren't influenced by it or that they don't absorb any of its messages about gender. The military affects gender roles and relations within society in myriad ways, the most basic of which may be channeling hundreds of billions of dollars of public money to an institution that mainly hires men. Beyond the more concrete effects, the military is also an important part of the culture and, through means such as recruiting materials, actively tries to shape it. Feminist scholars can't afford to ignore the military's role within popular culture. The military influences public perceptions of the masculine nature of military service and the nature of masculinity. How we see our military can affect how we see ourselves as men and women.

APPENDIX

Table 1: ACTIVE DUTY MILITARY PERSONNEL[1]

Year	Total	Army	Navy	Marines	Air Force
1789	718	718			
1801	7,108	4,051	2,700	357	
1810	11,554	5,956	5,149	449	
1812[2]	12,631	6,686	5,452	493	
1813	25,152	19,036	5,525	591	
1814	46,858	38,186	8,024	648	
1815	40,885	33,424	6,773	688	
1820	15,113	10,554	3,988	571	
1830	11,942	6,122	4,929	891	
1840	21,616	12,330	8,017	1,269	
1846[3]	39,165	27,867	10,131	1,167	
1847	57,761	44,736	11,193	1,832	
1848	60,308	47,319	11,238	1,751	
1850	20,824	10,929	8,794	1,101	
1860	27,958	16,215	9,942	1,801	
1861[4]	217,112	186,845	27,881	2,386	
1862	673,124	637,264	33,454	2,406	
1863	960,061	918,354	38,707	3,000	
1864	1,031,724	970,905	57,680	3,139	
1865	1,062,848	1,000,692	58,296	3,860	
1870	50,348	37,240	10,562	2,546	
1880	37,894	26,594	9,361	1,939	
1890	38,666	27,373	9,246	2,047	
1898[5]	235,785	209,714	22,492	3,579	
1900	125,923	101,713	18,796	5,414	
1910	139,344	81,251	48,533	9,560	
1917[6]	643,833	421,467	194,617	27,749	
1918	2,897,167	2,395,742	448,606	52,819	
1920	343,302	204,292	121,845	17,165	
1930	255,648	139,378	96,890	19,380	
1940	458,365	269,023	160,997	28,345	
1941[7]	1,801,101	1,462,315	284,427	54,359	
1942	3,858,791	3,075,608	640,570	142,613	
1943	9,044,745	6,994,472	1,741,750	308,523	
1944	11,451,719	7,994,750	2,981,365	475,604	
1945	12,055,884	8,266,373	3,319,586	469,925	

(*continued*)

Table 1: CONTINUED

Year	Total	Army	Navy	Marines	Air Force
1950[8]	1,459,462	593,167	380,739	74,279	411,277
1951	3,249,371	1,531,774	736,596	192,620	788,381
1952	3,635,912	1,596,419	824,265	231,967	983,261
1953	3,555,067	1,533,815	794,440	249,219	977,593
1960	2,475,438	873,078	616,987	170,621	814,752
1964[9]	2,685,782	973,238	665,969	189,777	856,798
1965	2,653,926	969,066	669,985	190,213	824,662
1966	3,092,175	1,199,784	743,322	261,716	887,353
1967	3,375,485	1,442,498	750,224	285,269	897,494
1968	3,546,071	1,570,343	763,626	307,252	904,850
1969	3,458,072	1,512,169	773,779	309,771	862,353
1970	3,064,760	1,322,548	691,126	259,737	791,349
1971	2,713,044	1,123,810	621,565	212,369	755,300
1972	2,321,959	810,960	586,923	198,238	725,838
1973	2,251,936	800,973	563,683	196,098	691,182
1975	2,128,120	784,333	535,085	195,951	612,751
1980	2,050,627	777,036	527,153	188,469	557,969
1985	2,151,032	780,787	570,705	198,025	601,515
1990	2,043,705	732,403	579,417	196,652	535,233
1991[10]	1,985,555	710,821	570,262	194,040	510,432
1995	1,518,224	508,559	434,617	174,639	400,409
2000	1,384,338	482,170	373,193	173,321	355,654
2001[11]	1,387,366	481,310	379,668	172,817	353,571
2002	1,411,634	486,542	383,108	173,733	368,251
2003[12]	1,434,377	499,301	382,235	177,779	375,062
2004	1,426,836	499,543	373,197	177,480	376,616
2005	1,389,394	492,728	362,941	180,029	353,696
2006	1,384,968	505,402	350,197	180,416	348,953
2007	1,379,551	522,017	337,547	186,492	333,495

1 Department of Defense Statistical Information Analysis Division, Personnel and Procurement Statistics, available at http://siadapp.dmdc.osd.mil/index.html.
2 War of 1812: 1812–1815.
3 Mexican American War: 1846–1848.
4 Civil War: 1861–1865.
5 Spanish-American War: 1898.
6 World War I: 1917–1918.
7 World War II: 1941–1945.
8 Korean Conflict: 1950–1953.
9 Vietnam Conflict: 1964–1973.
10 Operation Desert Storm/Persian Gulf War: 1991.
11 Operation Enduring Freedom in Afghanistan begins.
12 Operation Iraqi Freedom begins.

Table 2: FEMALE ENLISTED ACTIVE DUTY MILITARY PERSONNEL[13]

Year	Army %	Army #	Navy %	Navy #	Marines %	Marines #	Air Force %	Air Force #
1945		93,095		72,833		17,556		
1950		6,551		2,746		535		3,782
1955		7,716		5,707		2,113		8,282
1960		8,279		5,360		1,488		5,651
1965		8,520		5,261		1,441		4,741
1970	1.0	11,476	0.9	5,366	0.9	2,119	1.4	8,987
1973	2.4	16,448	1.8	8,835	1.1	1,973	2.6	15,022
1974	3.9	26,320	2.8	13,143	1.4	2,402	3.7	19,463
1975	5.6	37,703	3.7	17,357	1.6	2,841	5.0	25,232
1976	6.5	43,806	4.2	19,194	1.8	3,065	6.1	29,235
1977	6.8	46,093	4.2	19,210	2.0	3,509	7.4	34,609
1978	7.5	50,288	4.5	20,937	2.7	4,652	8.7	40,710
1979	8.3	54,815	5.4	24,751	3.3	5,501	10.0	45,954
1980	9.1	61,349	6.5	29,806	3.7	6,219	11.3	51,397
1981	9.6	64,877	7.3	34,348	4.1	7,090	11.5	53,902
1982	9.6	64,261	7.7	37,024	4.5	7,874	11.3	54,064
1983	9.9	66,056	8.3	39,873	4.7	8,286	11.4	54,864
1984	10.0	66,664	8.5	41,579	4.9	8,577	11.4	55,339
1985	10.2	67,930	9.0	44,492	5.1	9,041	11.8	57,586
1986	10.4	69,200	9.0	45,602	5.2	9,246	12.3	60,694
1987	10.6	71,136	9.0	45,938	5.1	9,140	12.7	62,666
1988	10.8	71,519	9.2	47,539	5.1	8,959	13.1	60,981
1989	11.2	73,780	9.6	49,602	5.1	8,975	13.7	63,175
1990	11.4	70,741	9.8	49,275	4.9	8,647	14.0	60,250
1991	11.2	67,229	9.7	48,172	4.8	8,278	14.3	58,540
1992	12.0	61,211	10.2	47,688	4.7	7,704	14.8	55,598
1993	12.4	59,668	10.5	45,919	4.5	7,228	15.1	53,940
1994	12.9	58,395	11.0	44,339	4.5	7,029	15.7	53,433
1995	13.4	56,666	12.0	44,375	4.7	7,402	16.2	51,478
1996	14.3	58,084	12.2	43,240	5.0	7,823	16.9	52,129
1997	15.1	61,661	12.4	41,309	5.4	8,499	17.8	53,167
1998	15.1	60,830	12.8	41,367	5.7	8,925	18.4	53,542
1999	15.2	60,283	13.2	41,399	6.0	9,276	18.9	53,968
2000	15.5	62,491	13.6	42,750	6.1	9,499	19.3	54,344
2001	15.7	62,827	14.0	44,630	6.2	9,552	19.6	54,856
2002	15.5	62,806	14.3	46,490	6.1	9,459	19.8	57,957
2003	15.2	62,943	14.5	46,535	6.0	9,560	20.0	59,354
2004	14.6	60,361	14.4	45,318	6.1	9,654	19.9	59,436
2005	14.1	57,196	14.3	43,698	6.1	9,849	19.9	54,906
2006	13.8	58,012	14.4	42,331	6.2	10,045	20.1	54,957
2007	13.4	58,117	14.7	41,114	6.3	10,568	20.0	52,595

[13] Department of Defense Statistical Information Analysis Division, Personnel and Procurement Statistics, available at http://siadapp.dmdc.osd.mil/index.html and Department of Defense Personnel and Readiness, *Population Representation in the Military Services* reports.

Table 3: FEMALE ACTIVE DUTY OFFICERS[14]

Year	Army	Navy	Marines	Air Force	Total
1945	62,775	19,188	809		82,772
1950	4,431	2,447	45	1,532	8,455
1955	5,222	2,936	135	3,080	11,373
1960	4,263	2,711	123	3,675	10,772
1965	3,806	2,601	140	4,100	10,647
1970	5,248	2,888	299	4,667	13,102
1973	4,279	3,454	315	4,727	12,775
1974	4,388	3,649	336	4,767	13,140
1975	4,594	3,676	345	4,981	13,596
1976	4,844	3,544	386	4,967	13,741
1977	5,696	3,791	422	5,383	15,292
1978	6,292	3,980	433	6,010	16,715
1979	6,866	4,358	459	7,276	18,959
1980	7,609	4,877	487	8,493	21,466
1981	8,349	5,345	526	9,106	23,326
1982	9,033	5,740	560	9,942	25,275
1983	9,490	6,300	623	10,560	26,973
1984	10,230	6,553	648	11,234	28,665
1985	10,828	6,913	654	11,927	30,322
1986	11,263	7,260	643	12,377	31,543
1987	11,569	7,223	649	12,642	32,083
1988	11,750	7,335	653	12,899	32,637
1989	12,197	7,453	696	13,403	33,749
1990	12,404	7,808	677	13,331	34,220
1991	12,532	7,981	685	13,323	34,521
1992	11,738	8,294	649	12,683	33,364
1993	11,140	8,265	639	12,251	32,295
1994	10,884	7,966	643	12,322	31,815
1995	10,786	7,899	690	12,068	31,443
1996	10,584	7,825	750	12,047	31,206
1997	10,389	7,796	788	12,008	30,981
1998	10,367	7,777	854	11,971	30,969
1999	10,522	7,699	889	11,840	30,950
2000	10,814	7,846	932	11,819	31,411
2001	11,034	8,038	979	12,034	32,085
2002	11,543	8,189	998	12,912	33,642
2003	11,982	8,248	1,087	13,479	34,796
2004	12,309	8,111	1,096	13,596	35,112
2005	12,475	7,825	1,098	13,471	34,869
2006	12,459	7,649	1,101	12,836	34,045
2007	12,963	7,617	1,135	11,835	33,550

14 Department of Defense Statistical Information Analysis Division, Personnel and Procurement Statistics, available at http://siadapp.dmdc.osd.mil/index.html.

Table 4: AFRICAN AMERICANS AS A PERCENTAGE OF ACTIVE DUTY ENLISTED FORCES[15]

Year	Army	Navy	Marines	Air Force	Total
1945	9.3	4.8			
1949	11.1	4.4	2.5	6.1	7.5
1964	11.8	5.9	8.7	10.0	9.7
1968	12.6	5.0	11.5	10.2	10.2
1970	13.5	5.4	11.2	11.7	11.0
1971	14.3	5.4	11.4	12.3	11.4
1972	17.0	6.4	13.7	12.6	12.6
1973	18.4	7.7	16.9	13.4	14.0
1974	21.3	8.4	18.1	14.2	15.7
1975	22.2	8.0	18.1	14.6	16.1
1976	24.3	8.1	17.0	14.7	16.9
1977	26.4	8.7	17.6	14.7	17.9
1978	29.2	9.4	19.0	14.9	19.3
1979	32.2	10.7	21.5	15.8	21.2
1980	32.9	11.5	22.4	16.2	21.9
1981	33.2	12.0	22.0	16.5	22.1
1982	32.7	12.4	21.4	16.9	22.0
1983	31.4	12.7	20.5	16.8	21.4
1984	30.5	13.1	19.9	16.9	21.2
1985	29.9	13.5	20.3	17.1	21.1
1986	29.7	14.2	20.6	17.3	21.2
1987	29.9	15.1	20.7	17.3	21.6
1988	30.5	15.9	20.9	17.6	22.1
1989	31.3	16.9	20.8	17.4	22.6
1990	32.1	17.7	20.7	17.7	23.2
1991	31.8	17.8	19.9	17.4	22.9
1992	31.5	17.9	18.9	17.1	22.4
1993	30.7	17.9	17.9	16.9	21.9
1994	30.3	18.1	17.3	16.8	21.8
1995	30.1	18.7	17.0	16.9	21.8
1996	29.9	19.1	16.8	17.0	21.9
1997	29.7	19.5	16.8	17.4	22.1
1998	29.5	19.9	16.6	17.8	22.2
1999	29.4	20.3	16.5	18.0	22.3
2000	29.1	20.6	16.2	18.4	22.4
2001	28.9	21.1	15.8	18.5	22.5
2002	27.5	21.0	15.2	18.1	21.8
2004[16]	25.1	21.5	13.0	17.3	20.6
2005	23.9	21.4	12.0	17.2	19.9
2006	22.7	21.0	11.2	16.9	19.3
2007	21.9	20.8	11.0	16.8	18.9

15 Binkin and Eitelberg (1982, 42; 1986, 75) and Department of Defense Personnel and Readiness, *Population Representation in the Military Services* reports.
16 The 2003 *Population Representation in the Military Services* provides racial data for new accessions (enlistees) but not for the existing enlisted forces, presumably because the Department of Defense made changes to its data collection methods for race and ethnicity (shifting the category "Hispanic" from race to ethnicity).

Table 5: AFRICAN AMERICANS AS A PERCENTAGE OF ACTIVE DUTY OFFICERS[17]

Year	Army	Navy	Marines	Air Force	Total
1945	0.8				
1949	1.9	0.05	0.05	0.6	0.9
1964	3.3	0.3	0.3	1.5	1.8
1968	3.3	0.4	0.9	1.8	2.1
1970	3.4	0.7	1.3	1.7	2.2
1971	3.6	0.7	1.3	1.7	2.3
1972	3.9	0.9	1.5	1.7	2.3
1973	4.0	1.1	1.9	2.0	2.5
1974	4.5	1.3	2.4	2.2	2.8
1975	4.8	1.4	3.0	2.5	3.1
1976	5.3	1.6	3.5	2.8	3.5
1977	6.1	1.9	3.6	3.2	4.0
1978	6.4	2.2	3.7	3.6	4.3
1979	6.8	2.3	3.9	4.3	4.7
1980	7.1	2.5	3.9	4.6	5.0
1981	7.8	2.7	4.0	4.8	5.3
1982	8.4	2.9	4.0	5.0	5.6
1983	8.6	3.0	4.3	5.2	5.8
1984	9.8	2.9	4.2	5.3	6.2
1985	10.2	3.2	4.4	5.4	6.4
1986	10.4	3.3	4.5	5.3	6.4
1987	10.5	3.3	4.5	5.4	6.5
1988	10.7	3.5	4.5	5.4	6.6
1989	10.9	3.7	4.8	5.5	6.8
1990	11.2	3.9	4.6	5.6	6.9
1991	11.3	4.1	4.6	5.7	7.1
1992	11.6	4.3	4.6	5.7	7.2
1993	11.2	4.5	4.6	5.7	7.0
1994	11.3	4.9	4.9	5.7	7.2
1995	11.3	5.3	5.8	5.6	7.4
1996	11.2	5.5	5.5	5.7	7.4
1997	11.0	5.8	5.9	5.9	7.5
1998	11.1	6.1	6.3	6.0	7.7
1999	11.3	6.3	6.5	6.2	7.9
2000	11.4	6.5	6.5	6.4	8.1
2001	11.9	6.8	6.5	6.6	8.3
2002	12.1	6.9	6.4	6.7	8.5
2004[18]	12.4	7.4	5.8	6.7	8.6
2005	12.5	7.5	5.6	6.6	8.7
2006	12.4	7.7	5.6	6.3	8.6
2007	12.3	7.7	5.3	6.1	8.6

17 Binkin and Eitelberg (1982, 42; 1986, 75) and Department of Defense Personnel and Readiness, *Population Representation in the Military Services* reports.

18 The 2003 *Population Representation in the Military Services* provides racial data for new officer accessions but not for the existing officer corps, presumably because the Department of Defense made changes to its data collection methods for race and ethnicity (shifting the category "Hispanic" from race to ethnicity).

Table 6: AFRICAN AMERICANS AS A PERCENTAGE OF FEMALE ACTIVE DUTY ENLISTED FORCES[19]

Year	Army	Navy	Marines	Air Force	Total
1972	17.7				15.1
1973	18.9				15.7
1974	19.8				16.9
1975	19.2				17.4
1976	22.4				18.0
1977	21.6				18.6
1978	30.3				20.8
1979	40.9				23.9
1980	39.6				26.1
1981	36.6				27.4
1982	29.9				28.1
1983	28.1				28.3
1984					28.9
1985					29.5
1986					30.3
1987					31.3
1988					32.4
1989	47.2	25.9	28.4	23.5	32.8
1990					
1991					
1992					
1993					
1994	48	28	26	24	33
1995					
1996	47.3	29.8	25.0	24.8	
1997	46.7	30.5	24.6	25.5	34.7
1998					
1999	46.6	31.1	23.5	26.9	34.9
2000	46.4	31.5	23.2	27.5	35.3
2001	46.5	31.6	22.8	27.7	35.3
2002	44.9	31.1	21.9	27.3	34.3
2003					
2004	42.7	31.4	19.1	26.3	32.9
2005	41.1	31.2	17.7	26.1	32.1
2006	39.6	30.7	16.9	25.6	31.3
2007	38.9	30.5	16.4	25.6	31.0

19 Binkin and Eitelberg (1986, 76); Office of the Deputy Assistant Secretary of Defense for Civilian Personnel Policy/Equal Opportunity (1991, 282); Department of Defense Personnel and Readiness, *Population Representation for the Military Services*, fiscal years 1997, 1999–2007 excluding 2003; Skaine (1999, 70); and Stiehm (1996, 66). The incompleteness of this table reflects the fact that minority participation in the armed forces is generally conceived in terms of "women" or "African Americans" (or another racial or ethnic minority group). Until recently, the intersections between categories were rarely considered or reported on, despite the fact that nonwhite women make up such a large proportion of women serving, especially in the Army.

NOTES

CHAPTER 1
1. By "feminist," I mean both the academic literature that uses gender as a category of analysis and the academic and nonacademic literature that seeks to improve the lives of women and, in some cases, to expand the opportunities for women in the military.
2. Technically, the Marine Corps is a part of the Navy and not a separate branch of the armed forces. However, the Marine Corps recruits as a separate branch, and so it will be treated as one for the purposes of this study.
3. The concept of masculinity is defined and discussed in chapter 2.
4. I sometimes use the term *soldier* in a generic sense to apply to members of all of the service branches—to sailors, Marines, and airmen, as well as Army soldiers.
5. Chapter 2 continues the discussion of the ties between the military and the nation in the United States in relation to citizenship. More broadly, however, since the American and French revolutions and Napoleon's development of the mass army, wars could be fought by national armies in the name of the people. As a result, "the male soldier hero is one of the main symbols of the nation" (Dudink 2002, 153). Also, see Hagemann (1997) on the forging of the link between the nation and its military.
6. For instance, the "Army of One" campaign emphasized the soldier as an individual, even though the Army depends on unit cohesion and teamwork. The Army wanted to recruit a young demographic that—based on other representations of Army life—feared it would lose its individuality in the Army (Dao 2001). The Army needed to counter those fears before it could sell potential recruits on Army life.
7. One potential question in examining recruitment materials is whether we can think of the ads as being created by the military branches or whether the images in the ads are dreamed up by civilians without much connection to and possibly even in opposition to the military officers and the service cultures. While Department of Defense civilians and advertisers play a large role in military recruiting, their influence shouldn't be overestimated. There seems to be both cooperation and struggle among the Pentagon, the branches, the advertising agencies, and even, occasionally, Congress, about the image of each service. At the beginning of the AVF, when the branches were less experienced with recruiting, I think the civilians were more likely to win the battles, but since then, the branches have gotten savvier. For instance, when Gen. Charles Krulak became commandant of the Marine Corps in 1995, he decided to pull all advertising and reshape the Corps' message based on his reading of the Pentagon's polling of young people (Freedberg 1999).

8. For example, "Citizens and Soldiers: Citizenship, Culture, and Military Service" October 2000, sponsored by the Institute for the Study of Economic Culture and the Center for International Relations, both of Boston University, and the Ethics and Public Policy Center of Washington, D.C. Select papers from the conference were published in the Summer 2001 issue of *Parameters: Journal of the US Army War College*.
9. Hearing on Sustaining the All Volunteer Force and Reserve Component Overview, Hearings on National Defense Authorization Act for Fiscal Year 2001—HR 4205 and Oversight of Previously Authorized Programs before the Committee on Armed Services, House of Representatives, Military Personnel Subcommittee, 106th Congress, 2nd session, March 17, 2000.
10. For example, Strother (1999) makes reference to the Navy's "women-in-charge" ads. As chapter 4 shows, this is a highly inaccurate characterization of Navy recruiting ads. Similarly, Bonat (1999) takes aim at a single ad—the only one in my Navy print ad sample that features a woman—and uses it to criticize the Navy's approach.
11. Jimmy Carter's Secretary of Defense Harold Brown ordered Navy Commander Dr. Richard W. Hunter to study the use of women to fill military manpower needs. According to Holm (1992), Hunter found that "the recruiting and advertising effort and expense that had to be put out in order to attract enough high quality men (i.e., high school graduates, upper mental categories) to meet the services' requirements for new recruits also attracted more women high school graduates, top mental categories, than the services planned to accept" (253). This implies that advertising meant to attract men to the military can also attract women, though I suspect the reverse isn't true.
12. The military shrank, but the conflicts in Iraq and Afghanistan increased the demands on it. To replicate the capabilities of a larger force, the military has had to rely on the Reserves and the National Guard, as well as on private military contractors. With the Reserves and Guard overseas, states may be left shorthanded in the case of natural disasters or other domestic emergencies. Reservists who signed on for a limited commitment near home but are then forced to leave behind jobs and families for extended tours bear serious costs, as do their communities. Recruiting for the Reserves becomes difficult. The use of military contractors, who aren't subject to the Uniform Code of Military Justice and may end up operating outside any binding legal frameworks, has led to a variety of problems and abuses. If the military can't recruit effectively, it must increase its reliance on contractors.
13. My sample lacks issues of *Popular Mechanics* from 1991 to 1994, and it is also missing intermittent issues of *Sports Illustrated* from the late 1980s. (Unsurprisingly, the annual *Sports Illustrated* swimsuit issue was usually missing from the libraries, both academic and public, that I visited.) In the case of *Life*, the magazine stopped publishing from 1973 to 1977, returning in 1978 as a monthly rather than a weekly publication, and it ceased publishing again in June 2000.
14. While the print ads were collected in a systematic fashion, and I know how frequently the service branches chose to publish a given print ad as well as in what publication, this is not the case with the television commercials. Some of the commercials I saw as they were being broadcast, some I found on the Internet, and some were in the collection of the Museum of Television and Radio. Each of the services also produces other kinds of recruiting materials, like brochures, but these are viewed mainly by people who have expressed interest in the armed

services by sending away for information or speaking to a recruiter. Although many World War I and World War II recruiting posters are famous, with changes in advertising practices, during the period of the AVF, military recruiting posters are most likely to be hung inside recruitment offices and thus are most likely to be seen by people who have already walked through the recruiter's door, rather than by the general public. The focus of this research is recruitment advertisements that are aimed at the general public, through mass-circulation magazines.

CHAPTER 2

1. See Connell (1995) for a discussion of the various meanings that have been ascribed to the term.
2. Scott illustrates this point with the example of nineteenth-century labor politics: "When middle-class reformers in France, for example, depicted workers in terms coded as feminine (subordinated, weak, sexually exploited like prostitutes), labor and socialist leaders replied by insisting on the masculine position of the working class (producers, strong, protectors of their women and children). The terms of this discourse were not explicitly about gender, but they relied on references to it, the gendered 'coding' of certain terms, to establish their meanings" (1986, 1073).
3. Connell uses the term *emphasized femininity* to refer to the most socially dominant ideal of femininity. He avoids the term *hegemonic femininity* because it would imply an equivalence between hegemonic masculinity and hegemonic femininity instead of recognizing the unequal status of the two in the gender order.
4. Note that while this set of missions was a change in terms of the military's immediate Cold War history and thus would alter the Cold War–influenced military culture, these types of tasks are not entirely new to the U.S. military. Historically, the U.S. military has engaged in a range of noncombat activities, including surveying and exploring the American West, thus opening it to settlement; surveying and exploring parts of Central and South America; scientific research; building economic infrastructure, including roadways, canals, and bridges; promoting public health; and governing colonies. For a discussion of the U.S. military's noncombat roles, see Huntington (1993).
5. The Cold War itself created a shift in the type of military professional that came to dominate the officer corps, from the combat leader to the managerial technician (Janowitz 1960). This change presumably also involved some alterations of masculine styles embodied by officers.
6. Working-class men, who could no longer be certain of their ability to support a family and their place in the social order, were particular subjects of the "crisis." They are also the men most likely to be a target of military recruiters, since they are less likely than middle- or upper-class men to go to college and more in need of the economic benefits provided by the military.
7. Kimmel is talking mainly about white, American manhood. His descriptions, for instance, of various eighteenth- and nineteenth-century transformations in masculinity were of hegemonic forms and did not impact African American slaves in the same way as white men; a male slave of the 1830s would not have looked back to his father's era as a time when masculinity was secure, though white men struggling with the emergence of "marketplace masculinity" in the cities would have. (Kimmel is sometimes explicit about issues of race and masculinity, and at

other times he is not and generalizes about American men in ways that seem to be relevant only to white men.) Men in various subordinate social categories may also face crises of masculinity, but they won't necessarily map neatly onto the crisis points of the dominant group.

8. The emblem of the fantasy of a reclaimed warriorhood is the figure of John Rambo—played by Sylvester Stallone—a Green Beret in Vietnam who is mistreated on his return to the United States. In the second film in the series, 1985's *Rambo: First Blood, Part 2*, when he is asked to return to Southeast Asia to find suspected POWs, Rambo responds with the now-famous question: "Do we get to win this time?"
9. For a further exploration of paramilitary culture and the fantasy of remasculinization through "New War," see Gibson (1994).
10. During the Gulf War, images of female soldiers were used as evidence of the superiority of Western culture and values to those of the Arab nations of the Middle East, whose inferiority was signaled in the subordination of women. American women in uniform were contrasted with veiled Arab women (Forde 1995).
11. The Selective Service System was discontinued during the Ford administration, but reinstated in 1980. Since then, within thirty days of their eighteenth birthday, young men (including undocumented immigrants who want to safeguard their chances for future U.S. citizenship) are required to register and remain registered until they are twenty-six. In *Rostker v. Goldberg*, the Supreme Court ruled in 1981 that since the purpose of registration is to create a pool of potential draftees for combat, and since women are barred from ground combat, women can be excluded from the Selective Service System.
12. For a discussion of the development and importance of the citizen-soldier tradition in the United States, see Snyder (1999).
13. A small number of black women were allowed to serve in the Army during World War II.
14. Israel is most often pointed to as the exception to this rule. It does draft women, but for a shorter term than men and for noncombat roles only. A few other states draft women, including Eritrea, Libya (for its People's Militia), and Peru. The vast majority of states with conscript armies draft only men.
15. Elsewhere in the same essay, he discuss the expansion of women's military roles, advising caution and expressing concern over whether women would be subject to a combat liability, as all men in the military theoretically are. In a December 2001 exchange in *American Enterprise* about whether the United States should reinstitute a draft in the wake of the September 11 terrorist attacks, Moskos is on the prodraft side. He advocates a demanding civilian alternative-service option, which could include such activities as airport baggage screening, for conscientious objectors and those who wouldn't perform well militarily. Despite the proposed nonmilitary options, the first principle on which he thinks the draft should be based is "males only, as combat would be a likelihood. Women should be allowed to volunteer as they do now" (Moskos and Korb 2001, 16). Without discussing it, he retains the idea that only men have an obligation to defend their country, and only their contribution is necessary.
16. One attempt to reframe the issue of women's participation to one of civic obligation is Snyder (2003).
17. The assumption that an appeal to a warrior spirit is ultimately the best way to recruit falters in the face of actual warfare. In January 2005, the Marines

missed a monthly recruiting goal for the first time in a decade and continued to have recruiting problems in the years that followed. The Iraq War dampened Marine and Army recruiting in the mid-2000s, and all the manliness of Marine Corps ads couldn't prevent the branch's death toll from dissuading young people from enlisting. The Navy and Air Force, which weren't suffering many casualties, did quite well at recruiting during the same time period.

CHAPTER 3

1. Builder does not examine the Marines. Although the Marine Corps has a unique service personality, as a part of the Navy, it doesn't play a strong independent institutional role in defense planning and strategy, his motivating concerns.
2. In my advertising sample, a little more than a third of all the ads that depicted people included an African American man. The same is not true for black women. Although African American women serve in proportionately greater numbers (and in some years greater absolute numbers) than white women, they appear in only a few recruiting ads. This is further discussed in chapter 8.
3. It worked well with target audiences, so the Army began using it despite strong resistance from within the Army itself. On being presented with the theme by advertisers, General Westmoreland asked, "Do you have to say it that way?" and General Palmer recalls, "God, I just wanted to vomit" (quoted in Griffith 1996, 142).
4. A benefits-based appeal isn't by definition masculine. However, many of the economic-track ads carry a masculine subtext, either in terms of the way the promise of economic advancement is framed or through other visual and textual markers, like references to "the guys."
5. The emphasis on feminine appearance, behavior, and image meant that until the end of the 1960s, WAC detachment commanders generally did not allow enlisted women to wear slacks or jeans outside their unit area, except to participate in sports, and they did not allow a woman in uniform to "enter a liquor store or a bar, smoke while walking, or chew gum in public" (Morden 2000, x). In 1970, the director of the WAC fought against changes to women's enlistment standards that would allow women with a history of sexually transmitted diseases or an out-of-wedlock pregnancy into the Army (separate from the question of whether women with minor children could enlist), factors that didn't prevent men from enlisting. She believed that military women needed to meet a higher moral standard and maintain a spotless public image (233–234).
6. According to Wolff (2005), in the United States, information workers have increased from 42 percent of the workforce in 1960 to 53 percent in 1980 and to 59 percent in 2000. In 1950, more than half of all jobs could be categorized as blue collar; by 2000, the proportion had declined to less than a quarter.
7. Men who lose high-paying blue-collar jobs may have trouble finding other jobs for which they are qualified and that give them comparable wages and status. According to the *New York Times*, many such men see the work that is available to them, often in the retail or service sectors, as being beneath their dignity and demeaning, as well as too low paid to be worth their time (Uchitelle and Leonhardt 2006). The blue-collar jobs had given men earning power and a sense of identity, and these disappeared along with the jobs. The *Times* has also reported that men without college degrees who lose factory jobs are likely to permanently fall out of the middle class (Egan 2005) and that men without college degrees have experienced the biggest decline of any group in marriage rates, in large

part because of economic insecurity and poor earning potential (Porter and O'Donnell 2006).

CHAPTER 4

1. Before the Navy restricted such practices in the 1990s, a shellback ceremony typically involved nudity, cross-dressing, and simulated sex acts (Shilts 1993). The absence of women and openly gay men allowed men to enjoy homoerotic activities while still having their heterosexual masculinity reinforced by an institution that confers militarized masculinity (Cohn 1998).
2. The posters are available on the Navy's military history Web site, www.history.navy.mil.
3. House Armed Services Committee Subcommittee on Military Personnel and Compensation, Gender Discrimination in the Military, 102nd Congress, 2nd Session, July 29 and 30, 1992. Other military commentators at the hearing claimed that "the Navy moved more slowly on social issues than did the other services" and that the Navy has a reputation as "the most conservative of the services."
4. For example, see Adler (1984) and Huntley (1984).
5. In addition to the transnational business masculinity described by Connell (1998; Connell and Wood 2005), Charlotte Hooper (2001) has similarly outlined the rise of a form of hegemonic masculinity associated with elite professionals working in a globalized economy.
6. In 1991, women could not fly combat aircraft and thus were not members of the Tailhook Association. Still, some female naval personnel attended the convention, which includes professional seminars, and many civilian women went to the associated parties. Cynthia Enloe has argued that women's participation in the social events was central to the annual convention; their objectification served to confirm the aviators' manliness (Enloe 1993, 195–196).
7. In 1997, one commentator for a technology publication complained about journalists calling high-technology firms "sexy" and referring to Microsoft founder Bill Gates as a "sex-symbol" (Benjamin 1997).
8. See Cooper (2000) for a discussion of how "new economy" high-tech work is framed as masculine through these traits.
9. See Hamm (1997) on the barriers women face in Silicon Valley and the high-tech sector.
10. Of course, the military did *not* lift the ban on gays in the military in 1993. It instituted the policy of "don't ask, don't tell," under which the military is not supposed to ask service members about their sexual orientation, and service members are not supposed to reveal it. The ban was not lifted, and gay service members continued to be kicked out of the military. Strother, however, presents the policy change as simply a lifting of the ban.
11. See Faludi (2007), Shepherd (2006), and Young (2003) on masculinity and foreign policy post–9/11.

CHAPTER 5

1. Throughout his discussion, Ricks seems to be talking about problems faced by African American men, though he seems unaware that he is neglecting to talk about African American women. I would guess that despite whatever specific problems nonwhite women face, because of combat restrictions and the fact that women are outsiders to Marine culture, any woman in the Marines is seen as female before she is seen as anything else.

2. One of the few exceptions to these limitations on the portrayal of Marines is an ad placed in *Sports Illustrated* in 1984 that makes a pitch to parents. The three-page spread is headlined "If there's one thing we teach your son it's ... Pride runs in the family." The first page shows the head and shoulders of a drill instructor. A large picture that runs across the second and third pages presents a Marine recruit with his parents. Smaller photos along the tops of the pages show a young man in a cap and gown with his parents, boot camp, Marines in dress uniforms posing for a photo at the foot of the Eiffel Tower, and a Marine in a dress uniform holding his hat in his gloved hand, leaning against a white picket fence and listening to the pretty young woman smiling at him from the other side. This ad presents a wider range of situations than a standard Marine ad, and it shows members of a Marine's family (and not just his Marine "family"). The text tells parents how the Corps can develop a young man's potential, and the imagery is less militarized than other ads from the same period. Warriorhood is not mentioned: the focus is on the Corps' ability to turn sons into men their parents will be proud of. The presence of the young woman behind the picket fence sends a presumably reassuring message to parents that the Marines produce fine young men who will someday settle down with a nice girl. Her femininity also emphasizes his masculinity and serves as a reminder of what he's protecting (see Goldstein 2001 on these feminine roles).
3. The familial imagery corresponds with the representations of male military "families" in military thriller genre fiction. Gibson (1991) analyzes post-Vietnam techno-thrillers that sought to heal the wounds to manhood inflicted by the Vietnam War. He finds that in these novels, which present the relationships among male characters as familial, older men—the fathers—create a new generation of warriors. This act of social reproduction is presented as the most important in society; the male military "families" that create warrior men from boys secure society so that actual families, with mothers and children, are possible.
4. The Army (Aberdeen Proving Grounds) and Navy (Tailhook) both faced major public scandals over the sexual abuse and harassment of women in the 1990s, but the Marines, which didn't suffer any scandals, have the largest percentage of women who have experienced sexual harassment, according to Defense Department surveys (Ricks 1997, 204).
5. As noted in the previous two chapters, the military's preoccupation with the feminine image of women service members was rooted in the perceived necessity that the women be feminine enough to highlight the masculinity of male service members (Enloe 2000).

CHAPTER 6

1. This is similar to the Navy's use of ships in its recruiting appeals in that the machinery that is central to the service's military purpose represents the service. However, in the Navy's presentation of ships, especially aircraft carriers, the ships embody power and might and take advantage of the ocean as a dramatic backdrop. Technological force isn't the most immediate impression given.
2. See Lohan and Faulkner (2004) for a review of the literature on the relationship between technology and masculinity.
3. The Navy, which also needs a lot of technical workers, placed slightly more ads in *Sports Illustrated* than in *Popular Mechanics*.
4. See Hafner and Meyer (1997) and Baker and Barrett (1997) on the shortage of information technology workers in the late 1990s.

5. For example, Stephanie Gutmann, an opponent of gender integration in the military, suggests strengthening the military by remasculinizing it, through such measures as reducing efforts to recruit women, separating men and women during basic training, and removing peacekeeping and humanitarian work from the military's jurisdiction. She argues: "If the United States continues to play social worker to the world, it is time to create a separate branch to dispense medicine, deliver bags of disposable diapers, show third-world mothers how to use them, inoculate animals, et cetera" (Gutmann 2000, 282). She feminizes relief work by focusing on diapers and mothers and by including it in a list of what the military needs to change if it's going to attract and retain suitable men.
6. "Cyclone Relief in Mozambique" is an excellent example of how a humanitarian mission can be recounted in the manner of an edge-of-your-seat thriller. The portion of the story included in the e-mail newsletter (the rest could be read by clicking on a link) proclaimed: "Forty airmen waited to hitch a ride home. After 64 days in Turkey supporting Operation Northern Watch, Naval Station Rota, Spain, was just one of several rest stops along the way. The calm before the storm interrupted, as rumors of another mission trickled through the crowd. Then a gust of urgency blew into the room. A cyclone had ravaged Mozambique, a country they couldn't spell without wiping the sleep out of their eyes. The possibility of redeployment home dissolved as motionless bodies woke to the surge of fragmented information."
7. DACOWITS, the Defense Advisory Committee on Women in the Services, was a body created by Secretary of Defense George Marshall in 1951, made up at the time of fifty prominent women, to advise the Pentagon on the recruitment and use of women in the military.
8. Some cadets who attempted to pursue complaints of assault found themselves being investigated for drinking or fraternization (see Janofsky with Schemo 2003; Schmitt 2003a; Schmitt with Moss 2003).

CHAPTER 7
1. While Operation Iraqi Freedom officially ended on August 31, 2010, 50,000 troops remained to provide training and support to the Iraqi military.
2. As mentioned in chapter 2, African Americans may have more fears than their white counterparts about being used as cannon fodder, based on perceptions of the conscription and combat assignments of black men in the Vietnam War (Moskos and Butler 1996; Segal 1989). The Army's knowledge of this concern, combined with the understanding that African Americans have turned to the Army for upward mobility that they can't always find in the civilian world, may be reasons that throughout the Iraq War period, African Americans seem especially likely to appear in ads that focus on job skills and civilian career success.
3. Most of these commercials were available at the Army Accessions Command's G7-Strategic Communications, Marketing, and Outreach Web site, www.usaac.army.mil/sod/.
4. One of the ads is called "Generations-Iraq," according to the Army Accessions Command's Web site, but a television viewer wouldn't see the title, and so the direct Iraq reference is not a part of the commercial.
5. A second version, with a young white man, was also produced and aired.
6. While Zeliff claims that Marine strategy was "[evolving] beyond transformation," "Leap," a commercial released during the summer of 2008, returns to the theme of transformation—a young man who can't swim conquers his fear of a high dive and turns into a Marine on an amphibious combat team.

CHAPTER 8

1. During the Cold War, two Army ads mention "Checkpoint Charlie" at the Berlin Wall, but in general the struggle between the United States and the Soviet Union, which formed the basis for military doctrine and practices, is ignored in recruiting advertisements.
2. While this study tracks how each service deploys constructions of gender, it does not claim that young men automatically internalize all of these constructions. I argue that these constructions contribute to the dominant culture, but some men will resist them.
3. The Navy, whose members are not playing a large role in the Iraq and Afghanistan wars, and which has not been at the forefront of reaching out to potential female recruits, may be taking the lead in portraying women as combatants. In 2010, the Navy Web site's "Navy for Women" section included a series of video clips in which Navy women describe their jobs and their lives, and they specifically discuss doing traditionally masculine work. A master at arms loads and fires a 50-caliber machine gun in one video, and the introduction to the page contains a list of roles that includes not only "mother," "sister," and "friend" but also "defender" and "warrior." The Navy has crossed a line that none of the other services has crossed in their depictions of women. However, while these pages aimed at women that will presumably be opened and viewed mainly by women do show women performing combat functions, the portrayals of sailors that are most likely to be seen by the wider public and by young men follow a more familiar script. The redesign of the Web site, which includes the new pages for women, was part of a new campaign that debuted in 2009 with the slogan, "America's Navy—A Global Force for Good." The debut television commercial barely included women at all and certainly didn't present them as warriors.
4. Since 1996, the Department of Defense Office of the Under Secretary of Defense, Personnel and Readiness, has published an online annual report, *Population Representation in the Military Services*, which includes data that break down women and men's military service by race and ethnicity. Some racially specific information on women's military participation can be found in Binkin and Eitelberg (1986), Office of the Deputy Assistant Secretary of Defense for Civilian Personnel Policy/Equal Opportunity (1991), Skaine (1999), and Stiehm (1996). Finding historical data on African American women's participation can be difficult because minority participation in the armed forces has generally been conceived in terms of "women" or "African Americans." The intersections between categories are not frequently considered or reported on.

BIBLIOGRAPHY

Abrams, Elliot, and Andrew J. Bacevich. 2001. "A Symposium on Citizenship and Military Service." *Parameters: Journal of the US Army War College* 31(2):18–22.
Adler, Jerry. 1984. "The Year of the Yuppie." *Newsweek*. December 31, p. 14.
Alvarez, Lizette. 2006. "Jane, We Hardly Knew Ye Died." *New York Times*. September 24, p. C1.
———. 2009a. "More Americans Joining Military as Jobs Dwindle." *New York Times*. January 19, p. A1.
———. 2009b. "GI Jane Breaks the Combat Barrier." *New York Times*. August 16, p. A1.
"Army's New Slogan Defies Common Sense." 2001. *VFW, Veterans of Foreign Wars Magazine*. March, p. 8.
Arndorfer, James B. 2005. "War Puts Damper on Army Minority Recruitment." *Advertising Age*. February 28, p. 18.
Baker, Paula. 1984. "The Domestication of Politics: Women and American Political Society, 1780–1920." *American Historical Review* 89(3):620–647.
Baker, Stephen, and Amy Barrett. 1997. "Calling All Nerds." *Business Week*. March 10, p. 36.
Barrett, Frank J. 1996. "The Organizational Construction of Hegemonic Masculinity: The Case of the US Navy." *Gender, Work, and Organization* 3(3):129–142.
Bender, Bryan. 2005. "Combat Support Ban Weighed for Women." *Boston.com (Boston Globe online edition)*. May 18. www.boston.com/news/nation/washington/articles/2005/05/18/combat_support_ban_weighed_for_women/.
Benjamin, David. 1997. "Is Silicon Valley Sexy? Not by My Standards." *Electronic Engineering Times*. April 28, p. 41.
Binkin, Martin, and Shirley J. Bach. 1977. *Women in the Military*. Washington, DC: Brookings Institution.
Binkin, Martin, and Mark J. Eitelberg. 1986. "Women and Minorities in the All-Volunteer Force." In *The All-Volunteer Force after a Decade: Retrospect and Prospect*, ed. William Bowman, Roger Little, and Thomas G. Sicilia. McLean, VA: Pergamon-Brassey's.
Binkin, Martin, and Mark J. Eitelberg with Alvin J. Schexnider and Marvin M. Smith. 1982. *Blacks and the Military*. Washington, DC: Brookings Institution.
Bly, Robert. 1990. *Iron John: A Book about Men*. Reading, MA: Addison-Wesley.
Bonat, Christian. 1999. "Is the Navy Sending the Right Message?" *United States Naval Institute Proceedings*. November, p. 96.
Bosker, A. J. 2000. "Air Force Studies Theme, Symbol." *Airman* 44(3):15.
Braudy, Leo. 2003. *From Chivalry to Terrorism: War and the Changing Nature of Masculinity*. New York: Alfred A. Knopf.

Brod, Harry, ed. 1987. *The Making of Masculinities: The New Men's Studies.* Boston: Allen & Unwin.

Brunner, Cornelia, Dorothy Bennett, and Margaret Honey. 1998. "Girl Games and Technological Desire." In *From Barbie to Mortal Kombat: Gender and Computer Games*, ed. Justine Cassell and Henry Jenkins. Cambridge, MA: MIT Press.

Builder, Carl H. 1989. *The Masks of War: American Military Styles in Strategy and Analysis.* Baltimore: Johns Hopkins University Press.

Burk, James. 2002. "Theories of Democratic Civil-Military Relations." *Armed Forces & Society* 29(1):7–29.

Burke, Carol. 1999. "Military Folk Culture." In *Beyond Zero Tolerance: Discrimination in Military Culture*, ed. Mary Fiansod Katzenstein and Judith Reppy. Lanham, MD: Rowman & Littlefield.

Cave, Damien. 2005. "Army Recruiters Say They Feel Pressure to Bend Rules." *New York Times.* May 3, p. A23.

Center for Strategic and International Studies, International Security Program. 2000. *American Military Culture in the Twenty-First Century.* Washington, DC: CSIS Press.

Chapkis, Wendy. 1981. *Loaded Questions: Women in the Military.* Amsterdam: Transnational Institute.

Chen, David W. 2001. "Armed Forces Stress Careers, Not Current War." *New York Times.* October 21, p. B10.

Christmas, Lt. Gen. George R. 1994. Prepared Testimony. House of Representatives, Committee on Armed Services, Military Forces and Personnel Subcommittee. Assignment of Army and Marine Corps Women under the New Definition of Ground Combat, 103rd Congress, 2nd Session, October 6.

Chura, Hillary, and Beth Snyder. 1999. "U.S. Air Force Rethinks Identity." *Advertising Age.* August 16, p. 8.

Clemons, Luis. 2005. "Profiting from the Bugle Call." *Multichannel News* 26(39):24.

Cockburn, Cynthia. 1985. *Machinery of Dominance: Women, Men, and Technical Know-How.* Boston: Northeastern University Press.

Cohen, Eliot A. 2001. "Twilight of the Citizen-Soldier." *Parameters: Journal of the US Army War College* 31(2):23–28.

Cohn, Carol. 1998. "Gays in the Military: Texts and Subtexts." In *The "Man" Question in International Relations*, ed. Marysia Zalewski and Jane Parpat. Boulder, CO: Westview.

Connell, R. W. 1985. "Masculinity, Violence, and War." In *War/Masculinity*, ed. Paul Patton and Ross Poole. Sydney, Australia: Intervention.

———. 1987. *Gender and Power: Society, the Person, and Sexual Politics.* Stanford, CA: Stanford University Press.

———. 1995. *Masculinities.* Berkeley: University of California Press.

———. 1998. "Masculinities and Globalization." *Men and Masculinities* 1(1): 3–23.

Connell, R. W., and James W. Messerschmidt. 2005. "Hegemonic Masculinity: Rethinking the Concept." *Gender & Society* 19(6): 829–859.

Connell, R. W., and Julian Wood. 2005. "Globalization and Business Masculinities." *Men and Masculinities* 7(4): 347–364.

Cooke, Kenneth R. 2002. "One Voice, One Force: Identity at the USAF." *Design Management Journal.* Winter. http://findarticles.com/p/articles/mi_qa4001/is_200201/ai_n9080138/.

Cooper, Marianne. 2000. "Being the 'Go-to Guy': Fatherhood, Masculinity, and the Organization of Work in Silicon Valley." *Qualitative Sociology* 23(4):379–405.

D'Amico, Francine, and Laurie Weinstein. 1999. *Gender Camouflage: Women and the US Military*. New York: New York University Press.

Daniels, Cynthia R., ed. 1998. *Lost Fathers: The Politics of Fatherlessness in America*. New York: St. Martin's.

Dao, James. 2001. "Ads Now Seek Recruits for an 'Army of One.'" *New York Times*. January 10, p. A1.

Department of Defense, Office of the Under Secretary of Defense, Personnel and Readiness. *Population Representation in the Military Services*. http://prhome.defense.gov/MPP/ACCESSION%20POLICY/poprep.aspx.

Department of Defense, Statistical Information Analysis Division. 2010. "Military Personnel Statistics." http://siadapp.dmdc.osd.mil/personnel/MILITARY/miltop.htm.

De Pauw, Linda Grant. 1998. *Battle Cries and Lullabies: Women in War from Prehistory to the Present*. Norman: University of Oklahoma Press.

Derbyshire, John. 2001. "Is This All We Can Be?" *National Review*. April 16, pp. 30–35.

"Digital Bridges Signs Licensing Agreement with Sports Illustrated for Branded Cell Phone Games." 2004. *Time Warner Press Releases*. November 22. www.timewarner.com/newsroom/press-releases/2004/11/Digital_Bridges_Signs_Licensing_Agreement_With_Sports_11-22-2004.php.

Dill, Mallorre. 1999. "Journey Out of Sea." *Adweek*. June 7, p. 22.

Dubbert, Joe L. 1979. *A Man's Place: Masculinity in Transition*. Englewood Cliffs, NJ: Prentice-Hall.

Dudink, Stefan. 2002. "The Unheroic Men of a Moral Nation: Masculinity and Nation in Modern Dutch History." In *The Postwar Moment: Militaries, Masculinities and International Peacekeeping*, ed. Cynthia Cockburn and Dubravka Zarkov. London: Lawrence & Wishart.

Dunnigan, James F., and Raymond M. Macedonia. 1993. *Getting It Right: American Military Reforms after Vietnam to the Persian Gulf and Beyond*. New York: William Morrow.

Dyer, Gillian. 1982. *Advertising as Communication*. London: Methuen.

Ebbert, Jean, and Marie-Beth Hall. 1993. *Crossed Currents: Navy Women from WWI to Tailhook*. Washington, DC: Brassey's.

Egan, Timothy. 2005. "No Degree, and No Way Back to the Middle." *New York Times*. May 24, p. A15.

Elliott, Stuart. 2003. "In Tense Times, Ad Placement Is a Strange and Fickle Thing." *New York Times*. March 21, p. C5.

———. 2006. "Army's New Battle Cry Aims at Potential Recruits." *New York Times*. November 9, p. C3.

Elshtain, Jean Bethke. 1987. *Women and War*. New York: Basic Books.

Enloe, Cynthia. 1983. *Does Khaki Become You? The Militarization of Women's Lives*. London: Pandora.

———. 1988. "Beyond 'Rambo': Women and the Varieties of Militarized Masculinity." In *Women and the Military System*, ed. Eva Isaksson. New York: St. Martin's.

———. 1989. *Bananas, Beaches, and Bases: Making Feminist Sense of International Politics*. Berkeley: University of California Press.

———. 1993. *The Morning After: Sexual Politics at the End of the Cold War*. Berkeley: University of California Press.

———. 1996. "Women, Men, and Soldiering after the Cold War." In *Professionals on the Front Line: Two Decades of the All-Volunteer Force*, ed. J. Eric Fredland, Curtis L. Gilroy, Roger D. Little, and W. S. Sellman. Washington, DC: Brassey's.

———. 2000. *Maneuvers: The International Politics of Militarizing Women's Lives*. Berkeley: University of California Press.
Evans, Marsha J. 1996. "Commentary." In *Professionals on the Front Line: Two Decades of the All-Volunteer Force*, ed. J. Eric Fredland, Curtis L. Gilroy, Roger D. Little, and W. S. Sellman. Washington, DC: Brassey's.
Faludi, Susan. 1999. *Stiffed: The Betrayal of the American Man*. New York: W. Morrow.
———. 2007. *The Terror Dream: Fear and Fantasy in Post-9/11 America*. New York: Metropolitan.
Faris, John H. 1984. "Economic and Noneconomic Factors of Personnel Recruitment and Retention in the AVF." *Armed Forces and Society* 10(2):251–275.
Fasteau, Marc Feigen. 1975. *The Male Machine*. New York: Delta.
Feirstein, Bruce. 1982. *Real Men Don't Eat Quiche*. New York: Warner.
Fiske, John. 1982. *Introduction to Communication Studies*. London: Methuen.
Forde, Christine. 1995. "'Women Warriors': Representations of Women Soldiers in British Daily Newspaper Photographs of the Gulf War (January to March 1991)." In *(Hetero)sexual Politics*, ed. Mary Maynard and June Purvis. London: Taylor & Francis.
Francke, Linda Bird. 1997. *Ground Zero: The Gender Wars in the Military*. New York: Simon & Schuster.
Freedberg, Sydney J., Jr. 1999. "Beyond the GI Bill." *National Journal*. August 21, pp. 2422–2428.
Garfield, Bob. 2001a. "Army's Latest Campaign Isn't All It Can Be and Rings False." *Advertising Age*. January 15, p. 43.
———. 2001b. "Navy Finds Ad Coordinates, Spots Speed Straight to Ego." *Advertising Age*. March 19, p. 49.
Getsy, R. R., and Ray Johnson. 2000. "Air Force Unveils New TV Commercials." *Airman*. October, p. 15.
Gibson, J. William. 1991. "Redeeming Vietnam: Techno-Thriller Novels of the 1980s." *Cultural Critique*. Fall, pp. 179–202.
———. 1994. *Warrior Dreams: Paramilitary Culture in Post-Vietnam America*. New York: Hill and Wang.
Gilder, George F. 1973. *Sexual Suicide*. New York: Quadrangle.
Goldman, Nancy Loring, ed. 1982. *Female Soldiers—Combatants or Noncombatants? Historical and Contemporary Perspectives*. Westport, CT: Greenwood.
Goldstein, Joshua S. 2001. *War and Gender: How Gender Shapes the War System and Vice Versa*. Cambridge: Cambridge University Press.
Griffith, Robert K., Jr. 1979. "Quality Not Quantity: The Volunteer Army during the Depression." *Military Affairs* 43(4):171–177.
———. 1982. *Men Wanted for the US Army: America's Experience with an All-Volunteer Army between the World Wars*. Westport, CT: Greenwood.
———. 1996. *The US Army's Transition to the All-Volunteer Force, 1968–1974*. Washington, DC: Center of Military History United States Army.
Gropman, Alan L. 1998. *The Air Force Integrates: 1945–1964*, 2nd ed. Washington, DC: Smithsonian Institution.
Gutmann, Stephanie. 2000. *The Kinder, Gentler Military*. New York: Scribner.
Hafner, Katie, and Michael Meyer. 1997. "Help Really Wanted." *Newsweek*. December 15, p. 44.
Hagemann, Karen. 1997. "Of 'Manly Valor' and 'German Honor': Nation, War and Masculinity in the Age of the Prussian Uprising against Napoleon." *Central European History* 30(2):187–220.

Hamm, Steve. 1997. "Why Women Are So Invisible." *Business Week*. August 25, p. 136.
Hanssens, Dominique M., and Henry A. Levien. 1983. "An Econometric Study of Recruitment Marketing in the US Navy." *Management Science* 29(10):1167–1184.
Harrod, Frederick S. 1978. *Manning the New Navy: The Development of a Modern Naval Enlisted Force, 1899–1940*. Westport, CT: Greenwood.
Hauk, Keith B., and Greg H. Parlier. 2000. "Recruiting: Crisis and Cures." *Military Review*. May–June, pp. 73–80.
"A Heart-Pumping Glimpse into the Marines' World." 2008. *Our Marines Editor's Blog*. April 4. http://our.marines.com/cms_content/show/type/blog/id/517.
Herbert, Melissa S. 1998. *Camouflage Isn't Only for Combat: Gender, Sexuality, and Women in the Military*. New York: New York University Press.
Higate, Paul R. 2003. *Military Masculinities: Identity and the State*. Westport, CT: Praeger.
Hodes, Jacob, and Emma Ruby-Sachs. 2002. "'America's Army' Targets Youth." *Nation (online version)*. August 23. www.thenation.com/article/americas-army-targets-youth.
Holm, Jeanne. 1992. *Women in the Military: An Unfinished Revolution*, rev. ed. Novato, CA: Presidio.
Hooper, Charlotte. 2001. *Manly States: Masculinities, International Relations, and Gender Politics*. New York: Columbia University Press.
House of Representatives, Committee on Armed Services, Military Forces and Personnel Subcommittee. 1994. Assignment of Army and Marine Corps Women under the New Definition of Ground Combat, 103rd Congress, 2nd Session, October 6.
Huntington, Samuel P. 1957. *The Soldier and the State*. Cambridge, MA: Harvard University Press.
———. 1993. "New Contingencies, Old Roles." *Joint Force Quarterly*. Autumn, pp. 38–43.
Huntley, Steve, with Gail Bronson and Kenneth T. Walsh. 1984. "Yumpies, YAP's, Yuppies: Who They Are." *US News & World Report*. April 16, p. 39.
Janofsky, Michael, with Diana Jean Schemo. 2003. "Women Recount Life as Cadets: Forced Sex, Fear and Silent Rage." *New York Times*. March 16, p. A1.
Janowitz, Morris. 1960. *The Professional Soldier*. Glencoe, IL: Free Press.
Jarvis, Christina S. 2004. *The Male Body at War: American Masculinity during World War II*. DeKalb: Northern Illinois University Press.
Jeffords, Susan. 1989. *The Remasculinization of America: Gender and the Vietnam War*. Bloomington: Indiana University Press.
Jenkins, Henry. 1998. "'Complete Freedom of Movement': Video Games as Gendered Play Spaces." In *From Barbie to Mortal Kombat: Gender and Computer Games*, ed. Justine Cassell and Henry Jenkins. Cambridge, MA: MIT Press.
Jensen, Trevor. 2005. "Navy Seas Smooth Sailing," *Brandweek*. June 20, p. 14.
Katzenstein, Mary Fainsod, and Judith Reppy, eds. 1999. *Beyond Zero Tolerance: Discrimination in Military Culture*. Lanham, MD: Rowman & Littlefield.
Keen, Sam. 1991. *Fire in the Belly: On Being a Man*. New York: Bantam.
Keene, R. R. 1999. "Can You Hack It?" *Leatherneck* 82(4): 40–43.
Kerber, Linda K. 1990. "May All Our Citizens Be Soldiers and All Our Soldiers Citizens: The Ambiguities of Female Citizenship in the New Nation." In *Women, Militarism, and War: Essays in History, Politics, and Social Theory*, ed. Jean Bethke Elshtain and Shelia Tobias. Savage, MD: Rowman & Littlefield.

Kiley, David. 2005. "Uncle Sam Wants You in the Worst Way." *Business Week*. August 22, p. 40.

Kimmel, Michael S. 1987. "The Contemporary 'Crisis' of Masculinity in Historical Perspective." In *The Making of Masculinities: The New Men's Studies*, ed. Harry Brod. Boston: Allen & Unwin.

———. 1996. *Manhood in America: A Cultural History*. New York: Free Press.

———. 2005. *The History of Men: Essays in the History of American and British Masculinities*. Albany: State University of New York Press.

Lauro, Patricia Winters. 2001. "The Media Business: Advertising—Addenda; Air Force Set to Run Recruiting Campaign." *New York Times*. November 2, p. C5.

Leo, John. 2001. "One Tin Slogan." *US News and World Report*. January 22, p. 13.

"Life, Liberty and the Pursuit of All Who Threaten It: The Perfect Slogan for Today's Navy." 2004. Military.com. August 2. www.military.com/NewContent/0,13190, 080204_Navy.00.html?ESRC=navy.nl.

Lohan, Maria, and Wendy Faulkner. 2004. "Masculinities and Technologies: Some Introductory Remarks." *Men and Masculinities* 6(4):319–329.

Malin, Brenton J. 2005. *American Masculinity under Clinton: Popular Media and the Nineties "Crisis of Masculinity."* New York: Peter Lang.

"Marines Far Surpass Recruiting Goal." 2008. Military.com. May 13. www.military.com;/news/article/marines-far-surpass-recruiting-goal.html?wh=wh.

"Marines Present New Facet to Advertising Campaign." 2005. *Marine Corps News*. Reprinted by military.com. September 28. www.military.com/NewsContent/0,13319,77857,00.html.

"Marines Smash Recruiting Records." 2008. *Dallas Morning News*. Reprinted by military.com. June 9. www.military.com/news/article/marines-smash-recruiting-records.html;?wh=wh.

Marks, Alexandra. 1997. "Women Flock to Armed Forces Despite Harassment Scandals." *Christian Science Monitor*. May 15, p. 3.

Marlowe, David H. 1983. "The Manning of the Force and the Structure of Battle: Part 2—Men and Women." In *Conscripts and Volunteers: Military Requirements, Social Justice, and the All-Volunteer Force*, ed. Robert K. Fullinwider. Totowa, NJ: Rowman & Allanheld.

Massey, Doreen. 1995. "Masculinity, Dualisms and High Technology." *Transactions of the Institute of British Geographers, New Series* 20(4):487–499.

McCarthy, Michael, and Darryl Haralson. 2003. "The Few. The Proud. The Ad: Marines Land Timely New Recruiting Pitch Tonight." *USA Today*. March 20, p. 3B.

McCormick, David. 1998. *The Downsized Warrior: America's Army in Transition*. New York: New York University Press.

Megens, Ine, and Mary Wings. 1981. "The Recruitment of Women." In *Loaded Questions: Women in the Military*, ed. Wendy Chapkis. Amsterdam: Transnational Institute.

Millet, Allan R. 1991. *Semper Fidelis: The History of the United States Marine Corps*, rev. ed. New York: Free Press.

Millis, Walter. 1956. *Arms and Men: A Study in American Military History*. New York: G. P. Putnam's Sons.

Minogue, Sara. 2002. "Protecting a Nation, Defining a Generation." *Boards*. June 1, p. 24.

Mitchell, Brian. 1989. *Weak Link: The Feminization of the American Military*. New York: Regnery Gateway.

———. 1998. *Women in the Military: Flirting with Disaster.* Washington, DC: Regnery.

Mitchell, John B. 1967. "Army Recruiters and Recruits between the World Wars." *Military Collector & Historian* 19(3):76–81.

Moniz, Dave. 2005. "Recruits Swamp Navy, Air Force." *USA Today.* January 24, p. 1A.

Morden, Bettie J. 2000. *The Women's Army Corps, 1945–1978.* Washington, DC: Center of Military History United States Army.

Morgan, David H. J. 1994. "Theater of War: Combat, the Military, and Masculinities." In *Theorizing Masculinities*, ed. Harry Brod and Michael Kaufman. Thousand Oaks, CA: Sage.

Moskos, Charles C. 1970. *The American Enlisted Man: The Rank and File in Today's Military.* New York: Russell Sage Foundation.

———. 1982. "Social Considerations of the All-Volunteer Force." In *Military Service in the United States*, ed. American Assembly, Columbia University. Englewood Cliffs, NJ: Prentice-Hall.

———. 1993. "From Citizen's Army to Social Laboratory." *Wilson Quarterly.* 17(1):83–95.

Moskos, Charles C., and John Sibley Butler. 1996. *All That We Can Be: Black Leadership and Racial Integration the Army Way.* New York: Basic Books.

Moskos, Charles C., and Lawrence Korb. 2001. "Time to Bring Back the Draft?" *American Enterprise* 12(8):16–17.

Mrozek, Donald J. 1987. "The Habit of Victory: The American Military and the Cult of Manliness." In *Manliness and Morality: Middle-Class Masculinity in Britain and America 1800–1940*, ed. J.A. Mangan and James Walvin. New York: St. Martin's.

Myers, Steven Lee. 1999. "Drop in Recruits Pushes Pentagon to New Strategy." *New York Times.* September 27, p. A1.

———. 2000. "Army, Its Recruiting Not All It Could Be, Decides to Overhaul Its Advertising." *New York Times.* January 8, p. A9.

Nalty, Bernard C. 1986. *Strength for the Fight: A History of Black Americans in the Military.* New York: Free Press.

"New Marine Corps Commercial Debuts; TV Spot Reflects the Courage of Those Who Put Country First." 2003. *PR Newswire.* Reprinted by Leatherneck.com. March 20. www.leatherneck.com/forums/showthread.php?t=5032.

Niva, Steve. 1998. "Tough and Tender: New World Order Masculinity and the Gulf War." In *The "Man" Question in International Relations*, ed. Marysia Zalewski and Jane Parpat. Boulder, CO: Westview.

Norton, Anne. 1993. *Republic of Signs: Liberal Theory and American Popular Culture.* Chicago: University of Chicago Press.

O'Brien, Timothy L. 2005. "Madison Avenue Wants You; How to Pitch the Military When a War Drags On?" *New York Times.* September 25, p. B1.

Office of the Deputy Assistant Secretary of Defense for Civilian Personnel Policy/Equal Opportunity. 1991. "Black Americans in Defense of Our Nation."

Peck, Michael. 2005. "Air Force's Latest Video Game Targets Potential Recruits." *National Defense.* January. www.nationaldefensemagazine.org/archive/2005/January/Pages/air_forces5899.aspx.

Peterson, Donald L. 2000. "Statement." House of Representatives, Committee on Armed Services, Military Personnel Subcommittee. Hearing on Sustaining the All Volunteer Force and Reserve Component Overview; Hearings on National Defense Authorization Act for Fiscal Year 2001—HR 4205 and Oversight of Previously Authorized Programs. 106th Congress, 2nd Session, March 17, 2000.

Skaine, Rosemarie. 1999. *Women at War: Gender Issues of Americans in Combat.* Jefforson, NC: McFarland.
Smart, John W. 2000. "Crisis in Military Recruiting." *VFW: Veterans of Foreign Wars Magazine.* February, p. 4.
Snyder, R. Claire. 1999. *Citizen-Soldiers and Manly Warriors.* Lanham, MD: Rowman & Littlefield.
———. 2003. "The Citizen-Soldier Tradition and Gender Integration of the US Military." *Armed Forces & Society* 29(2):185–204.
Stacey, Judith. 1998. "Dada-ism in the 1990s: Getting Past Baby Talk about Fatherlessness." In *Lost Fathers: The Politics of Fatherlessness in America*, ed. Cynthia R. Daniels. New York: St. Martin's.
Stiehm, Judith Hicks. 1981. *Bring Me Men and Women: Mandated Change at the US Air Force Academy.* Berkeley: University of California Press.
———. 1989. *Arms and the Enlisted Woman.* Philadelphia: Temple University Press.
———, ed. 1996. *It's Our Military, Too! Women and the US Military.* Philadelphia: Temple University Press.
Strother, Thomas. 1999. "The Recruiting Problem We Don't Talk About." *United States Naval Institute Proceedings.* May, p. 192.
Teinowitz, Ira. 2001. "Army Greens." *Advertising Age* 72(37):4.
Thurman, Maxwell R. 1996. "On Being All You Can Be: A Recruiting Perspective." In *Professionals on the Front Line: Two Decades of the All-Volunteer Force*, ed. J. Eric Fredland, Curtis L. Gilroy, Roger D. Little, and W. S. Sellman. Washington, DC: Brassey's.
Tilghman, Andrew. 2008. "Corps Premiers Its Latest Recruiting Ad." *Marine Corps Times.* January 21. www.marinecorpstimes.com/news/2008/01/marine_new_ad_080116/.
Tobias, Shelia. 1990. "Shifting Heroisms: The Uses of Military Service in Politics." In *Women, Militarism, and War: Essays in History, Politics, and Social Theory*, ed. Jean Bethke Elshtain and Shelia Tobias. Savage, MD: Rowman & Littlefield.
Tyson, Ann Scott. 2005. "Bid to Limit Women in Combat Withdrawn." *Washington Post.* May 26, p. A1.
———. 2008. "Woman Gains Silver Star—And Removal from Combat." *Washington Post.* May 1, p. A1.
Uchitelle, Louis, and David Leonhardt. 2006. "Not Working, and Not Wanting Just Any Job." *New York Times.* July 31, p. A1.
Van Creveld, Martin. 2000. "The Great Illusion: Women in the Military." *Millennium: Journal of International Studies* 29(2):429–442.
"The War in Military Ads? What War?" 1991. *New York Times.* March 8, p. D1.
Weinstein, Laurie, and Christie C. White. 1997. *Wives and Warriors: Women and the Military in the United States and Canada.* Westport, CT: Bergin & Garvey.
Williams, Christine L. 1989. *Gender Differences at Work: Women and Men in Nontraditional Occupations.* Berkeley: University of California Press.
Williams, Rudi. 1999. "Wartime Posters Drew Men, Women to Patriotic Duty." *American Forces Press Service.* April 7. www.defenselink.mil/news/newsarticle.aspx?id=42931.
Winter, Greg. 2000. "The Media Business: Advertising—Addenda; New Campaign Set by the Air Force." *New York Times.* August 25, p. C5.
Wolff, Edward N. 2005. "The Growth of Information Workers in the US Economy." *Communications of the ACM* 48(10):37–42.

Piot, Charles. 2003. "Heat on the Street: Video Violence in American Teen Culture." *Postcolonial Studies* 6(3):351–365.

Pitkin, Hannah Fenichel. 1984. *Fortune Is a Woman: Gender and Politics in the Thought of Niccolo Machiavelli*. Berkeley: University of California Press.

Porter, Eduardo. 2002. "Army's Hispanic-Recruitment Ads Cater to Mom." *Wall Street Journal*. May 24, p. B3.

Porter, Eduardo, and Michelle O'Donnell. 2006. "Facing Middle Age with No Degree, and No Wife." *New York Times*. August 6, p. A1.

Quenqua, Douglas. 2008. "Sending in the Marines (to Recruit Women)." *New York Times*. April 21, p. C1.

Ricks, Thomas E. 1997. *Making the Corps*. New York: Simon & Schuster.

Robb, David L. 2004. *Operation Hollywood: How the Pentagon Shapes and Censors the Movies*. Amherst, NY: Prometheus.

Rogan, Helen. 1981. *Mixed Company: Women in the Modern Army*. New York: Putnam.

Rostker, Bernard. 2006. *I Want You! The Evolution of the All-Volunteer Force*. Santa Monica, CA: RAND.

Rustad, Michael. 1982. *Women in Khaki: The American Enlisted Woman*. New York: Praeger.

Schmitt, Eric. 2003a. "Top Air Force General Backs Independent Inquiry in Rapes." *New York Times*. February 27, p. A1.

———. 2003b. "Soft Economy Aids Recruiting Effort, Army Leaders Say." *New York Times*. September 22, p. A1.

———. 2004. "Its Recruitment Goals Pressing, the Army Will Ease Some Standards." *New York Times*. October 1, p. A24.

———. 2005a. "Marines Miss January Goal for Recruits." *New York Times*. February 3, p. A12.

———. 2005b. "The Few and the Proud Fret about the 'Few.'" *New York Times*. February 25, p. A19.

Schmitt, Eric, with Michael Moss. 2003. "Air Force Investigated 54 Sex Assaults in 10 Years." *New York Times*. March 7, p. A1.

Schneider, Dorothy, and Carl J. Schneider. 1992. *Sound Off! American Military Women Speak Out*. New York: Paragon House.

Scott, Joan W. 1986. "Gender: A Useful Category of Historical Analysis." *American Historical Review* 91(5):1053–1075.

Segal, David R. 1989. *Recruiting for Uncle Sam: Citizenship and Military Manpower Policy*. Lawrence: University Press of Kansas.

Shanker, Thom. 2006. "Army and Other Ground Forces Meet '06 Recruiting Goals." *New York Times*. October 10, p. A19.

———. 2007. "Army, Shedding a Slump, Met July Recruiting Goal." *New York Times*. August 11, p. A8.

Shepherd, Laura. 2006. "Veiled References: Constructions of Gender in the Bush Administration Discourse on the Attacks on Afghanistan Post-9/11." *International Feminist Journal of Politics* 8(1):19–41.

Shilts, Randy. 1993. *Conduct Unbecoming: Gays and Lesbians in the US Military*. New York: St. Martin's.

Shulman, Mark Russell. 1995. *Navalism and the Emergence of American Sea Power, 1882–1893*. Annapolis, MD: Naval Institute Press.

Silverman, David. 2003. "Analyzing Talk and Text." In *Collecting and Interpreting Qualitative Materials*, 2nd ed., ed. Norman K. Denzin and Yvonna S. Lincoln. Thousand Oaks, CA: Sage.

Women's Research and Education Institute. 2003. "Chronology of Significant Legal and Policy Changes Affecting Women in the Military, 1947–2003." www.wrei.org/Women%20in%20the%20Military/Women%20in%20the%20Military%20Chronology%20of%20Legal%20Policy.pdf.
Young, Iris Marion. 2003. "The Logic of Masculinist Protection: Reflections on the Current Security State." *Signs: Journal of Women in Culture and Society* 29(1): 1–25.
Zimmerman, Jean. 1995. *Tailspin: Women at War in the Wake of Tailhook*. New York: Doubleday.

INDEX

Abrams, Elliot, masculinity and recruiting, 39
Active duty
   African American enlisted forces, 191
   African American female enlisted personnel, 193
   African American officers, 192
   female enlisted military personnel, 189
   female active duty officers, 190
   military personnel, 187–188
Adventure
   in Army ads, 48, 52, 53, 56, 57, 166, 167, 168
   in military recruiting, 5, 10, 180, 182
   in Navy ads, 15, 78, 82, 83, 90, 99, 101, 103, 179–180
Advertising. *See* Air Force; Army; Marine Corps; Navy
Advertising sample
   analysis of, 12–13
   composition of, 13–14
Advertising Age, Navy "Accelerate Your Life," 100
Afghanistan War
   Air Force, 173–175
   demands on military, 196n12
   deployment of women, 160
   Marine Corps, 169, 172–173
   recruiting, 158–159, 176–177
   recruiting advertisements, 17, 158–159, 169
African Americans
   active duty enlisted forces, 191
   active duty officers, 192
   Air Force, 132–133, 141, 184
   Army, 43–44, 63, 162, 165–166, 168, 184, 198n13, 199n2, 202n2
   Army recruiting problems, Iraq War, 162
   civil rights movement, 25
   female active duty enlisted forces, 193
   fight to serve in military, 30, 31
   Marine Corps, 106–107, 114, 123, 170, 184
   Navy, 80–81, 94, 101–102, 103, 184
   race and masculinity, 19, 31, 36–37, 101–102, 107, 197–198n7
   racial integration of military, 31, 43, 81, 107, 132
   Tuskegee Airmen, 133
   success of volunteer force, 36, 162, 184
   Vietnam War, 35, 107, 133, 202n2
   women, 63, 123, 183–184, 198n13, 199n2, 203n4
   World War I, 107
   World War II, 31, 81, 133, 198n13
Air Force
   active duty personnel, 187–188
   ads aimed at mechanically skilled, 137, 139, 140
   advertisements, number in sample, 14
   Afghanistan war, 173–175
   African American active duty enlisted forces, 191
   African American active duty officers, 192
   African American female active duty enlisted forces, 193
   African Americans, 132–133, 141, 184
   AFROTC, 152
   "Aim High," 138
   civilian world success, 134–135, 155

Air Force (continued)
    culture, 131–133
    "Cross into the Blue," 145, 147, 159
    "Do Something Amazing," 174–175
    family friendly, 148, 157
    female active duty officers, 190
    female enlisted active duty personnel, 189
    "flight plan" ads, 141–142
    glamorous reputation, 130, 133–134, 138–139, 156, 181–182
    humanitarian missions and recruitment, 143, 146–147, 156, 157, 174
    "Lullaby," commercial, 143
    Iraq war, 173–175
    masculinity and, 16, 130, 131, 134, 137, 141–142, 143, 145, 146, 155–157, 179, 180
    new world order masculinity, 131, 145, 146, 156–157, 180
    "No One Comes Close," 142
    patriotism in ads, 138
    recruiting advertisements, 133–148, 152–155, 173–175
    recruiting background, 133–134
    recruiting needs, 11–12, 138, 140
    recruiting problems, 3, 141
    skills training, 130, 134–135, 137, 138, 141, 152, 155, 157
    slogans, 135, 137, 138, 142, 145, 174
    technology, 16, 130–131, 134, 139, 141, 142, 143, 144–145, 146–147, 156–157, 173, 175, 180
    television commercials, 3, 141, 142–143, 145, 174, 175
    transition to all-volunteer force (AVF), 133–134
    travel, 141, 144, 147, 148
    video games, 131, 144–146, 156, 174, 181–182
    Vietnam, 133, 151–152
    warrior masculinity and culture, lack of, 133, 137, 138–139, 141–142, 142, 155, 157, 180
    warrior masculinity, technologically mediated, 144, 147, 175
    Web site, 143–145, 146–148, 155, 156, 174–175
    "We've Been Waiting for You," 145, 146, 154, 174
    women and, 12, 141, 147–148, 148–155, 156, 157, 173, 174, 175, 183, 184
    women WAF, 150
    working-class masculinity, 16, 130, 137, 139–141, 152, 155
Air Force Academy, sexual assaults, 154
All-volunteer force (AVF)
    Air Force transition to, 133–134
    Army transition to, 45–46, 65–66
    gay people, 33
    gender, 32, 33
    hearing on sustaining, 196n8, 196n9
    history, 34–40
    Iraq and Afghanistan wars, 158–159
    Marine Corps transition to, 111
    military pay, 35, 36
    Navy transition to, 77–78, 81
    transition of military to, 3–4, 28
    women, 21, 66, 158
American Enterprise, conscription debate, 198n15
American society and the military, 6, 185
"America's Army," video game, 60–62, 181–182
Antifeminist literature on the military, 4
Armed forces
    American attitudes towards, 20–21
    citizenship and naturalization, 30
Armed Forces Qualifying Test, 38
Army
    "12 Matches," ad, 48
    accessible version of masculinity, 15, 41, 47, 48, 73, 117, 179
    active duty personnel, 187–188
    ads in 1970s, 47–49
    ads in 1980s, 50–52
    ads in 1990s, 52–57
    ads in 2000s, 57–62
    adventure, 48, 52, 53, 56, 57, 166, 167, 168
    advertisements, number in sample 14
    African American active duty enlisted forces, 191
    African American active duty officers, 192
    African American female active duty enlisted forces, 193
    African Americans, 43–44, 63, 162, 165–166, 168, 184, 198n13, 199n2, 202n2

[216] Index

"America's Army" video game, 60–62, 181–182
"Army of One" campaign, 57–60, 71, 99, 159, 162, 164
"Army Strong" campaign, 166–168
"Be All You Can Be" campaign, 50, 57, 58
character development, 41, 47, 48, 49, 52, 53, 59, 73, 162, 166, 167, 179
civilian-world job success, 53–54, 56, 166
commercials aimed at parents, 164–166
culture, 42–44
"Cut from the Same Cloth," commercial 163–164
"Dinner Conversation," commercial, 165–166
female active duty officers, 190
female enlisted active duty personnel, 189
"Freedom Isn't Free," commercial, 155
gender integration, 43, 67
high-tech training, 51, 51–52, 53, 56, 68–70
Iraq War recruiting, 161–168
masculinity and, 15, 41, 46–47, 48, 49, 50, 52, 53–54, 56–57, 59, 71–73, 165–166, 168, 179
militarized imagery, 15, 50, 53–54, 55, 56, 59, 60, 73, 162, 163, 164, 167, 179
patriotism in ads, 54–55, 64, 163
recruiting advertisements, 46–62, 66–71, 162–168
recruiting background, 44–46
recruiting needs, 11–12, 41, 45, 73
recruiting problems, 49, 57, 161–162, 198–199n17
"Responsible Choice," commercial, 165
"The Right Thing," commercial, 163–164
soldier as defender, 47, 54–56, 163
TEAMS concept (Training, Education, Adventure, Money, and Service), 56, 57
technology, 15, 51, 53, 56, 70, 162
television commercials, 50–51, 53, 55, 58, 162–167
"Think Enormous," ad, 48
transition to all-volunteer force (AVF), 45–46, 65–66
warrior masculinity, 15, 48, 56, 59, 71–73, 179
Web site, 56–57, 60, 61 164, 165
women and, 41–42, 43, 51, 52, 55, 61, 62–71, 72, 163, 165, 167, 168, 183, 184, 199n2, 201n4
Army Accessions Command, 163, 166, 167, 202n3
Army Air Force (AAF), women, 149
"Army of One"
  campaign, 57–60, 99, 159
  commercials, 164
  print ads, 59–60, 71, 162
  retirement of slogan, 166
  soldier as individual, 195n6
  women in print ads, 71
Army Research Institute, 49

Bacevich, Andrew J., masculinity and recruiting, 39
Bach, Shirley J., women in military, 85
Baggerly, Captain Tim, Air Force Web site, 147
Bammies, 123
BAMS (Broad-Assed Marines), 123
Bangladesh, Air Force humanitarian mission, 143
Barrow, Gen. Robert H., women in Marine Corps, 124
BBDO, Navy advertising agency, 94, 97
Binkin, Martin, women in military, 85
Bly, *Iron John*, 26
Bonat, Lieutenant Christian, Navy, 97–99, 128
Books, masculinity crisis, 23
Boy's Life magazine, 100
Bridges, Master Sergeant Marialena, Marine ad, 127
Brown, Harold, study of women in military, 196n11
Brown, PFC Monica, Silver Star recipient, 161
Builder, Carl
  Air Force culture, 131–132
  Army culture, 42–43
  Marine Corps culture, 105–106, 199n1
  Navy culture, 75

Index [217]

Butler, Lieutenant Colonel Jack, women in Army, 65

Caldera, Louis, individualism in the Army, 57–58
Campbell-Ewald, Navy advertising agency, 100
Camp Lejeune, Marine Corps racial incidents, 107
Carter, Jimmy, study of women in military, 196n11
Center for Strategic and International Studies, 43, 133
Charlie Company, women in Marine Corps, 124
Charlie's Angels, women in Marine Corps, 124
Christian Science Monitor, Navy recruitment of women, 93
Christmas, Lt. Gen. George R., women in Marine Corps, 126
Christy, Howard Chandler, Navy recruiting, 84, 89
Citizenship
  absence of concept from ads, 180–181
  link with military service, 30, 33–34, 184–185
  military, gender, and, 28–34
  military, nation, and, 195n5
  military service and, literature, 31–32
  military service, masculinity and, 14, 28–30, 31
Citizen-soldiers, 20, 29–30, 32, 33, 42, 198n12
Civil-military gap, 10
Civil rights movement, 25, 31, 81
Clinton, President Bill
  hybrid masculinity, 27
  women in Army, 70
  women in aviation, 153–154
Cochran, Jacqueline, women in Air Force (WAF) program, 150
Cohen, Eliot, citizen-soldiers, 32
Cold War
  Air Force in post-, 139
  Air Force women, 150
  Checkpoint Charlie ad, 56, 203n1
  end of, 21
  Marines and conscription, 110
  Marine Corps women, 124

Navy women, 85–86
  officers, military types, 197n5
  standing force, 34
  soldier as defender, 56
Collins, Kevin, Air Force ad, 141–142
Co-location, women and combat units, 160–161
Combat
  Army ads, 53–54, 163–164
  definitions, 160
  Marine Corps, 15–16, 169–171
  women and, 17, 29, 42, 61, 67, 70, 71, 86, 92, 96–97, 106, 150, 153–154, 158, 160–161, 163, 167, 168, 177, 183, 185, 198n11, 203n3
Committee on Equality of Treatment and Opportunity, African Americans, 132–133
Congress
  Cold War draft authorization, 133
  creation of the all-volunteer force (AVF), 36
  hearings on the military, 10, 65, 126, 196n9, 200n3
  investigation of sexual assaults at Air Force Academy, 154
  policies on women's military service, 63, 65, 67, 70, 85, 86, 92, 153, 154, 160–161
  post-Revolutionary War Army, 44
  restrictions on service, 33
  role in recruiting campaign creation, 195n7
  Vietnam War draft, 35
Connell, R. W., hegemonic masculinity, 19, 27–28 (*see also* hegemonic masculinity)
Conscription
  all-volunteer force (AVF), 20–21, 31, 34–37
  Cold War, 110
  end of, 45, 77, 86, 180, 182
  gender and, 31–32, 36, 182, 198n14, 198n15
  reinstitution, 62–63
  Vietnam, 35, 202n2
  World War II, 34, 110
Constellation, race riots, 81
Copland, Aaron, "Fanfare for the Common Man," 92

Culture
  Air Force, 131–133
  Army, 42–44
  Marine Corps, 105–107, 128–129
  Navy, 75–76

DACOWITS (Defense Advisory Committee on Women in the Services), 202n7
Defense Advisory Committee on Women in the Services (DACOWITS), 202n7
Defense Authorization Act (1979), women, 86
Democratization of war, 29
Department of Defense. *See also* Pentagon
  influence on recruiting campaigns, 195n7
  Risk Rule, 67, 70, 126, 153
  study of draft, 34–35
  women in Marine Corps, 124–125
Desert Storm, 38, 139, 143 (*see also* Gulf War)
"Don't ask, don't tell" rule, 29, 38, 200n10
Draft. *See* Conscription
Drone aircraft, 133, 173, 174, 175, 182
Dubbert, Joe L., *A Man's Place: Masculinity in Transition*, 23

Economy
  1920s, 45
  1990s, 38
  deindustrialization, 23
  effects on recruitment, 60, 141, 159, 161, 162, 169
  shift from manufacturing to knowledge-based, 73, 84, 181
Education
  Air Force, 130, 132, 135, 137, 141, 147, 151
  Army, 41, 44–45, 47, 51, 53, 56–57, 66, 68, 72–73, 162, 167
  draft deferments, 34–35
  GI bill, 49
  Marine Corps, 112
  Navy, 80, 90, 93–95, 98, 101, 176
  recruiting standards, 9, 36, 63, 64, 86, 132, 151

Eisenhower, President, "New Look" defense policy, 151
Elections, military spectacles, 20
Elshtain, Jean Bethke, soldier as protector, 55
Emphasized femininity, term, 197n3
Enloe, Cynthia
  Does Khaki Become You?, 8–9
  femininity of military women to support masculine military culture, 64–65, 66–67, 86, 151, 201n2, 201n5
  guidelines on women's participation in the military, 160
  militarized national loyalty and identity, 6
  role of women at Tailhook convention, 200n6
Entertainment Weekly magazine, 14, 100
Equal Rights Amendment, 26, 86
Evans, Rear Admiral Marsha Johnson, Navy recruitment of women, 89–90
Executive Order Number 9981, 31

Fahy Committee, Air Force, 132
Falluja effect, Marine Corps, 168
Fatherlessness, concern about, 26
Femininity
  analysis of in advertising sample, 12–13
  appearance and behavior of women in the military, 64–65, 66, 86, 124, 127, 199n5, 201n5
  definition, 18–19
  emphasized, 197n3
  race and, 184
  reinforcement in ads, 66, 68, 70, 127, 173
Feminism, as threat to military, 4
Feminist, definition, 195n1
Fire in the Belly, Keen, 26

Garfield, Bob, Navy's "Accelerate Your Life," 100
Gates Commission
  marketplace model of recruitment, 35, 37
  plan for volunteer force, 35, 36, 46
Gays in the military, 9, 29, 30, 33, 38, 96–97, 106, 200n1, 200n10

Index [219]

Gender. *See also* masculinity, femininity
  as code to signify power, 19, 197n2
  endorsement of equity in
    transnational business masculinity, 28, 96
  interrelationship with constructions of soldiering, 21, 185
  intersections with race in ads, 183–184
  literature of military recruiting and, 8–9
  military, citizenship, and, 28–34
  options for use of in recruiting ads, 11
  progressiveness of military as part of national identity, 185
  progressiveness of new world order masculinity, 27, 156–157
  recruitment images of, relationship to civilian world, 7
  use of concept in analysis of the military, 4
Gender integration
  Army, 43
  critics of, 39–40, 72, 76, 96–97, 202n5
  of basic training, concerns about, 70
  Navy, 76, 81, 183
GI bill
  impact on recruiting, 37–38, 49
  New, Plus the New Army College Fund, 51
Gibson, J. William
  challenges to military values, 25
  paramilitary culture, 25–26, 198n9
  techno-thrillers, 26, 83, 201n3
Gilder, George, *Sexual Suicide*, 23
Glamour, Air Force, 130, 133–134, 138–139, 156, 181–182
Goblettes, term for Navy women, 85
Goldwater, Barry, promise to end draft, 34
Great Depression, effect on recruiting, 45
Greene, Gen. Wallace M., Jr., Women Marines program, 124
Grenada, participation of Army women, 70
Griffith, Robert K. Jr., Air Force, 134
Gulf War, 56, 159 (*see also* Desert Storm)
  Air Force, 156–157
  images of female soldiers, 198n10
  masculinity, 27
  women, 70

new world order masculinity, 156–157

Harrod, Frederick, Navy man-of-warsman, 77
Heck, Major Fritz, Air Force Web site, 147
Hegemonic femininity, term, 197n3
Hegemonic masculinity
  Air Force, 130–131, 156
  Army, 41, 46–47, 53, 72, 179
  career status and, 53, 72, 84, 179
  definition, 19
  Gulf War new world order masculinity as, 27, 156
  middle- and upper-class white men and, 36–37
  military's relationship to, 19–20, 37
  Navy, 22, 84
  race and, 19, 36–37, 107, 197–198n7
  relationship to femininity, 197n
  technology and, 130–131
  transnational business masculinity as, 28, 200n5
Hirschmann, Lieutenant Commander Loree "Rowdy," Navy ad, 93–94, 97–98
Hispanics
  Air Force ad, 141
  Army efforts to recruit, 58, 162–163, 168
  Navy ad, 94
Holcomb, Lt. Gen. Thomas, women Marines, 123
Holm, Maj. Gen. Jeanne, women in military, 64, 67, 122, 124, 150, 151, 153
Humanitarian missions, 21
  Air Force, 143, 146–147, 156, 157, 174, 202n6
  gendering of, 146, 202n5
Human rights, effect on military masculinities, 22
Hunter, Dr. Richard W., study of women in military, 196n11
Hunter, Rep. Duncan, women's military roles, 160–161
Hussein, Saddam, hypermasculinity, 27
Hybrid masculinity
  Air Force use of, 143

[220] *Index*

description, 5
dominant in 1990s, 27
as model that military branches can utilize, 17, 181
new world order masculinity a form of, 27, 40
Hypermasculinity, 27, 156

Individual Ready Reserves program, Army, 161
Internet. *See* Web Sites
Iraq War
African Americans, 162, 202n2
Air Force, 173–175
Army, 161–168
demands on military, 196n12
deployment of women, 160
Marine Corps, 168–169, 172–173
Navy, 176–177
recruiting, 158–160, 176–177
recruiting advertisements, 17, 163–164, 167, 176
Iron John, Bly, 26
Israel, conscription of women, 198n14

Jay, John, treaty negotiator, 29
Jay, Sarah Livingston, toast to citizen-soldiers, 29
J. Walter Thompson, Marine ad agency, 169

Kaneohe Naval Air Station, Marine Corps racial incidents, 107
Keen, Sam, *Fire in the Belly*, 26
Kitty Hawk, race riots, 81
Kohn, Richard H., Marines and combat, 129
Korean War
Air Force women, 150–151
footage in ads, 163–164
Marine Corps, 107
recruitment of women, 64, 150–151
size of standing force and, 34
Kosovo air war, participation of Air Force women, 154
Krulak, General Charles, Marine Corps advertising, 195n7

Lee, Spike, Navy commercials, 94
Leo Burnett USA, Army advertising agency, 57

Lesbian, labeling of military women, 122–123
Life magazine, 13, 51, 79, 140
Literature
citizenship and military service, 31–32
masculinity and the military, 4, 8
recruitment, 9
women and the military, 8

McCartney, Bill, Promise Keepers, 26
Machiavelli, Niccolò, citizen-soldier ideal, 20
Magazines, recruitment advertising sample, 13–14
The Making of a Man-o'-Warsman, Navy recruiting brochure, 77
Making the Corps, Ricks, 105
Manhood. *See* masculinity
Man's Place: Masculinity in Transition, Dubbert, 23
Marine Corps
active duty personnel, 187–188
ad agency, J. Walter Thompson, 169
advertisements, number in sample, 14
Afghanistan war, 169, 172–173
African American active duty enlisted forces, 191
African American active duty officers, 192
African American female active duty enlisted forces, 193
African Americans, 106–107, 114, 123, 184
"America's Marines," commercial, 171, 172
"Applications," commercial, 170–171
brotherhood, 16, 104, 105, 117, 118, 119, 127, 169, 178
challenge, 104, 109, 112, 114, 117–118, 121, 126, 127, 128
"The Climb," commercial, 118, 126
culture, 105–107, 117, 128–129
"Devil Dogs," commercial, 169–170
"Diamond," commercial, 169
elitism, 16, 38, 104, 108, 111, 112–113, 117–118, 169, 170
Falluja effect, 168
as family, 119, 120, 201n3
female active duty officers, 190

Index [221]

Marine Corps (*continued*)
  female enlisted active duty personnel, 189
  "A few good men," 40, 112, 113–114, 121
  "The few, the proud, the Marines," 114, 169, 171
  focus on combat, 15–16, 106, 108, 110, 120, 169, 181
  "For Country," commercial, 169
  identity as all-encompassing, 117
  Iraq war, 168–169, 172–173
  "Leap" commercial, 202n6
  masculinity and, 10, 15–16, 47, 73, 104, 107, 108, 110, 111, 113–114, 117, 119–120, 121, 128–129, 178–179, 185
  as model for other services, 10, 38–39, 58–59, 96–99, 108
  part of Navy, 121, 123, 195n2, 199n1
  recruiting advertisements, 111–121, 126–127, 169–171, 171–172
  recruiting background, 108–110
  recruiting needs, 12, 108, 129, 159, 178
  recruiting problems, 108–109, 111, 168, 198–199n17
  rite of passage, 16, 104, 119–120, 178, 180–181
  semper fidelis (always faithful), 105
  separate-but-equal approach to women, 121
  slogans, 105, 110, 112, 114
  television commercials, 117–118, 169–171, 202n6
  transformation theme, 114, 117–120, 170, 171 202n6
  transition to all-volunteer force (AVF), 111
  turnover of personnel, 12
  uniforms, 104, 113, 117
  warrior masculinity, 5, 10, 16, 104, 106, 107, 108, 110, 111, 117, 118, 128, 129, 185
  Web site, 105, 118–121, 122
  women and, 12, 104, 106, 113–114, 118, 120, 121–128, 169, 170, 171–172, 183, 184, 200n1, 201n4
  "Women Marines," 121, 123
  World War I, 107, 110, 123
  World War II, 110, 111, 170

Marinettes, term for women Marines, 123
Marketplace masculinity, 197–198n7
Masculinity. *See also* Hegemonic masculinity
  analysis of in advertising sample, 12–13
  Air Force, 16, 130, 131, 134, 137, 141–142, 143, 145, 146, 155–157, 179, 180
  anxiety over, 10, 23–24, 26, 40, 129
  Army, 15, 41, 46–47, 48, 49, 50, 52, 53–54, 56–57, 59, 71–73, 165–166, 168, 179
  crisis, 3, 23–28, 77, 110
  definition, 18–19
  historical ties to military service, 3–4, 19–20
  hybrid, 5, 17, 27, 40, 143, 181
  hypermasculinity, 27, 156
  Marine Corps, 10, 15 16, 47, 73, 104, 107, 108, 110, 111, 113–114, 117, 119–120, 121, 128–129, 178–179, 185
  marketplace, 197–198n7
  military, 5, 10, 19–23, 29, 181–182
  military service, citizenship, and, 28–31
  military's options in relation to, 4, 11
  Navy, 15, 74, 80, 82, 83–84, 92, 96, 99–100, 101, 102–103, 179–180
  new world order, 16, 27, 40, 131, 145, 146, 156–157, 180
  as solution to recruiting problems, 10, 39–40, 96, 108, 202n5
  study of, 18
  race and, 19, 31, 36–37, 101–102, 107, 197–198n7
  technology and, 10, 11, 26, 27, 130–131, 134, 145, 179, 181–182, 183, 200n8, 201n2
  transnational business, 28, 54, 96, 200n5
  warrior, 3, 4, 5, 10, 11, 16, 17, 20, 23, 26, 39, 48, 50, 56–57, 59, 71–73, 74, 99, 101, 102, 103, 104, 106, 107, 108, 110, 111, 117, 118, 128, 129, 144, 147, 175, 178, 179, 181, 182–183, 185
  women's access to, 11, 52, 62, 70, 71, 155, 182–183, 203n3

[222] *Index*

Military
    changing roles, 21–22
    citizenship, and gender, 28–34
    operations other than war, 21–22
Military Academy at West Point, 49
Military masculinities, 19–23 (*see also* Masculinity)
Military pay, all-volunteer force, 35, 36, 37–38, 47, 49
Military personnel
    active duty, 187–188
    African American enlisted active duty, 191
    African American female enlisted active duty, 193
    African American officers active duty, 192
    drop in number due to post-Cold War cuts, 12
    female enlisted active duty, 189
    female officers active duty, 190
    number of women in 2010, 21
    size of forces in 2010, 21
Military recruiting. *See* Recruiting
Military service
    ties to masculinity, 3–4, 19–23, 27, 178, 181, 182
    link with citizenship, 33–34
    literature of citizenship and, 31–32
    as preparation for politics, 30
Militias, masculinity and, 20
Millet, Allan R., Marine history, 109
Milošević, Slobodan, 3
Mitchell, Brian
    soldier as protector, 55
    history of women in the Marines, 122
    women in military, 39–40
Modern Volunteer Army Program, 46
Morgan, David H. J., military service and masculinity, 21
Moskos, Charles
    Air Force, 132
    military service, 30, 31–32, 35–36
    reputation of each service, 45–46
Mozambique, humanitarian mission, 202n6
Museum of Television and Radio, 196n14
Myers, Colonel John, Army Recruiting Command, 159

National Defense Act of 1920, 34
National Defense Authorization Act, women in aviation, 153
National identity, military as a source of, 6
National Military Strategy, 1995 changes, 22
Naturalization, incentive for military service, 30
Naval Act (1916), 84
Naval Coast Defense Reserve Force, 30, 84
Naval Reserve, women, 85
Naval Reserve Act of 1925, women, 85
Naval Reserve Act of 1938, women, 85
Navy
    "Accelerate Your Life," 99–102, 159, 175–176
    active duty personnel, 187–188
    adventure, 15, 78, 82, 83, 90, 99, 101, 103, 179–180
    African American active duty enlisted forces, 191
    African American active duty officers, 192
    African American female active duty enlisted forces, 193
    African Americans, 80–81, 94, 101–102, 103, 184
    "Band," commercial, 94
    "be someone special" theme, 78–81
    career opportunities and high-tech training, 15, 82–83, 84, 90, 94–96
    culture, 75–76
    female active duty officers, 190
    female enlisted active duty personnel, 189
    hegemonic masculinity, 22
    "Homecoming," commercial, 94
    "It's not just a job, it's an adventure," 82
    job training and skill development, 78–80
    "Let the Journey Begin," 90, 93–94
    "Live the adventure," 83
    "Life, Liberty, and the Pursuit of All Who Threaten It," 100–101, 159, 176
    masculinity and, 15, 74, 80, 82, 83–84, 92, 96, 99–100, 101, 102–103, 179–180

Index [223]

Navy (*continued*)
  "Minivan," commercial, 101
  recruiting advertisements, 78–84, 86–89, 90–102, 175–176
  recruiting background, 76–78
  recruiting needs, 11, 12
  recruiting problems, 93, 96–97
  "SEALs," commercial, 94
  slogans, 78, 82, 90, 93, 99, 100, 159, 203n3
  social issues, 200n3
  Tailhook scandal, 92–93, 201n4
  television commercials, 83, 92, 94, 176, 203n3
  transition to all-volunteer force (AVF), 77–78, 81
  travel, 78, 83, 87, 88, 94, 95, 139
  "Travel," commercial, 94
  warrior masculinity, 15, 74, 99, 101, 102, 103
  Web site, 90, 94, 95, 96, 99, 176, 203n3
  women and, 30, 74, 76, 81, 84–90, 92, 93, 94, 95, 96–99, 102, 103, 176, 183, 184, 196n10, 201n4, 203n3
  "You and the Navy, full speed ahead," 90
  "You are tomorrow. You are the Navy," 83
New world order masculinity, 16, 27, 40, 131, 145, 146, 156–157, 180
New York Times
  blue-collar jobs and men's status, 199–200n7
  Marine Corps, 169, 172
  recruiters, 159
Nineteenth Amendment, women's war work, 31
Niva, Steve, new world order masculinity, 16, 27, 40, 131, 156–157, 180
Nixon, Richard, 35, 46

Office of Personnel Operations, recommendations on women in Army, 65–66
Operation Allied Force, 3, 143
Operation Enduring Freedom, 158, 169 (*see also* Afghanistan War)
Operation Iraqi Freedom, 158, 164, 202n1 (*see also* Iraq War)
Operation Just Cause, 70
Operation Northern Watch, 202n6
Operation Urgent Fury, 70

Panama, participation of Army women, 70
Paramilitary culture, reaction to masculinity crisis, 25–26
Parents, Army commercials aimed at, 164–166
Parker, Technical Sergeant Tom, Air Force Web site, 147
Parris Island, Marine training, 98, 118–119, 121
Patriotism
  Air Force ads, 138
  Army ads, 54–55, 64, 163
  as potential basis for recruiting, 8, 180
  recruitment of women and, 64
The Peacemakers, Marine recruiting film, 110
Peace of Paris, 29
Peace operations and peacekeeping
  in Air Force recruiting, 146
  gendering of, 146, 202n5
  post-Cold War military roles, 21–22
  in recruiting, 55
  relationship to military masculinities, 22
  women's participation, 70
Pentagon. *See also* Department of Defense
  Air Force Academy investigations, 154
  influence on recruiting campaigns, 195n7
  National Military Strategy, 22
  Risk Rule, 67, 70, 126, 153
  women, 160, 161
Persian Gulf War. *See* Gulf War
Philippines, Air Force humanitarian mission, 143
Political parties, military spectacles and elections, 20–21
Political science
  study of citizenship and military service, 9, 31–32
  study of gender and recruiting, 8
  study of military, 5–6
  study of recruiting, 9

Pool, Senior Airman Marilyn, Air Force Web site 148
Popular Mechanics magazine, 13–14, 73, 113, 116, 136, 196n13
  Air Force ads aimed at mechanically skilled, 137, 139, 140
  Army ads featuring military hardware, 51–52
  Navy, 82
Predator drone, 173, 175 (*see also* Drone aircraft)
Prisoners of war, political value of experience, 30
Proceedings, U.S. Naval Institute journal, 96, 97–99, 111
Project Ahead program, Army, 47
Project VOLAR, voluntary Army field experiment, 13
Project Volunteer, Navy, 77
Project Volunteer in Defense of the Nation (PROVIDE), 46, 65
Promise Keepers, 26
Prostitute, labeling of military women, 64, 122–123
PROVIDE (Project Volunteer in Defense of the Nation), 46, 65

Race. *See also* African Americans; Hispanics
  Air Force, 132–133, 151
  Army, 43–44, 164
  integration of military, 31, 43, 81, 107, 132
  intersections with gender in recruiting ads, 183–184
  Gates Commission, 36
  Marines, 107, 169
  military service and diversity, 31–32
  Navy, 81, 103
  relationship to hegemonic masculinity, 19, 36–37, 107, 197–198n7
  in study of recruitment, 9
Race riots and racial incidents
  Air Force, 133
  Marine Corps, 107
  Navy, 81
Rambo movies and masculinity, 25, 27, 156, 198n8
Rand, Brig. Gen. Ron, Air Force director of public affairs, 142

RAND Corporation, Army study, 49
Rangers, Army, 52, 57, 164
Reagan, Ronald, 26, 67, 84
Recruiters
  Air Force's outnumbered by other services', 141
  as factor in recruitment decisions, 8
  helping Army recruits cheat, 161
  hostility to women in World War II, 63
  Iraq War, 159, 161, 168, 169
  targeting of working-class men, 197n6
Recruiting
  advertisement sample, 12–14
  during Afghanistan war, 158–177
  Air Force advertisements, 133–148, 152–155, 173–175
  Army advertisements, 46–62, 66–71, 162–168
  audience for, 6, 7, 199n3
  background for Air Force, 133–134
  background for Army, 44–46
  background for Marine Corps, 108–110
  background for Navy, 76–78
  crisis of late 1990s, 3, 10, 38–39, 57, 93, 96–97, 141
  during Iraq war, 158–177
  Marine Corps advertisements, 111–121, 126–127, 169–171, 171–172
  masculinity as basis for, 4, 5, 8, 10, 11, 33, 36–37, 39, 178, 181
  Navy advertisements, 78–84, 86–89, 90–102, 175–176
  needs of military branches, 11–12, 178–179
  posters, 3, 45, 78, 80–81, 84, 89, 110, 180, 197n14
  purposes of, 6–7
  representations of military service in, 7, 9, 33, 180–181, 185
  study of, 5–10
  television commercials, 3, 50–51, 53, 55, 58, 83, 92, 94, 117–118, 141, 142–143, 145, 162–167, 169–171, 174, 175, 176, 202n6, 203n3
  women and the Air Force, 141, 147–148, 148–155, 156, 157, 173, 174, 175, 183, 184
  women and the Army, 41–42, 51, 52, 55, 61, 62–71, 72, 163, 165, 167, 168, 183, 184, 199n2

Index [225]

Recruiting (*continued*)
  women and the Marine Corps, 104, 113–114, 118, 121–128, 169, 170, 171–172, 183, 184
  women and the Navy, 74, 81, 84–90, 92, 93, 94, 95, 96–99, 102, 103, 176, 183, 184, 196n10, 203n3
Relief missions. *See* Humanitarian missions
Reserve Officer Training Corps (ROTC)
  advertising campaigns, 6
  Air Force (AFROTC) women, 149, 152, 154
  Navy women, 86, 93, 98
Revolutionary War, 29, 30, 44
Ricks, Thomas E.
  Marine culture, 105–107
  Vietnam and Marine Corps, 111
  Separation of women in Marine Corps, 121
Risk Rule, 67, 70, 126, 153
Rolling Stone magazine, 14
Rostker v. Goldberg, women and Selective Service court case, 198n11

Sailorettes, term for Navy women, 85
Segal, David R., social composition of all-volunteer force, 36
Selective Service System, 29, 110, 133, 198n11
September 11, 2001 terrorist attacks, 20, 60, 100, 198n15
Seventeen magazine, 14
  Air Force ads, 152, 154, 154–155, 156, 173
  "Army of One" ads, 71
  Marine ads, 113, 126, 127
  Navy's absence from, 93
Sexual abuse and harassment scandals, 70, 92–93, 154, 201n4
Sexual Suicide, Gilder, 23
Sharpe, Captain Roma, Marine ad, 127
Siegel & Gale, Air Force study and commercials, 142, 143
Slogans
  Air Force, 135, 137, 138, 142, 145, 174
  Army, 46, 50, 57–58, 166
  Army, bilingual, 58
  Korean War recruitment of women, 64
  Marine Corps, 105, 110, 112, 114

  Navy, 78, 82, 90, 93, 99, 159, 203n3
Social networking, Marine use of, 168–169
Soldier, use of term, 195n4
Soldiering
  defender and protector role, 54–56
  images of, 6, 52
  masculinity, 18, 48, 50–51 73, 179
Somalia, Air Force humanitarian mission, 143
Spanish-American War, articles about Marines, 110
Special Forces
  Army ads, 59
  "America's Army," video game 60–61
Sports Illustrated magazine, 13, 73, 196n13
  Air Force, 140, 154
  Army, 49, 51, 54, 69, 71
  Marine Corps, 115, 201n2
  Navy, 80, 88, 91, 128
State power, military as embodiment, 6
Steihm, Judith Hicks, Marine culture, 106
Stock market crash, effects on recruiting, 45
Strother, Navy Commander Thomas, Navy recruiting, 96–97
Super Bowl, ad placement, 58–59, 118

Tailhook Association, 92–93, 200n6
Tailhook scandal, Navy, 92–93, 201n4
Technology
  Air Force, 16, 130–131, 131–132, 133, 134, 137–138, 139, 141, 142, 143, 144–145, 146–147, 156–157, 173, 175, 180
  Army, 15, 51, 53, 56, 70, 162
  element of recruiting appeals, 5, 10, 179, 181–182
  masculinity and, 10, 11, 26, 27, 130–131, 134, 145, 179, 181–182, 183, 200n8, 201n2
  Navy, 15, 82–83, 84, 90, 94–96, 102, 175–176
  as part of military's overall image, 185
Telemundo, Army ad placement, 58
Television commercials
  Air Force, 3, 141, 142–143, 145, 174, 175

[226] *Index*

Army, 50–51, 53, 55, 58, 162–167
Marine Corps, 117–118, 169–171, 202n6
Navy, 83, 92, 94, 176, 203n3
Television shows, ad placement, 58, 117
Thurman, Maxwell A., volunteer force, 37–38
Timmerman, Airman Genis, Air Force Web site, 147
Tobias, Sheila, political value of military service, 30
Top Gun, movie, 92, 94
Transnational business masculinity, 28, 54, 96, 200n5
Travel
   Air Force, 141, 144, 147, 148
   Navy, 78, 83, 87, 88, 94, 95, 139
   Marine Corps, 110, 112, 201n2
Truman, President
   racial integration of military, 31, 43, 81, 107, 132
   Committee on Equality of Treatment and Opportunity, 132
   Executive Order Number 9981, 31
   Korean War recruitment of women, 64
Tuskegee Airmen, World War II, 133
Twenty-Sixth Amendment, U.S. Constitution, 30

Uniforms
   in Air Force ads, 130, 155
   in Army ads, 45, 50, 59, 66, 71, 72, 73, 117
   in Marine Corps ads, 104, 113, 117
   in Navy ads, 87, 89
   item of analysis, 13
   warrior masculinity and, 20, 50, 117
   women's, 63, 64, 66, 89, 163, 198n10
Univision, Army ad placement, 58
"USAF: Air Dominance," video game, 174
U.S. Constitution
   Nineteenth Amendment, 31
   Twenty-Sixth Amendment, 30
USS *Constitution*, first woman in Marines, 122
USS *Sanctuary*, Navy women, 86

Van Antwerp, Lt. General Robert L., Army Accessions Command, 166–167

van Creveld, Martin, women as cause of recruiting problems, 39
VFW, Veterans of Foreign Wars Magazine, critique of Army slogan, 58
Video games
   Air Force, 131, 144–146, 156, 174, 181–182
   "America's Army," 60–62, 181–182
Vietnam War
   1990s recruiting problems and, 38
   African Americans, 35, 107, 133, 202n2
   Air Force, 133, 151–152
   combat footage in ads, 163–164
   cultural representations of, 26, 156, 198n8
   defeat, 23, 25
   draft, 35
   draft and voting rights, 30
   Marine Corps, 110, 111
   masculinity crisis and, 3, 23, 25, 26, 201n3
   military masculinity and, 25, 27, 156, 178, 198n8
   political value of service, 30
   size of U.S. forces, 34
   women's participation, 65, 86, 124, 151–152
Volunteer force. *See* All-volunteer force

WAC (Women's Army Corp), 63–65, 67, 199n5
WAF (women in the Air Force), 150, 151–152
War. *See also* Afghanistan War; Gulf War; Iraq War; Korean War; Vietnam War; World War I; World War II
   democratization of, 29
   masculinity and, 19–20, 22, 23, 25, 27, 55, 156
   political value of participation, 30
   as solution to masculinity crisis, 25
   references in Army ads, 163–164, 165, 167, 177
War of 1812, Marine Corps, 109
Warrior masculinity
   Air Force, technologically mediated, 144, 147, 175
   Air Force, lack of, 133, 137, 142, 155, 157, 180

Warrior masculinity (*continued*)
  Army ads, 15, 48, 56–57, 59, 71–73, 179
  Marines, 5, 10, 16, 104, 106, 107, 108, 110, 111, 117, 118, 128, 129, 185
  Navy, 15, 74, 99, 101, 102, 103
  as solution to masculinity crisis, 26
  as traditional form of military masculinity, 3, 4, 5, 10, 11, 17, 20, 23, 39, 178, 181, 182–183, 185
  uniforms and, 20, 50, 117
Washington, George, discharge of Continental Army, 44
WASPs (Women's Airforce Service Pilots), 149, 150
WAVES (Women Accepted for Volunteer Emergency Service), Navy 85–86
Web sites
  Air Force, 143–145, 146–148, 155, 156, 174–175
  "America's Army," 61
  Army, 56–57, 60, 61, 164, 165
  Army Accessions Command, 167, 202n3
  Marine Corps, 105, 118–121, 122
  Navy, 90, 94–95, 96, 99, 176, 203n3
  recruiting, 14
  social networking, 168
Westmoreland, Gen. William, Army recruiting, 65, 199n3
West Point, 44, 49
Williams, Christine, women in Marine Corps, 125
Wilson, Gen. Louis H., Marine Corps, 111, 124
Women
  access to masculine characteristics in ads, 5, 11, 52, 62, 70, 71, 155, 182–183, 203n3
  active duty officers, 190
  African American female active duty enlisted forces, 193
  African Americans, 63, 123, 183–184, 198n13, 199n2, 203n4
  Air Force, 12, 141, 147–148, 148–155, 156, 157, 173, 174, 175, 183, 184
  all-volunteer force's (AVF) reliance on, 21, 36, 67, 158

  appearance and behavior, concerns about, 64–65, 66, 86, 124, 127, 199n5, 201n5
  Army, 41–42, 43, 51, 52, 55, 61, 62–71, 72, 163, 165, 168, 183, 184, 199n2, 201n4
  combat and, 17, 29, 42, 61, 67, 70, 71, 86, 92, 96–97, 106, 150, 153–154, 158, 160–161, 163, 167, 168, 177, 183, 185, 198n11, 203n3
  conscription and, 31–32, 182, 198n11, 198n14, 198n15
  expansion of military roles in wartime, 158, 63, 70, 160–161
  female enlisted active duty military personnel, 189
  influence on military masculinities, 22, 158
  Iraq and Afghanistan deployment, 160–161
  labeled as lesbians, 122–123
  labeled as prostitutes, 64, 122–123
  Marine Corps, 12, 104, 106, 113–114, 118, 120, 121–128, 169, 170, 171–172, 183, 184, 200n1, 201n4
  Navy, 30, 74, 81, 84–90, 92, 93, 94, 95, 96–99, 102, 103, 176, 183, 184, 196n10, 201n4, 203n3
  Nineteenth Amendment, 31
  protection of as motivation for men, 55, 164, 201n2
  reinforcement of femininity in ads, 66, 68, 70, 127, 173
  restriction of military roles, 64, 67, 85, 125, 150, 151, 153
  as reward for men's service, 74, 87–88, 89, 103, 164, 200n6
  Risk Rule, 67, 70, 126, 153
  sexual abuse and harassment in military, 4, 70, 92–93, 154, 201n4
  studies of women in military, 65–66, 67, 124–125, 196n11
  uniforms, 63, 64, 66, 89, 163, 198n10
  Vietnam War, 65, 86, 124, 151–152
  World War I, 62–63, 84–85, 123
  World War II, 62–63, 85, 123, 148–149, 198n13
Women Accepted for Volunteer Emergency Service (WAVES), Navy, 85–86
Women in the Army Study, 67

"Women Marines," 121, 123
Women's Airforce Service Pilots (WASPs), 149, 150
Women's Armed Services Integration Act, 63–64
   Air Force, 150
   Army, 63–64
   Marine Corps, 123
   Navy, 85, 86
Women's Army Auxiliary Corp, 63
Women's Army Corp (WAC), 63–65, 67, 199n5
Women's League for Self Defense, 62
Women's movement
   masculinity crisis and, 3, 23, 25
   women's participation in military, 36, 65, 151
World War I
   African Americans, 107
   Army and women, 62–63
   Marine Corps, 107, 110, 123
   Marines and women, 123
   Navy and women, 84–85
   recruiting posters, 81, 84, 110, 180, 197n14
   women's suffrage, 30–31
World War II
   African Americans, 31, 81, 133, 198n13
   Air Force and women, 148–149
   Army and women, 62–63, 149, 198n13
   civil rights, 31
   combat footage in ads, 163–164, 170
   conscription, 34, 110
   Marine Corps, 110, 111, 170
   Marines and women, 123
   masculinity and, 20
   Navy and women, 85, 149
   political value of service, 30
   recruiting posters, 3, 110, 180, 197n14
   Tuskegee Airmen, 133

XXL magazine, 14

"Yeomanettes," term for Navy women, 85
Young Women's Christian Association, 62
Youth Attitudinal Tracking Survey, Army research, 49
Yugoslavia, Air Force military operation, 143

Zeliff, Lt. Col. Mike, Marine advertising, 171
Zumwalt, Admiral Elmo, Navy, 81, 86

Enlisting Masculinity

OXFORD STUDIES IN GENDER AND INTERNATIONAL RELATIONS

SERIES EDITORS
J. Ann Tickner, University of Southern California, Laura Sjoberg, University of Florida